Crime

Altho
This
racy.
socie
the m
balan

David Blunkett, MP

Media clamour on issues relating to crime, justice and civil liberties has never been more insistent. Whether on the murder of James Bulger or detaining terrorist suspects for long periods without trial, mediated comment has grown immeasurably over the last twenty years. So, how does it interact with and shape policy in these fields? How do the politicians both respond to and try to manipulate the media which permeates our society and culture?

Crime, Policy and the Media is the first academic text to map the relationship between a rapidly changing media and policymaking in criminal justice. Spanning the period 1989–2010, it examines a number of case studies – terrorism, drugs, sentencing, policing and public protection, amongst others – and interrogates key policymakers (including six former Home Secretaries, a former Lord Chief Justice, Attorney-General, senior police officers, government advisers and leading commentators) about the impact of the media on their thinking and practice.

Bolstered by content and framing analysis, it argues that, especially in the last decade, fear of media criticism and the *Daily Mail* effect has restricted the policymaking agenda in crime and justice, concluding that the expanding influence of the Internet and Web 2.0 has begun to undermine some of the ways in which agencies such as the police have gained and held a presentational advantage.

Written by a former BBC Home Affairs Correspondent, with unrivalled access to the highest reaches of policymaking, it is both academically rigorous and accessible and will be of interest to both scholars and practitioners in media and criminal justice.

Jon Silverman has been Professor of Media and Criminal Justice at the University of Bedfordshire since July 2007. He is a leading criminal justice analyst and authority on international war crimes tribunals and from 1989 to 2002 was the BBC Home Affairs Correspondent. His earlier BBC career included a spell in Paris as a correspondent (1987–89) and at Westminster as a political correspondent. In 1996, he won the Sony Radio Gold Award for his reporting of war crimes issues on Radio 4.

Crime, Policy and the Media

The shaping of criminal justice, 1989–2010

Jon Silverman

Routledge
Taylor & Francis Group

LONDON AND NEW YORK

First published 2012
by Routledge
2 Park Square, Milton Park, Abingdon, Oxon, OX14 4RN

Simultaneously published in the USA and Canada
by Routledge
711 Third Avenue, New York, NY 10017

Routledge is an imprint of the Taylor & Francis Group, an informa business

British Library Cataloguing in Publication Data
A catalogue record for this book is available from the British Library

Library of Congress Cataloging in Publication Data
Crime, policy and the media : the shaping of criminal justice, 1989–2010 /
Jon Silverman.
   p. cm.
   Includes bibliographical references.
   1. Mass media and criminal justice–Great Britain. 2. Crime–Great
Britain. 3. Criminal justice, Administration of–Great Britain. 4. Crime
in mass media. I. Title.
   P96.C742G775 2012   364.94109'049–dc23
   2011022612

ISBN: 978-0-415-67231-3 (hbk)
ISBN: 978-0-415-67232-0 (pbk)
ISBN: 978-0-203-15693-3 (ebk)

Typeset in Times New Roman
by Bookcraft Ltd, Stroud, Gloucestershire

To mum and dad, Len and Lili Silverman.
For everything.

Contents

Acknowledgements

When I left the BBC in 2002, it was with the intention of exploring some fresh avenues, although I had only the haziest idea what they might be. Regular chairing of public policy conferences was one because, although it is sometimes a comfort as a broadcaster not to be able to see your audience, more often you feel like a horse wearing blinkers, racing towards a deadline but closed off from the crowd. So, in 2007, when my good friend and colleague, Ivor Gaber, suggested that the University of Bedfordshire might be willing to offer me a (part-time) home, I realized that it was just the intellectual spur I needed. So, my first debt of gratitude is to Ivor, Professor Alexis Weedon and my other colleagues at UoB, on both the media and social science sides, for providing me with the opportunity to develop and refine my ideas. Without that platform, this book would not have been written.

I am grateful to all those people who agreed to be interviewed, many giving up an hour or so of busy lives to be probed. The legendary American journalist, Bob Woodward, says he approaches his books in the spirit of 'neutral inquiry' and that you should take people as seriously as they take themselves. I concur. Anyway, with politicians, it is a necessity if you want to get past first base!

Thanks are due to Brian Willan for his positive response when I proposed a book on this theme at a British Society of Criminology conference in 2007 and for granting me an extra year to complete when I realized that the outcome of the 2010 election, while almost certainly dismal for New Labour, might unlock a few ex-ministerial (and other) doors for me. Julia Willan at Routledge has been an exemplary editor, reassuring and supportive.

As a technophobe, I leaned heavily on computer support while I was at the BBC. That role has been unofficially assumed by my son, Alex, and he has got me out of more scrapes than I care to reflect on. Thanks. His brother, Daniel, has provided welcome distraction with tales from the worlds of recruitment, football and trips to the US. And to my wife, Jackie, who retains only the haziest idea of what I look like after two years and more locked away with my laptop, I can only echo the Terminator by promising: 'I'll be back' (and all my love and gratitude).

Finally, no words of praise are high enough for my research assistant and PhD student, Lisa Thomas, with whom I have shared an office, a dodgy printer and all the stresses and strains of this enterprise. Her cheerfulness and resourcefulness have seen me over the finishing line and I look forward with confidence to her own dissertation which will be a distinguished contribution to scholarship. Lisa, you're a star.

Preface

Does a book need a preface when it is followed by an introduction which explains the purpose and context of the study with, one trusts, sufficient clarity? Self-evidently, I have decided that this one does and these few lines are intended to convey the spirit with which I approached this inquiry, to stake out, as it were, how I propose to cross that contested territory which divides the journalist from the academic, often the source of mutual suspicion and misunderstanding.

The *Times* columnist, Alice Miles, who returned to university after two decades to pursue a Master's course, wrote in the *New Statesman* (29 November 2010) that too much of what she was required to study 'was clothed in the abstruse and impenetrable discourse of academia'. Whilst acknowledging that journalism often 'goes too far the other way, prioritizing simplification over accuracy, opinion over fact', she concludes that, if nothing else, journalists are good at 'talking human'.

Since this is a book about the colliding and overlapping worlds of media and policymakers, the frequently fractious, sometimes collusive, relationship they share as they both, in their own ways, seek to capture either the attention or the votes of ordinary people, it seems to me incumbent to 'talk human' throughout. This does not, of course, absolve me of the requirement to be intellectually rigorous in my thesis, to build it on evidence and not conjecture, and to acknowledge and source the work of others who have toiled in this field. But in writing a book which, I hope, will be of interest to students, academics, journalists, policymakers, think tanks and those with no affiliation but merely an abiding preoccupation with the media, criminal justice and governance, accessibility has been my watchword throughout.

Only you, the reader, can decide whether I have been as good as my word.

1 Introduction

This book is about the interlocking relationships between the media and policymakers and shapers and the impact on criminal justice. Journalists, politicians, police officers and others in public life are fish that swim in the same
sea. Occasionally, it is true, they eat each other but, on the whole, the ecological
balance is maintained. But in July 2011, a fortnight before this manuscript was
sent for typesetting, that balance was disturbed by a tide of effluence flowing
from revelations about phone hacking and other 'dark arts' practised by those
employed by, or on behalf of, the *News of the World*. So toxic was this outpouring
of admitted fact and credible allegation that the newspaper, 168 years old and
thriving on the country's biggest circulation, was closed.

This book spans a period of 21 years, 1989–2010. Neither date was chosen
at random. The year 2010 is a natural bookend because New Labour's election
defeat lends a necessary perspective to many of the shibboleths and strategies –
from anti-social behaviour orders (ASBOs) to control orders – which sustained
it in office. But why start in 1989, almost midway through the eighteen years
of Conservative rule? There are three compelling reasons and one has a linear
bearing on the tumultuous events of 2011 at Rupert Murdoch's News Corporation.

Mr Murdoch's current priority, at time of writing, is to purchase that portion of
the highly lucrative satellite broadcast company, BSkyB, which News Corporation
does not already own. Although the outcome of this story is impossible to predict,
we know that it began in February 1989 with the inaugural broadcast of Sky
News, the UK's first 24-hour news service.

To many of today's ravenous producer-consumers of Twitter, YouTube and
Facebook, the arrival of satellite television is merely a cultural fossil, of interest
only to media palaeontologists. But it was the start of something more significant
than a new 'licence to print money'.[1] It ushered in rolling news which brought
with it a more intensive invigilation of politics, which, however tentative, and,
many would say, over-focused on surface drama, is slowly transforming the relationship between state and citizen and underpinning what has been called a 'moni-
tory democracy' (Keane 2009: xxvii). We are still witnessing the evolution of
this process but some of the developments of 2010, such as the scrutiny of public
order policing via camera phone and YouTube, real-time dissemination of information on Twitter, and the disclosure of state secrets by Wikileaks, are helping to
map a new landscape which this book explores.

The second reason for starting this study in 1989 is a more personal one. In the summer of that year, I became Home Affairs Correspondent for the BBC and was thus obliged to confront, for the first time, the issues dealt with in this book. And by 1993, feeling like a veteran in the post, I was sufficiently emboldened to offer some thoughts to the fresh-faced shadow Home Secretary, one Tony Blair, over lunch in Pimlico, when he probed the weaknesses of government policy on crime and justice. As it turned out, home affairs was merely a launch pad to greater things for Mr Blair, but it is significant that, alone among post-war Prime Ministers, he would have chosen the job of Home Secretary rather than any of the other great offices of state had he not made it to the very top. Indeed, one of the themes of this book is the way in which the Home Office, especially in New Labour's second term, often found itself dancing to the tune emanating from Downing Street. As Huw Evans, special adviser to David Blunkett in that post-2001 period comments: 'Tony always considered that he was the best Home Secretary this country never had' (Interview with author, 10 February 2010).[2]

It would be immodest to claim that my induction into the masonry of crime/home affairs specialists was of any media significance, though it gave me a privileged view of many of the events which left an indelible mark on the 1990s: the quashing of the convictions of the Guildford Four and the Birmingham Six, the response to the killing of James Bulger, the Stephen Lawrence murder, the IRA's mainland bombing campaign, and so on. But many of the ideas which have come to maturity in this study sprang from this background of reporting and analysis.

A third reason for viewing 1989 as a landmark is that it was the last shout of a style of governance in home affairs which believed in party consensus rather than confrontation, and reflection rather than rapid response. As Garland, writing in 2001, put it: 'criminal policy has ceased to be a bipartisan matter that can be left to professional experts and has become a prominent issue in electoral competition' (Garland 2001: 13). Douglas Hurd left the Home Office in October 1989, after more than four years in the post, and with him went a set of assumptions about the discharging of the role of Home Secretary which have never made a comeback. As will be explained, this, too, can be linked to the changing media of the 1990s.

Hurd is one of six former Home Secretaries who submitted to semi-structured interviews for this research along with a former Lord Chief Justice, a former Attorney-General, a former head of UK Counter-Terrorism, the current president of the Association of Chief Police Officers, two former heads of the National Offender Management Service, a number of government special advisers and other policy actors over this 21-year period. Quotations from one or two have been anonymized at their own request because they are still working in government. Forty-four of the interviewees, most of whom were recorded digitally, are listed towards the back of the book. (The recordings will be housed in a Special Collections archive at the University of Bedfordshire and made available to other researchers.)

Some of these people – Douglas Hurd, David Blunkett, the former counter-terrorism chief, Andy Hayman, former Assistant Commissioner, Brian Paddick – have written their own accounts of this period. But memoirs are almost, by definition, self-serving, while an interview, testing their account of key episodes, illuminated by analysis of relevant documentary material, can provide a form of triangulation (journalists might be more comfortable with the term 'second source'), regarded as the minimum requirement for arriving at a well-grounded judgment.

Taming the feral beast

The starting point for this inquiry was the last major speech delivered by Tony Blair before he handed over the prime ministerial reins to Gordon Brown in June 2007. On 12 June, he spoke to an invited audience at the headquarters of Reuters, the long-established international media organization. It is the speech in which he referred to the media as 'like a feral beast, just tearing people and reputation to bits' (Blair 2007a). Blair's analysis is worth examining in a little detail here:

> The media world ... is becoming more fragmented, more diverse and, above all, transformed by technology. ... When I fought the 1997 election ... we could take an issue a day. At the last election, in 2005, we had to have one [issue] for the morning, another for the afternoon, and by the evening, the agenda had already moved on ... the relationship between politics, public life and the media is changing as a result of the changing context of communication in which we all operate: no-one is at fault – this change is a fact; but it is my view that the effect of this change is seriously adverse to the way public life is conducted; and that we need, at the least, a proper and considered debate about how we manage the future, in which it is in all our interests that the public is properly and accurately informed.
>
> ibid.

Perhaps predictably, that 'debate' was both short-lived and framed largely in terms of New Labour's relentless focus on media presentation, both before and during its years in power. Typical was the response of the former *New Statesman* editor, Peter Wilby: 'The difficulty with Blair's speech is one of chicken and egg. Did the pressures of 24-hour news come first, or the politicians' more manipulative approach to supplying news?' (*Guardian*, 13 June 2007).

But it is all too easy to get trapped in a somewhat circular argument which serves only one purpose – that of attaching blame. Another of Blair's thoughts offers a more fruitful line of inquiry:

> I am going to say something that few people in public life will say, but most know is absolutely true: a vast aspect of our jobs today – outside of the really major decisions, as big as anything else – is coping with the media, its sheer scale, weight and constant hyperactivity. At points, it literally overwhelms.
>
> Blair 2007a

If media watchers and practitioners found plenty of red meat in Blair's speech, those more interested in governance would have found it tantalizingly incomplete. After all, he does not spell out what 'coping' with the media means, other than to imply that feeding the voracious appetite of a 24/7 news machine – satisfying what the *Newsnight* presenter, Jeremy Paxman, has called the 'expectation infla-tion'[3] – places strains on ministers and officials which did not exist in the less frenzied political environment enjoyed by some of his predecessors. Bearing in mind the exponential growth in information sources in the four years since that speech, and, if it is true, that, taking into account the many and varied influences on a government – parliament, the business community, organized labour, inter-national obligations and partnerships, think tanks, pressure groups and so on – the outpouring of the media is 'as big as anything else', then the question of what this means for the making of policy and taking of crucial decisions must merit close attention.

This may seem like a statement of the obvious but some of those working inside government to devise and mould policy would not necessarily agree. Dr Geoff Mulgan provided intellectual ballast to many of the innovative programmes of the Blair premiership as director of the PM's Strategy Unit. In a discursive analysis of the intersection between knowledge and policymaking, delivered at a conference in Australia, he mentions the media only once, two lines from the end (Mulgan 2003: 11). Even in 'policy fields in flux ... where the knowledge base is contested', among which he includes crime, he concedes no role for the influence of the media in acting, either as a conduit for the unfettered filtering of knowledge or the wilful distortion of it.

Douglas Hurd, however, is prepared to give due weight to the impact which the media can have on ministers and their advisers:

> Because the media is a more hectic and feverish thing now, the quality of analysis is cruder and it is more difficult to take decisions based on thought and proper reflection. Ted Heath [former Conservative Prime Minister] used to say 'the first account of anything is always wrong – 48 hours later it will look different'. Well, today you have not got 48 hours.
>
> Interview with author, 21 July 2008

Today's media increasingly exhibits two tendencies which, at first glance, can strike one as contradictory. On the one hand, it suffers from a form of attention deficit disorder which drives it to constantly search for something 'new' (or at least different) to report on the hour every hour. While on the other, it is able to direct an unwavering and merciless focus on a story of perceived wrongdoing (think MPs' expenses) or incompetence (the demise of Charles Clarke as Home Secretary over the foreign prisoners debacle – see Chapter 6) which bears out Alastair Campbell's dictum that a minister cannot survive more than eleven days of hostile headlines. The question for this study is: how does Mulgan's purist notion of a knowledge-based policymaking, incubated in a strategy hothouse, fit into this framework? As Koch-Baumgarten and Voltmer rightly point out: 'The policy agenda develops over long time spans, often involving several different legislative terms'. Whereas, 'the substance of the media agenda ... is driven by newsworthy events rather than structural problems' (2010: 2). How, then, to map the contours of this turbulent and shifting relationship between media and policy?

Indexing, agenda-setting and attention allocation

If not quite virgin territory, the way that media and policymakers interact bears relatively few academic footprints. Koch-Baumgarten and Voltmer express 'surprise' that neither political science nor communication studies have given this field much attention (ibid.: 1). For Walgrave and Van Aelst, 'the field of media and political agenda-setting is disparate and under-theorized' (Walgrave and Van Aelst 2006: 89). While it is true that the impact of the media on US foreign policy has been the subject of a celebrated study which has spawned its own theory, 'the CNN Effect' (Robinson 2002), there is comparatively little research into the media's role in the domestic policy nexus and nothing of note on the subject of this research – criminal justice; though some attempt has been made to correlate the media's influence on crime policy in the US in the 1980s and 1990s (see Jones and Wolfe 2010: 35–7).

That is one reason why this book will lean heavily towards practical case studies from the fields of crime and justice to make its points. Nevertheless, as the unnamed French philosopher memorably (and perhaps apocryphally) said: 'Yes, it works in practice, but will it work in theory?' Well, there is certainly no shortage of theories to sift through. Jones and Wolfe (ibid.) suggest that the role of the media in the public policy process can be characterized by three established theories. These are:

1 Influence theory: the media tell the politicians what to think.
2 Agenda-setting theory: the media tell the politicians what to think about.
3 Indexing theory: the politicians tell the media what to write about.

And a fourth model which they propose:

4 Detection theory: politicians and the media struggle to identify, characterize and prioritize complex multiple information streams.

This last is a refinement of the theory of 'information processing' developed by Jones and Baumgartner (2005). Jones and Wolfe ascribe a key role to the allocation of attention to an issue: 'By ... highlighting particular aspects of the information stream, the media may help to set the tone for subsequent policy action' (2010: 19).

All of the above theories have been modelled on what we can call 'traditional' mass media and if anything seems clear in an often opaque and contested field, it is that a great deal of fresh theorizing will have to be done in the light of the sudden impact of 'new media' on events and policy developments around the world. These range from the overthrow of authoritarian rulers in the Middle East (so-called 'Twitter revolutions') to the suppression of free speech in China to the strategy adopted in public order policing in London. Where the onrush of these developments is leading us 'only time will tell' (the clichéd payoff of many a broadcast news report). Thus, this review of a 21-year period, in which politicians have focused their attention chiefly on mass circulation newspapers and mainstream broadcast outlets, will also concentrate on 'old' media, while pointing up, where appropriate, how technology is changing the rules and learned behaviour of the relationship.

It is important at this early stage to make it clear that the case studies which follow this introduction have not been chosen because they are round pegs to be fitted neatly into the round theoretical holes already outlined. Counter-terrorism, sentencing, drugs policy, public order policing and so on, reflect some of the major criminal justice challenges for government over the past 21 years and, as such, have been the subject of intense media scrutiny. Although facets of Jones and Wolfe's four theories can be found in the intersection of media and policy in each of these areas, it is apparent that no off-the-shelf model will provide us with the means to fully understand the relationship.

Take the example of drugs strategy, where, arguably, agenda-setting might be thought to be most strongly at work in corralling the policymakers within a narrow legislative space which refuses to countenance decriminalization or legalization. It is true that the agenda of certain influential newspapers like the *Daily Mail* seems to have weighed heavily with Prime Minister, Gordon Brown, and his Home Secretaries. But how does one explain the Blair administration's general inflexibility on drugs even at a time (admittedly a fairly brief period) when a majority of newspapers, including the *Mail*, were receptive to reform, if not actively advocating it?

Or, to take another issue, there is the theorizing on the 'populist punitiveness' (Bottoms 1995) which followed the murder of James Bulger. Was the media to blame for generating a discourse and thereby creating a 'manufactured and manipulated climate' (Scraton 2004: 138) which took it for granted that society's moral compass had gone askew? Or is this an example of indexing theory (Bennett 1990) writ large, with Tony Blair, a rising politician on the make, stamping his political vision on a media which had grown weary of a four-term Tory administration and was ripe for a new star to follow? His carefully crafted, faux lyrical, description of crimes such as the Bulger murder as 'hammer blows struck against the sleeping conscience of the country' was intended to be picked over in newspaper leaders and op-ed columns and it duly was.[4] It is equally true that the media demonization of youth, some no older than the Bulger killers, had begun well before Blair's emergence, as will be seen in Chapter 2.

This is not to suggest that criminal justice somehow defies the theoretical patterns which have helped to define this area of research. There appears to be much evidence for Koch-Baumgarten and Voltmer's contention that 'less established policy fields provide plenty of opportunities for new actors to enter the arena and they usually do this by mobilizing the media for their cause' (2010: 5). In the realm of public protection, especially dealing with sex offenders, there was undoubtedly a policy vacuum when New Labour came to power in 1997, which enabled 'new actors' (for example, Sara Payne, later to be appointed Victims Champion), in alliance with sections of the media (the *News of the World*), to galvanize legislative change in the form of the Criminal Justice and Court Services Act, 2000, which introduced Multi Agency Public Protection Arrangements (Silverman and Wilson 2002).

The corollary of this is that in policy fields where there is a 'high degree of path dependency and the dominance of civil servants, there is probably less media influence [on policy]' (Koch-Baumgarten and Voltmer 2010: 5). This is an accurate characterization of the Home Office of the early 1990s, where Oxbridge-educated mandarins such as David Faulkner[5] held sway. It took the arrival of Michael Howard and a tabloid media seeking to discredit some of the liberal certainties underpinning the Criminal Justice Act 1991 to clear a pathway for policy change of the 'prison works' variety[6] (see Chapter 5 for a more detailed exposition).

This period of the 1990s is also a good example of what Koch-Baumgarten and Voltmer call 'interpretative communities', in which a two-way interaction between policymakers and 'elite' journalists influences the formation of policy (ibid.: 4). Michael Howard admits to exploiting newspaper revelations about 'lax' offender supervision to impose more stringent requirements on the probation service (Interview with author, 9 July 2008). While the commentator, Nick Cohen, found to his surprise that what had been intended as an ironic comment during a phone conversation in 1996 with the then shadow Home Secretary, Jack Straw, about curfews for 10-year-olds, quickly transmuted into official New Labour policy (Cohen 1999: 2–3).

Mediating emotional governance

In its methodology, this research – a thesis based on a series of semi-structured interviews with policy 'actors' – is in the spirit of some of the work done by Aeron Davis on the media–politics nexus (Davis 2007a, Davis 2007b). Davis concludes that:

> Politicians use news and their interactions with journalists to get other sorts of information that are relevant to the political process on a day-to-day level. The two also combine, sometimes consciously in alliances and sometimes by playing off each other, to influence political agendas and the search for policy solutions.
>
> Davis 2007a: 194

There are any number of examples from the recent history of criminal justice which bear witness to this media–politics symbiosis. But underlying the surface arguments over ASBOs, control orders and DNA databases, one can often detect deeper currents. Adopting a psychological approach and writing in the context of terrorism, Barry Richards uses the term 'emotional governance' to describe the deliberate attention paid by politicians to the emotional 'dynamics' of the public (Richards 2007). It is a useful theme which will be explored in more depth later in this book. The reason for highlighting it here is that, under New Labour, there was an almost perfect congruence between the empathic style of leadership – Blair as Prime Minister and, during 2001–4, David Blunkett as Home Secretary – and a media increasingly confessional in tone, in which opinion, no matter how rancorously ill-informed, lorded it over fact-telling. As Blunkett puts it: 'almost imperceptibly, the British print media (and gradually, the broadcast media) had moved away from reporting fact and moved instead into opinion. I am afraid that democracy is the worse for it' (Blunkett 2006: 293).

Like the dinosaurs, the Douglas Hurds of politics had no chance of surviving the media climate change. In this new ecology, the way to prosper was by 'feeling the pain' of the voter or citizen, as David Blunkett explains in interview. And although he, too, had a limited lifespan and could not cheat the avenging media when his tangled love life became the story rather than his policies, he did, at least, enjoy the satisfaction of purveying opinion himself when he was employed as a columnist for the *Sun* in 2005.

One of the earliest policy expressions of 'feeling the pain' was almost a literal one – the rise to prominence of the 'victim' in criminal justice thinking. Like many developments which are associated chiefly with New Labour, victim discourse began to be taken seriously in the Home Office towards the end of the Major premiership (the Victims Charter was introduced in February 1996).[7] As Home Secretary, Michael Howard consistently presented himself as the champion of the victim of crime but his perceived lack of empathy failed to carry the message much beyond Tory Party conferences. So, like a rough diamond, the idea of privileging the victim in policy formation awaited refining by those better equipped to exploit its potential political allure. No one was more adept at that than Tony Blair.

Putting victims 'at the heart of the criminal justice system' – by, for example, introducing into court proceedings victim impact statements and the appointment of a Victims Commissioner (the aforementioned Sara Payne) – is about public confidence rather than a means of making the system run more efficiently. It is an illustration of the 'message-sending' aspect of governing, which has run alongside the stated commitment to evidence-based policymaking. For Geoff Mulgan, it is a proper function of democracy that governments should sometimes ignore sound evidence and follow a contrary route. He cites the issue of police numbers, where there is little of substance to suggest that more officers on the beat will help cut crime, but a clearly expressed desire by the public for more visible policing (Mulgan 2003: 10).

In the early 1990s, Conservative Home Secretaries were faced with what appeared to be the same choice between evidence and 'emotion' when presented with findings from the Audit Commission that police officers on foot patrol were not a cost-effective form of deployment, even if they reassured the public (Audit Commission 1990). The politically significant aspect of this finding was public confidence. Yet, despite a plethora of media stories that the police were losing control of the streets, the government opted to surrender the power to set numbers in the Police and Magistrates Court Act 1994, and to put budgets in the hands of Chief Constables, who gave priority to updating their fleets of patrol cars and other hardware.

Given the centrality of police numbers to the party political debate post-2000, this policy phenomenon, so different from the route taken by New Labour, is puzzling. It is only part of the answer to say that, deep in a recession, the Tories were counting the pennies and looking primarily at the bottom line. The larger truth is that the administration of John Major had used up the 'emotional govern-ance' capital which had given Mrs Thatcher such longevity and could not spot an issue which might help re-connect it with a disillusioned populace. By contrast, at the end of the 1990s, Home Secretary Jack Straw was making profligate pledges to boost police numbers to record levels, notwithstanding knowing, as a statistician, that they would have little or no bearing on the crime figures.[8] (This issue is dealt with more fully in Chapter 9.) But what goes around comes around, and a decade later, when Gordon Brown encountered a mildly disillusioned Labour voter while campaigning in Rochdale and called her 'that bigoted woman', the world realized that New Labour's hard-won capital had also drained away to nothing.[9]

Conclusion

Anyone who has worked in the media during the last decade will almost certainly have spent a great deal of time navel-gazing. In such a notoriously self-obsessed world, this is not new. But what is different is that, in the face of a devastating series of mainly technological and economic changes, practitioners have been forced to lift their eyes from the perennial argument about whether journalism is a trade or a profession, to consider larger, more fundamental questions about the place of reporting in a democratic society. If any one book seems to have caught this zeitgeist it is *Flat Earth News*, a broadside against what the author terms 'churnalism', the unreflective regurgitation by overworked reporters of press releases and handouts in place of independent inquiry (Davies 2009).

Davies's analysis is certainly correct but it raises a pertinent question of aeti-ology. Did changes in the media make inevitable this relentless spewing out of 'soft' stories and spin, which news outlets greedily lap up? Or has the policy diar-rhoea of government helped change the character of the media, making it more difficult for it to see the wood for the trees, to separate the significant from the ephemeral? 'A good day to bury bad news' may have been one of those sugges-tions dashed off unthinkingly in an email, but it carried a toxic legacy for New Labour.[10] One example is that in 2006, frustration that the Home Office was in the habit of issuing a deluge of research reports on the same day each month boiled over into a rare letter of complaint from the Home Affairs 'lobby' of correspond-ents. It is worth quoting from:

> Yesterday [March 30 2006], there were eight papers published on your website, including major sets of figures on race, crime and motoring offences. They totalled 550 pages of complex data – all, of course paid for by the taxpayer. The documents were issued just half an hour before the Home Secretary held a press conference on the Identity Cards Bill gaining Royal Assent. ... Additionally, your department issued material on the extension of drug testing on arrest to 14 more police forces, and on controversial restructuring of the probation service ... This leads many of us to fear that the practice has been instituted deliberately to 'bury bad news'.
> Confidential letter from the Home Affairs lobby to Julia Simpson, Home Office Director of Communications, 31 March 2006[11]

As part of the research for this book, the Home Office was asked to supply a copy of every press notice it had issued between 2001 and 2009. The several large boxes which arrived contained 3,214 releases and probably would have been at least double that had the department not been divested of many of its functions – prisons, offender management, sentencing and so on – when the Ministry of Justice was formed in May 2006. Many of these press notices are repeat announcements of something the Home Office had already publicized in one form or another. Whether this over-feeding was intended to give Tony Blair's 'feral beast' bulimia and skew its judgment about what was important and what was not is a matter of conjecture. But, sometimes, too much information can be as unsettling as too little.

2　The media and the punitive gene

Where did it all begin ?

Asked to choose a single year on which late modern UK policy on crime and justice pivoted, many criminologists would plump unhesitatingly for 1993 and the lurch into 'populist punitiveness' (Bottoms 1995) precipitated by the murder of James Bulger. This study is not an exercise in revisionism but it is an attempt to frame a fresh policy equation, with the media as one of the constituent variables. In that light, just as a later chapter holds up a lens to the responses to 9/11 and argues that they were rooted in a distinctive New Labour paradigm about crime and society, so it is necessary to begin with the 'back story' to the political and social response to the Bulger killing. In that story, the media played a role which has not always been given due weight. In some ways, this is surprising, given that the stridency of media representation of youth crime is clearly evident in the 'emerging ground-tone of state attitudes towards young people', which noticeably began to change post-1990 (Wayne *et al.* 2008: 76).

For Wayne *et al.* 'the early 1990s saw a significant shift in the framing of young people in news media – notably the linkage of youth and crime within the British news media' (ibid.: 76). Tim Newburn and Beatrix Campbell are more precise in identifying both the time and place at which this phenomenon emerged. Campbell locates the catalyst as the Ely estate in Cardiff where there was a serious confrontation between local youth and the police in August 1991. Like a chain reaction, other estates, previously unfamiliar to the national media, where there was a high concentration of disaffected young people – for example, Blackbird Leys (Oxford) and Meadow Well (Tyneside) – also had their spasms of violence.

Newburn writes: 'From mid-1991 onwards, stories started to appear in the press about youngsters who, it was believed, were so involved in crime that they accounted for a significant proportion of juvenile crime in the areas in which they lived' (Newburn 1996: 69). The high-water mark of what he calls 'open season in the press' (ibid.: 70) on young – in many cases, very young – miscreants was the autumn of 1992. And what is most notable is that the newspapers, both tabloid and broadsheet, began to focus on individual offenders and their misdeeds. Typical was this offering from the *Daily Mail*, under the headline, 'One-boy crime wave': 'He was only 11 when his life of crime began with the theft of chocolate bars from a corner shop ... within two years, he had become a one-boy crime wave' (*Daily Mail*, 10 September 1992).

Suddenly, there was a media vogue for publishing photographs and describing the offending history of 11- and 12-year-olds in balaclavas, waving two fingers at the camera. The accompanying headlines left no doubt that these children, relatively few of whom were guilty of acts of serious violence, were somehow representative of a much wider social anomie. As the *Daily Star* put it, with typical understatement: 'Much of Britain is now facing a truly frightening explosion of kiddie crime' (*Daily Star*, 30 November 1992).

Neither should the impact of television news imagery be under-estimated. *BBC News* bulletins took to routinely illustrating stories about car crime with menacing shots of a youngster putting a brick through a vehicle window in order to steal valuables inside. The net effect was that the aforementioned 'ground-tone' had become an insistent drumbeat, which the policymakers could not ignore. The Home Secretary, Kenneth Clarke, told the Police Federation in October 1992 that 'there was a case for increasing court powers to lock up, educate and train them [i.e. juvenile offenders] for their own and everyone else's interest' (cited in Newburn 1996: 70). As Robert Reiner has argued: 'media representations tend to exaggerate the threat of crime and to promote policing and punishment as the antidote. This is likely to accentuate fear, and thus support for law and order policies' (Reiner 2002: 407).

Although the kind of reportage of juvenile offending which emerged in the early 1990s has become commonplace in the two decades since, one has only to rewind the clock by the same length of time, to the early 1970s, to notice a different tone and a different impact. As Bob Roshier points out in a study of newspaper coverage, in that period, despite a growing media preoccupation with crime, 'very little information was usually given about offenders ... there certainly seems to be very little evidence of any direct influence by the newspapers on their readers' views' (Roshier 1973: 33–8).

But by the end of 1992, the potency of media images of young joyriders and youthful ram-raiders, had, in a sense, overwhelmed a more mature consideration of crime. It had certainly marginalized a debate taking place within the Home Office about the official recorded crime statistics. In 1989, the TV executive, Michael Grade, in an unfamiliar role as government-appointed chair of a committee on fear of crime, recommended that one way of diluting the impact of media 'simplification, over-dramatisation and sensationalism' was to release the official figures half yearly instead of quarterly. His reasoning was that the more frequent publication of the figures was an excuse for the media to indulge in another bout of scaremongering (Home Office Standing Conference on Crime Prevention 1989: 23–4).

By 1992, the commentator Simon Jenkins, provoked by what he considered alarmist reaction to the latest recorded statistics, was writing: 'I repeat, these figures are rubbish. They mean nothing. They are devoid of sense. They should not be collected' (*The Times*, 30 September 1992).

He was partly right. It was not that the statistics were totally unreliable (though neither were they wholly reliable). It was that the media tended to cherry-pick those elements of the figures which accorded with its own narrative on crime. Thus, the received version was that youth crime was out of control even though the recorded police figures 'suggested that recorded crime by young people was actually going down at this time' (Hagell *et al.* 2000: 11).

The plotlines for a policy response having been laid out, in November 1992 the Commons All-Party Home Affairs Committee instigated an inquiry into juvenile offending. From that point, there is a clear linear connection to the announcement by the Home Secretary Kenneth Clarke, in March 1993, that the government was introducing a new Secure Training Order for 12–15-year olds who were 'a menace to the community'.[1]

The media-led identification of early years teenagers with lawless amorality, encapsulated in the label 'feral youth', clearly made a big impact on Tony Blair; and a long-lasting one. The 2007 speech, in which he called the media 'feral', discussed in the previous chapter, was an echo of this preoccupation, which in the early 1990s had nourished New Labour's gestating Project. Seven months before the murder of James Bulger, while he was still shadowing the employment brief, Blair had written a two-thousand-word opinion piece in the *Mail on Sunday*, headlined 'If society doesn't care, who will?' In what amounts to an early manifesto for communitarianism (*pace* the American social scientist, Amitai Etzioni), he yoked together the latest 'horrendous' crime figures and what he called an 'atomised' society:

> Many people of an older generation in my constituency are appalled at the level of crime: that they can't leave their back door open as they used to; or walk down a street without abuse ... But the issue of rising crime is merely a symptom of a deeper failure to think of ourselves as, and to act as, a community ... Crucial to a modern idea of community are the rights and the responsibilities of the individual that accompany it.
>
> *Mail on Sunday*, 28 June 1992

It has been established that there was a significant media 'ground-tone' before the murder of James Bulger, which paved the way for radical policy change. But it takes what Dearing and Rogers call the 'trigger event' to push a policy to the top of the Whitehall agenda (Dearing and Rogers 1996). Ed Owen started working as Jack Straw's policy adviser in 1993. With Tony Blair's office only feet away on the other side of the Commons corridor, he observed how the two began to stitch together a coherent strategy for government:

> There is no doubt that Tony [Blair] changed the terms of the debate on crime and anti-social behaviour as shadow Home Secretary, although it is interesting that he told Jack that, for the first year in the post, he found it hard to get any traction with the media on issues he wanted to raise. After the Bulger murder, that all changed. But Tony is a big picture person, whereas Jack is most effective with the detail. And it was Jack who did all the detailed groundwork on youth justice – with Alun Michael, Ruth Allan and Norman Warner – and on changing the civil rules of evidence to

tackle persistent low-level offenders, which eventually became the Crime and Disorder Act 1998.

Interview with author, 1 October 2008

That Act abolished the ancient legal principle of *doli incapax*, a significant statement of New Labour's intent to apply the notion of 'responsibility' even to children as young as ten.[2] It was a reform which the Conservatives did not get around to making, even though it had been aired through the media, and it prompts again the question which has intrigued some criminologists: who fired the starting pistol which set off the penal arms race between the parties post-1993? Was it Straw and Blair or Michael Howard (Downes and Morgan 2002: 296–7)? For those, like Ed Owen, at the heart of the policy battle, the lines of cause and effect are inevitably blurred:

> It is very hard to say who influenced whom. Nothing operates in a vacuum and all of these influences are connected. Politicians like Blair and Straw were influenced by the media but also by public opinion, which they were continually gauging through constituency surgeries and so on. It is true that some newspapers were trying to lead popular opinion but it seemed to me at the time that the press and the political system were reflecting a real sense of unease about lawlessness and Jack tapped into this – even more than Tony actually.

ibid.

Straw himself, who, like Owen, had been a special adviser (to Barbara Castle, in his case) believes that addressing these concerns was a sign that New Labour was at last facing outwards to the 'community' (a term freighted with significance for his party, to which we shall return) and, in so doing, ridding itself of some unhelpful baggage:

> In opposition, we had become the clients of some articulate pressure groups. It is a great temptation for oppositions because bodies like the NCCL [later to become Liberty] and the Howard League had more research resources than we did in the 1980s, and would serve up position papers and so on, which we adopted. That is very dangerous for parties in opposition. For example, we opposed a reform like the Police and Criminal Evidence Act, even though it was a huge improvement on the Judge's Rules which had existed previously. ... By the 1990s, I had identified that English criminal law had a gap in it. It was very good at dealing with individual, acute incidents of criminality – like murder or robbery – but what it was no good at was addressing lower-level but continuous criminality, where any one incident would be regarded as relatively trivial but added together, they could wreak even greater misery on the victims than robbery or burglary.

Interview with author, 21 September 2010

Straw distilled his thinking on this issue into an important consultation paper, 'A quiet life – tough action on criminal neighbours' in the summer of 1995. What was to become the Anti-Social Behaviour Order is here called a Community Safety Order and critics would argue that this marks the start of New Labour's steady disavowal of due process, which was to lead to an unprecedented expansion of 'summary' justice after 2000, along with more corrosive consequences for civil liberties. This, for many, is one of the hallmarks of Tony Blair's legacy. Jack Straw has a more nuanced take on it:

> If you read Tony's book [*Tony Blair: A Journey*], it is evident that he is impatient with due process because it takes time. I have great admiration for him, and that's not flannel, but he and I had a difference of view about the importance of process. I believe that process gives you legitimacy. However, I completely reject the suggestion that ASBOs do not have process attached to them.
>
> ibid.

Jack Straw's defence of the ASBO in response to a question about respect for 'due process' is, perhaps, a clue to New Labour's casual attitude towards long-held legal precepts. As the former Lord Chief Justice, Lord Bingham, points out: 'The expression "due process", all but sacrosanct in American jurisprudence, derives from later translations of chapter 39 of Magna Carta'. As an aside, one can speculate that, although both Blair and Straw were barristers, the fact that Blair did not practise in criminal law put a distance between him and customary juridical procedure which was later mirrored by David Blunkett (a non-lawyer). By contrast, Jack Straw, notwithstanding the occasional sideswipe at lawyers and fellow 'Hampstead liberals', generally eschewed eye-catching shortcuts to achieve his ends.[3]

Exploiting crime

By 1995, home affairs had become a fiercely contested policy arena, perhaps the only one in which a fast-fading Conservative government was still not merely fighting its corner, but going on the attack with a stream of initiatives of its own. Mike Grannatt, a Whitehall veteran who served both Conservative and Labour administrations in sensitive roles, became head of communications at the Home Office in 1995:

> Michael Howard's inclination as Home Secretary was completely different from predecessors such as Willie Whitelaw and Douglas Hurd, who were said to have 'great bottom'. Their instinct was to sit back and see how far an issue rippled the political pond. Howard's instinct was to get on top of it straight away. He was a political animal to his toes. He was not a man who would recognize a 'state policy' – for example, like Northern Ireland. Everything was political. Crime was a big political issue because it resonated on the doorsteps and for him, if you made an impact on crime, you made an impact on politics.
>
> Interview with author, 12 October 2010

Perhaps not surprisingly, Grannatt views ministerial effectiveness through a presentational lens. By contrast, Douglas Hurd adhered to the convention that parliament had primacy over the media: 'I could not go on the *Today* programme and announce something before parliament knew. It just would not have happened then' (Interview with author, 21 July 2008).

The former *Times* lobby correspondent, Sheila Gunn – later to become John Major's personal press adviser – recalls an example of this scrupulousness working to her advantage:

> I was covering Home Office questions in the Commons during the miners' strike when Hurd suddenly announced a whole new raft of policing measures. I came out and told my political editor that I had a very good story. In fact it was my first front page splash. But at that time [1985], if MPs heard an announcement being made on the *Today* programme or indeed, anywhere outside parliament, points of order would be raised and there would be a huge fuss.
>
> Interview with author, 29 September 2008

But the key issue is the evident politicization of crime between the Hurd era and that of Michael Howard. Douglas Hurd has no regrets about what would now be considered his air of almost Olympian detachment:

> I remember making a speech about fear of crime being an evil in itself. I certainly didn't think of crime as a legislative or a party political matter ... We thought the law [on crime and justice matters] was about right.
>
> Interview with author, 21 July 2008

In 2010, at the end of an era in which more than fifty criminal justice bills were presented to parliament, the notion that a Home Secretary thought that the law 'was about right' and didn't need amending, is quite breathtaking – and refreshing. But Hurd's 'insouciance' was partly because, unlike his successors, he did not have the Prime Minister breathing down his neck on crime issues: 'To an extent which surprises me, the PM left me alone to cope with problems of law and order' (Hurd 2003: 341). A year after he moved to the Foreign Office, John Major became Prime Minister and 'he used to ring me at 7am on big issues. Mrs Thatcher did not' (Interview with author, 21 July 2008).

Interventionism from Number 10 is a factor which previous studies on the relationship between media and policy have not taken into account. If Robin Brown is correct in concluding that: 'The real significance of the media lies in what they tell policy actors and potential policy actors about the state of the politically relevant world' (Brown 2010: 138), then the fact that the Prime Minister or the Number 10 Strategy Unit has taken a direct hand or, at least, active interest, in a departmental policy area has an effect like a feedback loop. In other words, the PM's intervention gets picked up by – or, more usually, is deliberately leaked to – the media, whose reporting of the issue becomes part of the 'politically relevant world' and is an element in determining the urgency of a policy formulation. The street crime initiative instigated by Tony Blair in 2000, discussed in Chapter 6, is a good example of this syndrome at work.

This melding together of the interests of politicians and the reflexes of the media, which is not necessarily the same as 'collusion', is a phenomenon which came of age during the 1990s and has had profound consequences for public policy on crime and justice in the UK. As Alastair Campbell pointed out while still in government, the sheer growth of media has changed the nature of the media itself:

> In a noisy competitive [media] marketplace, it usually means that the noisiest is likely to get heard the most ... so papers do best, or feel they do best, to adopt positions and postures. I also think there's been a breakdown of the barriers between broadcasters, broadsheets and tabloids ... now they are very much in the same marketplace for news.
>
> Campbell 2002: 16

In the same critique, Campbell cited the wise observation made by the veteran Labour politician – and sometime Home Affairs spokesman – Gerald Kaufman: 'In government, you wake up and say: "What am I going to do today?". In opposition, you wake up and say: "What am I going to say today?"' (ibid.: 18).

In 1994, when he became New Labour leader, Tony Blair, in partnership with Campbell and Peter Mandelson, not only determined that he was going to say something but that, unlike his immediate predecessor Neil Kinnock, the way he said it would make him fireproof against the scepticism, mockery (and worse) of a largely hostile press. 'Competence with the media conveyed a general competence that was important to us in establishing ourselves as a competent government' (ibid.: 17).

As Blair battled, first against Michael Howard, and then against John Major, to establish his presentational competence (indeed, before long, his utter supremacy), there was an equally significant conflict going on behind the scenes in the respective news operations to take advantage of this expanding media, hungry for exclusives, previews of forthcoming attractions, and the odd bit of blatant manipulation. From 1995, Mike Grannatt, in the Home Office, was at the heart of this struggle:

> It is always said that New Labour invented the famous news grid to manage communications and a forward diary. They did not. We invented it in the Home Office under Michael Howard in 1995. I suggested it to Mandelson after the election in 1997 when he was in charge of the Cabinet Office and he adopted it. But it began in government two years earlier and it was driven by Howard's wish to ensure that we were on top of the news agenda at all times.
>
> Interview with author, 12 October 2010

In government, 'success has a thousand fathers'[4] and paternity for a slicker, more pro-active news operation in the dying days of the Major administration can also be claimed by the deputy Prime Minister, Michael Heseltine. In 1995, the former *Times* parliamentary correspondent, Sheila Gunn, was plucked from the lobby to become John Major's personal press adviser:

Michael Heseltine had such good instincts about which stories were going to make waves and which would not and he decided that the Home Office would henceforth have to co-ordinate its announcements with Number 10. Every morning, at 8.30, he would chair a Cabinet committee that focused on news management. I was a member of it. And on Wednesdays, we would have a meeting in the ministerial office at the House of Commons, down in the basement, to plan the week ahead. This was the real beginning of press co-ordination right across Whitehall.

Interview with author, 29 September 2008

For the Home Office press operation, the triple alliance of Michael Howard and Mike Grannatt within, and Michael Heseltine without, had the electric impact of a cattle prod jolting it out of its previous torpor. And it had got into bad habits, as Sheila Gunn recalls from her time as a lobby journalist:

There used to be this dreadful business of press officers going home at half past five. There would be a duty person but often he or she would be travelling, so you could not reach them until nearly seven. These are crucial times for daily newspaper journalists. And if you did get hold of someone to put your query to, they would say 'that comes under the police desk, not my remit' ... And their general attitude to the media, well, it may be going too far to say they thought of journalists as the enemy but they were very nervous of them. ... The point is that none of them had had formal training as press officers. They had tended to come from regional papers or the Press Association. And their idea of strategy was to track down the right person to provide a comment to a journalist's inquiry but to say as little as possible really.

ibid.

Thus, despite Michael Howard's best efforts to go on the front foot, with legislation such as the Crime Sentences Bill (characterized by the tag, 'three strikes and you're out'), New Labour made considerable headway with the media, as Ed Owen acknowledges:

Was it easy to get coverage? No, we still had to work pretty hard. I can't say that there were a whole lot of journalists willing to regurgitate stuff fed to them by us. But inevitably, because there was a general feeling that we were going to win the election, which was only two years away, people were more interested in what Labour had to say than maybe they had been two or three years earlier. In that sense, I had a ready audience.

Interview with author, 1 October 2008

And the audience was more receptive because the expansive, opinion-driven media which had been developing through the 1990s was an ideal platform for New Labour's apparently more holistic prescription for addressing crime, disorder and social breakdown.

English exceptionalism explained?

The Cambridge-based American criminologist, Michael Tonry, begins his book *Punishment and Politics* with this question: 'Why is England the only major Western country whose government has chosen to emulate American crime-control policies and politics of the past quarter century? It is puzzling' (Tonry 2004: vii).

On one level, it is not so puzzling. When New Labour strategists returned from observing and, in some cases, participating in Bill Clinton's triumphant presiden-tial campaign in 1992, they packed one important lesson in their bags: 'never be outflanked on the right'. As a core principle, it may not have been written into the constitution like Clause Four but henceforth, it became a boilerplate of every policy of The Project. Tony Blair's essential contribution was to smoothe off some of the flintier edges of Clintonian crime policy – Clinton's authorizing of the execution of a mentally ill felon in his home state of Arkansas during the prima-ries was perhaps the most egregious example – and convert it into an appealing sales pitch for the British electorate, under the mantra 'tough on crime, tough on the causes of crime'.[5]

But in case 'tough on crime …' seemed just a little too much like a sound-bite in search of a Big Idea to give it some heft, another American proposition, with a more substantial pedigree, was available to re-tool for Middle England – communitarianism. The value of this concept, conceived by Amitai Etzioni, was its political malleability. For John Major, it dovetailed with his own belief in 'social responsibility'. In Blair's hands, it transmuted into The Third Way, strongly influenced by the Scottish theorist, John Macmurray, who combined 'Christian socialism and a conservative critique of the individualistic worldview of liberalism' (Fairclough 2000: 37–8).

Reduced to its core elements of 'rights and responsibilities', it found a welcoming home in a wide spectrum of the British press. But those who both-ered to read Etzioni's original 'sacred text' ('The Responsive Community: Rights and Responsibilities' cited in *The Spirit of Community* 1995), might have had a foretaste of the punitive medicine which New Labour would prescribe when in government. Here is Etzioni, warning that the UK was sliding towards the 'levels of moral anarchy' of the United States:

> Increases in rates of violent crime, illegitimacy, drug abuse, children who kill and show no more remorse, and yes, political corruption, are all indications … The best time to reinforce the moral and social foundations of institutions is not after they have collapsed but when they are cracking. Does anyone truly believe that they have not yet cracked in the United Kingdom?
>
> Etzioni 1995: xxi

A dependence on such an alarmist diagnosis could lead in only one direction. And it is difficult to disagree with Bill Jordan when he writes that New Labour policy 'was forged in an atmosphere of moral condemnation and mistrust', relying on 'top-down, authoritarian methods to achieve its ends' (Jordan 1999: 203).

So, to return to Michael Tonry's question, it is not surprising that Etzioni's analysis of Britain's ills, applied first by the Conservatives and then, with more intensity, by New Labour, led to an apeing of many US policies, such as harsher prison regimes and mandatory minimum sentences. But quite reasonably, Tonry also wants to know why: 'England's [sic] government employs the most hyperbolic anti-crime rhetoric of any in Europe, language that elsewhere characterizes xenophobic right-wing fringe parties' (Tonry 2004: vii–viii).

Tonry terms this phenomenon 'English exceptionalism', and he posits the argument that what unites British and American culture is 'a deeper strain of moralistic self-righteousness and punitiveness towards deviance and deviants' (ibid.: 64). He describes this thesis as 'speculative' but the argument advanced in the opening chapter of this study should give him retrospective comfort. He has hit on something and it is only a surprise that he did not follow the trail further to see where the media fitted into this essentialist tableau.

Pick up any copy of the *Daily Mail* or the *Sun* and you will be confronted by a parade of Jungian archetypes – the family as nurturing, the jobless as 'workshy' and so on – which cannot be detached from the 'politically relevant world' of today's Britain (Brown 2010). True, the United States has a tabloid press but its role in policy debates cannot be compared to that of the UK, which, if not unique – Australia's runs it close (students of Rupert Murdoch's career will not be surprised at the parallel) – undoubtedly serves as an influential artery of public discourse. In conjunction with an adversarial justice system and an electoral politics that was played to a winner-takes-all set of rules, its framing of issues has to be taken into account.

If the thesis advanced in this study is correct, then the crucible for the 'English exceptionalism' of which Tonry writes is the period of the early to mid-1990s when the media was expanding and evolving rapidly and the political class was searching for a new philosophy to underpin policy. Given Michael Howard's own 'obsession with the United States' (Crick 2005: 96), it is tempting to speculate about what would have happened had the Conservatives, against the odds, won the 1997 election and remained in power. After all, despite New Labour's attempt to re-write history, the steady downturn in recorded crime began in 1995. Would the hypothetically victorious Tories have also 'discovered, so to speak, a new territory of concern, and a beguiled public found a new crime-wave replacing the old'? (Mooney and Young 2006: 399). In other words, would anti-social behaviour have had the same totemic significance for the Conservatives as it did for New Labour?

We will never know the answer to that 'what if?' question. But we do know the pattern of policy from the mid-1990s onwards and can make some interpretative judgments based upon it. And reading the emerging policy on crime and disorder, one can detect the palimpsest of a new contract between society and the individual, which has had profound consequences. The work that Michael Howard sketched in outline was developed more fully by Blair and Straw, and the result was the re-drawing of the contours of civil rights around the notion of community.

For most of the twentieth century, politicians on both Left and Right would, if pressed, have been happy to stand four-square behind the former Master of the Rolls, Lord Donaldson of Lymington, when he declared: 'We have all been brought up to believe, and do believe, that the liberty of the citizen under the law is the most fundamental of all freedoms'.[6] Note the singularity of the word 'citizen'. It is not the community of citizens but the individual. Even in the most extreme of circumstances – global war or an ongoing terrorist threat from the IRA – it was accepted that the citizen was owed a duty of protection which, if not quite a cast-iron guarantee along the lines of Thomas Jefferson's 'unalienable rights',[7] was bolstered by three centuries of certitude in the central importance of individual liberties.

But faced with rising crime levels and mediatized pressure, a new equation of liberty was modified for the 1990s. In the hands of Howard, Straw and Blair, it can be defined as the right of the 'community' to be protected from the activities of the aberrant or suspect individual. It is evident in the Criminal Justice and Public Order Act 1994; achieves fuller expression in the Crime and Disorder Act 1998; and flowers exuberantly after 2000 with the Regulation of Investigatory Power Act, the Terrorism Act (Section 44) of that year, the Proceeds of Crime Act 2002 and a host of other legislation throughout the decade. Thus, by 2007, writing in the context of terrorism, Tony Blair could declare, with the same conviction as Lord Donaldson, that it was a 'dangerous misjudgment' to put civil liberties before security (Blair 2007b).

If Tony Blair is correct in labelling the media a 'feral beast', then it is an animal, which, with a few honourable exceptions, has shown its claws in fights of transient significance – and behaved like a tame pussy cat where erosion of fundamental civil liberties is concerned.

3   Politicians, media and judges

They fought the law – and who won?

The term 'judicial review' tiptoed into the media lexicon in the early 1980s when lawyers began to exploit new and simplified procedures for challenging administrative decisions on grounds of fairness. By the early 1990s, Home Secretaries, such as Kenneth Baker and Michael Howard, were being forced to respond to the admonishment of judges over departmental unlawfulness, and the seeds of a growing tension between the executive and judiciary were sown. In the field of crime and terrorism it has been an undercurrent of British policy discourse for the past twenty years. The Lord Chief Justice at time of writing, Lord Judge, has said 'a degree of tension is healthy' (House of Lords Select Committee on the Constitution 2007: 16), while the former Lord Chancellor, Lord Mackay of Clashfern, believes 'a certain degree of tension … is inevitable and healthy' (ibid.). But tension, some of it expressed via the media, some of it exacerbated by the media, has undoubtedly strained the constitutional relationship between judges and politicians.

From the judicial bench, there is resentment at what is viewed as an ill-informed 'running commentary' from certain Home Secretaries on sentencing decisions. The former Lord Chief Justice and senior law lord, Lord Bingham, was no doubt speaking for the majority of his judicial brethren when he wrote, with studied understatement, that 'public and political comment are not a sure guide' to the challenge of a sentence (Bingham 2010: 54).

From the politicians, as we shall hear, there was a gathering conviction during the New Labour years that it was not merely an expedience to vent their concerns through the media but a duty on behalf of society as its elected representatives. From this conflict, there is a bundle of 'grievances' to be separated and examined but one unifying thread is the media framing of issues around its own preoccupations – the weakening of parliament's sovereignty, the perceived bias of the courts towards the human rights of convicted prisoners, asylum seekers and suspected terrorists, the inadequacies of legal due process in the face of new and unprecedented security threats, and so on.

Two examples illustrate the first two of these preoccupations. When the High Court ruled in May 2006 that nine Afghan nationals should have discretionary leave to remain in the UK under the Human Rights Act, the following day's *Daily Express* ran this leader:

Using the European Convention on Human Rights as cover, Mr Justice Sullivan made a ruling which many will regard as tantamount to a judicial coup against Parliament. ... Britain's out-of-touch judges are increasingly using the Human Rights Act as a means of asserting their will over our elected representatives.

Daily Express, 11 May 2006

Three years earlier, the *Daily Mail* carried an editorial asserting that:

Britain's unaccountable and unelected judges are openly, and with increasing arrogance and perversity, usurping the role of Parliament, setting the wishes of the people at nought and pursuing a liberal, politically correct agenda of their own, in their zeal to interpret European legislation.

Daily Mail, 20 February 2003

Even the most cursory discourse analysis of those extracts captures certain words and phrases, which stand out as signifiers of a whole set of prejudices dear to sections of the press. 'European legislation' maliciously confuses, for many readers, the European Convention on Human Rights with the 'tyranny' of the European Union, which has its own court (of Justice) but is not a court of last resort in criminal or immigration cases. 'Liberal, politically correct agenda' is invariably cast as a counterpoint to the 'plain common sense' of British citizens frustrated by legalistic obfuscation. 'Judicial coup' attributes to the courts an overarching plan to subvert the will of parliament rather than an interpretative ruling by a professional adjudicator, paid to do precisely that.

It is hard to take issue with the House of Lords Select Committee on the Constitution when it recommended that: 'If the media object to a judgment or sentencing decision, we suggest they focus their efforts on persuading the government to rectify the legal and policy framework rather than "treating judges as fair game"' (House of Lords Select Committee on the Constitution 2007: 46). However, in acknowledging that the judiciary has 'assumed a more distinct identity' (ibid.: 15) as a result of both the Constitutional Reform Act and the Human Rights Act, the committee has given a partial explanation of why judges are increasingly 'treated as fair game' by the media.

It is also evident that, over the period covered by this study, the role of the judge has come under much greater and closer scrutiny and that senior judicial figures have emerged from the shadows to play a more prominent role in public discourse. The Lord Chief Justice in 1989, Lord Lane, while willing to hold 'regular meetings' with Douglas Hurd at the Home Office (Rozenberg 1994: 284), saw no need to engage with the media. Indeed, during his eleven years in post, he never gave a single media interview. By contrast, his successor, Lord Taylor, held a press conference on the day his appointment was announced in 1992 and spoke of 'making the judiciary more user-friendly' (*Guardian*, 26 February 1992).

Thereafter, successive Lord Chief Justices felt free to speak out on issues ranging from legal aid to minimum sentences, and in March 2011 the senior judge responsible for sentencing in England and Wales, Sir Brian Leveson, even took part in a radio phone-in programme to explain new sentencing guidelines.[1] Inevitably, as judicial figures emerged from the anonymity of their wigs and gowns, so, in turn, the media felt freer to put their decisions, whether on asylum seekers or inebriated drivers, under an increasingly harsh spotlight.

Perhaps that explains why some Home Secretaries have been unable to resist criticizing individual sentencing decisions; but does it exculpate them? David Blunkett places this trend in a larger context, which relates to the concept of 'emotional governance' outlined in the Introduction:

> I defend the right of the Home Secretary to speak on behalf of the people. After all, the judges have the Lord Chancellor at the Cabinet table to advocate on their behalf. But who do the public have, if not the Home Secretary? On the issue of crime, I was getting it in the neck at community meetings in Sheffield and the local papers were picking up on that and asking 'who is on our side?' That was the thing that touched me most. I would reply: 'I am on your side'.
>
> Interview with author, 8 October 2008

In one sense, by dividing representative functions into 'sides', Blunkett is mirroring the adversarial contest which takes place in any courtroom. But at a deeper level, it expresses what Robert Reiner has called a 'zero-sum contest between victims and offenders … a key feature of the currently dominant politics of law and order' (Reiner 2007: 19). By zero-sum is meant the assumption that what benefits the offender is inevitably detrimental to the victim. As an aside, this may be one reason why the more consensual approach of restorative justice has not made the headway which its advocates had hoped for under New Labour: because it sits uneasily with the shared instinct of media (not all media, obviously) and politicians to clearly attribute 'moral responsibility … and condemnation' (ibid.).

The commentator, Peter Oborne, argues that Blunkett fundamentally misunderstood the role of Home Secretary:

> Blunkett's view about sending messages is a really frightening thing. It is a confusion. His job is to make sure that law and order works. It is not to put himself at odds with the law, which is what he often did. When I was political editor of the *Spectator*, I was once at a dinner with Blunkett and Norman Tebbit [a leading right-wing member of Mrs Thatcher's government]. They got on so well, it was untrue. Neither understood the British concept of independent institutions – especially the judiciary.
>
> Interview with author, 14 December 2010

Certainly, within the delicate balance of Britain's unwritten constitution, Blunkett's argument carries risks. And it breaks down entirely when the judges, or an individual judge, is left with no one to 'advocate on his behalf': when the Lord Chancellor has joined forces with the Home Secretary and sections of the media to undermine the independence of the bench in order to tap into popular disapproval of a sentence. And, following the enactment of the Constitutional Reform Act in

2005, the case of the convicted paedophile, Craig Sweeney, exposed exactly this faultline in the relationship between executive and judiciary.

On 12 June 2006, Sweeney was sentenced to life at Cardiff Crown Court after pleading guilty to abducting and sexually assaulting a 3-year-old girl. It was an Indeterminate Sentence for Public Protection (IPP) and Judge Griffith Williams spelled out, in open court, that the minimum tariff (that portion of the sentence awarded for punishment and deterrence) would be five years and 108 days. He told Sweeney that he would be released only 'when and if there is no risk of you reoffending' (*Independent*, 13 June 2006). Two things then happened to provoke a *cause célèbre*. Within hours, the Home Secretary, John Reid, asked the Attorney-General to examine the sentence with a view to referral to the Court of Appeal on the grounds that the tariff 'does not reflect the seriousness of the crime' (ibid.). The following day's tabloid newspapers, their ire stoked up by Reid's response, launched a concerted broadside against the particular judge, and judges in general.

The *Sun* attacked: 'the arrogance of judges in their mink-lined ivory towers who leave the rest of us to cope with the real crisis of soaring crime' (*Sun*, 13 June 2006). The *Daily Express* described the judiciary as: 'deluded, out-of-touch and frankly deranged' and 'combining arrogance with downright wickedness ... [sentencing] now bears no relation at all to the seriousness of the crime' (*Daily Express*, 13 June 2006).

It would be easy to treat this simply as an egregious example of bad faith and to endorse the Lord Chief Justice's description of media comment as 'intemperate, offensive and unfair' (House of Lords Select Committee on the Constitution 2007: 19). After all, the leader writers on the *Sun* and *Express* knew full well that the IPP was designed with serious cases like Sweeney's in mind, where release was out of the question until the Parole Board was satisfied that the offender no longer posed a risk to the public. Moreover, as the judge explained, he was bound by sentencing law to give Sweeney a discount on the tariff for a guilty plea.

But it should not be forgotten that it was the Home Secretary who was first off the blocks with his attack on the sentence and his invitation to the Attorney-General, Lord Goldsmith, to intervene. Lord Woolf, the former Lord Chief Justice, was a member of the House of Lords Select Committee on the Constitution, which considered the Sweeney case during its inquiry:

> It takes a minimum of 36 hours, I would say, to get the full transcript from a trial so that you have the facts of a case and you can respond authoritatively. In fairness to Reid, he intervened without seeing the transcript so he didn't know that the judge had applied the legislation absolutely meticulously. The judge was right on the ball but you couldn't expect a politician to be on the ball. Neither did Reid know the consequences of legislation which his own government had passed. This is why talking about individual sentences is always a mistake for a politician.
>
> Interview with author, 11 May 2009

It would be an understatement to say that Lord Goldsmith was disturbed by this encroachment of the executive onto judicial territory:

I thought it was utterly inappropriate for a political minister to have made statements about an individual sentence. Separation of powers means you stay out of that. It is perfectly open to the Home Secretary, if he is unhappy about something, to refer it quietly to the law office and ask them to look at it. Then, it is approached on a dispassionate basis. But once a Home Office spokesman had briefed [the media], that raised it to a political level.

Interview with author, 14 November 2008[2]

Reid's predecessor, Jack Straw, was also perturbed about his heavy-handed comments on the Sweeney sentence:

It was ridiculous and I am highly critical of John for that. When I became Justice Secretary, I asked Gordon [Brown] for his support that no minister should go out and criticize judges. And I got it. This was for two reasons. In a democracy, the judiciary is independent of the executive and we had to respect that. But also, if we did start criticizing judges, or encouraged media criticism of them, then osmotically, that would start to be reflected in sentencing policy. And while I am in favour of firm sentencing, I am not in favour of filling up the prisons just for the sake of it.

Interview with author, 21 September 2010

John Reid's refusal to be interviewed for this book, noted elsewhere, means that it is not possible to hear his reasons for intervening in the Sweeney case so publicly. But there are several factors which clearly had a bearing. It was barely five weeks since he had replaced Charles Clarke in charge of a Home Office, which, famously, 'was not fit for purpose'.[3] Those who observed him at close quarters have commented (privately) that media presentation was at the forefront of his priorities. He even created a 'rapid reaction team' of mainly youngish press officers and installed them in a meeting room immediately outside his own office, so that his response to a breaking news story could be perceived to be immediate and dynamic.[4] And perhaps crucially, the day of the Sweeney sentencing was the same day that the *Sun* launched a campaign to sack ten judges who, it claimed, were guilty of being 'soft' on 'killers, child sex beasts and rapists' (*Sun*, 12 June 2006).

This will be discussed in more detail in Chapter 4, which deals with public protection. Suffice to say, at this point, that the Sweeney sentence provided the new Home Secretary with an irresistible opportunity to show that he was on the side of the tabloid media and 'public' by taking to task an 'out-of-touch' judge.

Contrary to the impression frequently given by sections of the media, the modern judiciary is not so unworldly that it is completely unprepared for Home Secretaries to comment on sentencing issues, with a public audience in mind. Sir David Latham was vice-president of the Court of Appeal Criminal Division from 2006 to 2009:

I do not criticize politicians for saying things about sentencing policy. They must have this right because parliament lays down the parameters in which sentencing takes place. But there is a problem when they comment on individual sentences when it is not entirely clear that they have understood what the case is all about. Indeed, I cannot remember a really critical comment by a politician about a sentence where they have actually understood what the case was about. The Sweeney case was a classic example of this. It is partly to do with the soundbite mentality. A soundbite tends to be just a reaction, not a thought-through comment.

Interview with author, 17 November 2010

But as the *Sunday Mirror* columnist Richard Stott pointed out, considered comment, let alone considered action, is increasingly seen as an unaffordable luxury in our mediated age:

Politicians surviving in a 24-hour, news-hungry, wall-to-wall goldfish bowl feel the pressure of immediate reaction that inevitably means a rush to judgment. Doing nothing is not an option, calm reflection a sign of weakness. Instant solution is all. Always be seen to be doing something, even if it is a 'wrong' something.

Sunday Mirror, 18 June 2006

There is another element to the Sweeney controversy which provides a measure of the remorseless advance of mediatized politics into the application of the law. This might be described as the case of 'the dog which didn't bark'.[5] Despite John Reid's widely reported comments on the day that Sweeney was sentenced, and remarks the following day by the Prime Minister's spokesman that Reid had been right 'to articulate the concern the public has', there was a deafening silence from the person whom the judges believed had a constitutional duty to defend their integrity and independence, the Lord Chancellor, Lord Falconer. It was three days before he made a public reference to the case, and even then, his defence of judicial independence was tempered by the curious claim that the Home Secretary 'did not attack the judge'.[6]

Commenting on this period in which the judges appeared to have been without a single high-level protector, the legal editor of the *Daily Telegraph*, Joshua Rozenberg, said that the Lord Chancellor had left them 'to swing in the wind' (House of Lords Select Committee on the Constitution 2007: 21). It is hard to disagree.

If one were entering pleas of mitigation on behalf of John Reid and Lord Falconer, it might be said that the one intervened in the Sweeney case almost as a reflex response, while the other stayed silent because he was still adjusting to the changes to the role of Lord Chancellor brought about by the Constitutional Reform Act 2005. What, then, of the performance of Lord Falconer's parliamentary secretary of state in the Department for Constitutional Affairs, Vera Baird QC? A full four days after the furore provoked by comments about the Sweeney sentence, and, presumably, after sufficient time for cool reflection, she was on a radio programme, maintaining that:

this judge has just got this formula wrong, so I am critical of the judge for three reasons – one, starting too low [on the tariff scale]; two, deducting too much for the guilty plea; and three, getting the formula wrong.

Any Questions, Radio 4, 17 June 2006

Three days after that onslaught, Ms Baird was obliged to apologize for her comments, all of which were incorrect – although, even four years later, she was prepared to argue the point, with some vigour:

I felt that the judge, a resourceful, intelligent and experienced judge, should have expected the outcry which followed his sentencing. And he could have done more to explain the technicalities so that the public would have a better understanding of why he sentenced as he did. But the way the question was put to me on radio was: there is something wrong with the IPP sentence. And I must say that when I was told what Judge Williams had said in court, it appeared to me that he was actually having a go at the Labour government by implying that his hands were tied by the IPP sentence, which we had introduced.

Interview with author, 5 July 2010

Vera Baird's justification is worth interrogating. It gives succour to David Blunkett's attitude that the interests of executive and judiciary were (are) somehow inimical to each other. And it is a demonstration that, in Whitehall, attack is invariably seen as the best form of defence: in other words, accuse the judge of playing politics in questioning the structure of a sentence he was obliged to hand out, rather than admit that it was the Home Secretary's hasty intervention which had raised the stakes. She also – perhaps inadvertently, perhaps not – tinkers with the timeline so that it appears that John Reid was responding to press comment: 'I don't remember why [the issue] became so prominent but I think it was because it was so prominent in the media that there was a ministerial response' (ibid.).

Where Ms Baird has a point, though, is in suggesting that the judge 'could have done more to explain the technicalities'. Sir David Latham, too, argues that judges have a civic duty to explain, though he believes this battle was largely fought and won in the early 1990s:

It became apparent around 1992–3 that we would have to explain what we were doing, and why we were doing it, with much greater clarity than before. This was a lesson which most judges learned from unhappy experience. In other words, they would pass a sentence which was misunderstood by the press, or a sentence which was justified but nobody understood why you had passed it. So, although the general influence of the media has been malign, drawing the judiciary out of the shadows, so to speak, was a beneficial thing.

Interview with author, 17 November 2010

Sense, sentencing and sentiment

There is a compelling reason why, even when sentences have been carefully explained, influential sections of the media prefer their own narrative about crime and justice above any other. The newspaper with probably the surest touch in giving its 'core demographic' what it wants to read is the *Daily Mail*. Its long-serving editor, Paul Dacre, believes that, when it comes to sentencing, the public 'still have great faith in the judiciary but there are worries that it is not reflecting their values and instincts' (House of Lords Select Committee on the Constitution 2007: 45). That judges are expected to reflect something as amorphous as values and instincts (which, in any case, can hardly be shared by a population of some 62 million people) might strike one as perverse; except that this is quite frequently the language of modernist politics, artfully designed to fit into a newspaper head-line and to strike a popular chord.

'Rebalancing the criminal justice system' would surely appeal to any handyman who sees the point of a spirit level. And what decent citizen would argue with 'putting the sense back into sentencing'? The foremost authority on sentencing practice, Dr David Thomas QC, calls these 'meaningless slogans which have driven legislation for more than a decade' (Thomas 2010).

Several years earlier, Michael Tonry came to much the same conclusion by examining the unusually demotic language of the White Paper that preceded the Criminal Justice Act 2003 (Tonry 2004: 25–6). The chapter on sentencing begins: 'The public is sick and tired of a sentencing system which does not make sense' (Home Office 2002a: 86). As Tonry points out: 'Nowhere does the White Paper say why, or in what ways, the public believes sentencing "does not make sense" (Tonry 2004: 30). One assumes their disquiet is reflected mainly through the media, which is why his next observation, though correct in a narrow vein, perhaps misses a wider and more significant truth: 'In most ways, the English system of processing criminal cases closely resembles those of every Western country – the same kinds of functionaries, procedures, criminal laws, punishment options … If the English system doesn't make sense nor does that of any country' (ibid.).

A sentencing system which develops out of political contrivance is never going 'to make sense', if that term is considered semantically. A mathematical formula makes sense, once and always. A formula for delivering 'justice' is necessarily fluid, as one prevailing concern – whether it is abolishing the 'double jeopardy' rule or criminalizing forced marriage – gives way to another, and so on. But that is self-evident. The question to answer is this: Is there a factor which makes the English (or British) justice system more vulnerable to public dissatisfaction than its Continental counterparts? The commentator, Simon Jenkins, believes there is:

> In the UK and US, because of the jury system and a particularly lurid press [more so in the UK], we have got stuck in a 'lynch mob' rut over sentencing. In the US, the issue is capital punishment. In the UK, it is pressure for a very high rate of incarceration. But in both cases, it is a mildly hysterical reaction, fostered between the press and politicians. Whereas in most of Europe, juris-prudence tends to be regarded as a technical matter. It is dealt with almost

entirely within the judicial and penological profession. You don't get this hysteria in Scandinavia, Holland, Germany, etc. And it is because they don't have this adversarial judicial system. In the UK, the courts are so arranged that there is no fuzzy line between guilt and innocence.

Interview with author, 21 June 2010

Allowing for the Scottish verdict of 'not proven', it is a valid observation – up to a point. Jenkins believes that the jury system 'is disastrous and feeds a much higher profile for crime in public discourse, to which politicians tend to respond and on which the media plays' (ibid.). One can agree with the second part of that sentence without endorsing the conclusion in the first part, which is that we should scrap juries. Even if their verdicts do not always make sense, juries validate the delivery of 'justice' in a way which a professional judge sitting alone cannot do because of the constraints of statute and precedent.[7]

But the issue is not whether the jury is a good or a bad thing. Nor is it whether the adversarial process is more inimical to what Thomas calls a 'dispassionate rational analysis of the problems' (Thomas 2010) than an inquisitorial one. It is that the combination of a binary system of justice, a binary form of politics (until 2010) and media which often delight in binary archetypes is going to place inordinate strain on the task of applying sense to sentencing. If that analysis is sound, then who should take responsibility for leading us out of this maze? Simon Jenkins is in no doubt:

It is the politicians' duty to take the media as it is and bend it to their will. Politicians know this to be true. But they're scared of the press. Look at all those ministers who used to be members of civil liberties groups but now will not confront the tabloid press on crime and justice issues. I've had this conversation with Jack Straw about drugs. He says: 'Better talk to the *Daily Mail* not me'.

Interview with author, 21 June 2010

But real cases present politicians, whatever their intentions, with hard choices. In the Sweeney controversy, Vera Baird insists that her intervention was not motivated by the same populist instinct as that of John Reid:

My position was not his, which was simply: 'this is a soft sentence which is making people in my constituency angry'. My take on it was different. By the time I made my comments, the issue was no longer an outcry against a judge but on the IPP sentence which the *Daily Mail* would have spun as, 'only a small amount of time in prison, with the rest of the sentence in the hands of unspecified social worker types' who are not necessarily representative of 'white van man'. I intervened because I thought the judge was not doing what he should have done to safeguard the integrity of the IPP sentence against cheap attack by the media.

Interview with author, 5 July 2010

We will return to the problematic issue of the Indeterminate Sentence for Public Protection in the next chapter.

It is good to talk?

Generations of democratic politicians have, from time to time, grappled with Benjamin Franklin's (crudely paraphrased) observation that those willing to trade liberty for security deserve neither. But after the events of 9/11, the nettle had to be grasped almost as a daily test by Home Secretaries. David Blunkett calls it a 'continuing theme' of his time as Home Secretary and finds it incomprehensible that senior judges refused to engage in discussions about finding the correct balance between the nation's security and the provisions of the European Convention on Human Rights (Blunkett 2006: 323). Charles Clarke regarded it 'as disgraceful that no Law Lord is prepared to discuss in any forum with the Home Secretary of the day the issues of principle involved in these matters. The idea that their independence would be corrupted by such discussions is risible' (House of Lords Select Committee on the Constitution 2007: 26).

The case which brought this deadlock fully out into the open was the so-called 'Belmarsh ruling' by the Law Lords in December 2004 that declared unlawful the indefinite detention without trial of twelve foreign-born terror suspects.[8] Coming only twenty-four hours after Charles Clarke became Home Secretary, the judgment found that Part 4 of the Anti-Terrorism, Crime and Security Act 2001 was incompatible with Article 5 of the European Convention on Human Rights. Not surprisingly, Clarke made his most urgent priority the rescue of a centrepiece of his government's anti-terrorism strategy. As he explained in a press interview, given after the 7/7 bombings:

> [Being] unable to defend ourselves against a potential terrorist would create an almost unstoppable pressure on politicians. People would ask whether we were really saying that adherence to the European Convention was more important than Joe Bloggs blowing up a Tube train. In those circumstances, there would be immense pressure to change our relationship with the European Convention on Human Rights.
>
> *New Statesman*, 26 September 2005

A superficial reading would suggest that this was framing the issue in very much the way it had been framed by a large section of the media – from which the 'unstoppable pressure' was continuing to come. He could have posited the puzzlement of the ordinary citizen rather differently and asked whether 'we were really saying' that adherence to MI5's refusal to countenance the use of intercept evidence in a criminal trial was 'more important than Joe Bloggs blowing up a Tube train'. Yet Clarke was anything but an unashamed populist and in his later evidence to the House of Lords Select Committee on the Constitution, one can see a more nuanced approach. He says that the attitude of the Law Lords (to entering into a dialogue with the government over tackling terrorism) has to change because: 'It fuels the dangerously confused and ill-informed debate which challenges Britain's adherence to the European Convention on Human Rights' (House of Lords Select Committee on the Constitution 2007: 26).

At the time he gave his evidence, the debate, fuelled by sections of the media, had led the Conservatives to take up the mantle of a British Bill of Rights, which was 'cover' for an onslaught against the European Convention on Human Rights (ECHR). But this particular genie had been uncorked from the bottle by Clarke's predecessor, David Blunkett, who had consciously fostered a media profile as the 'People's Home Secretary' in opposition to a judiciary which was presented as wilfully snubbing popular sentiment. Clarke's comments were aimed as much at him as anyone.

While he was still in post, Clarke attempted to square the circle of keeping the UK within the ECHR, without imperilling the nation's security, by opening up a private channel of communication to the Law Lords. The approach was rebuffed on the grounds that it undermined the doctrine of separation of powers between executive and judiciary. Even five years later, with plenty of time for reappraisal, Clarke felt he was on the right side of the argument.

This is Clarke's account of what happened:

> After the Belmarsh ruling, I did try and meet Lord Bingham [the senior Law Lord] to discuss the principles involved. It was suggested to me that it would be OK if I went to a Law Courts dinner and was sat next to him 'socially'. I thought that was quite wrong and demeaning and I refused to go down that line. There were various soundings because I was advised that I should not make a direct request. The suggestion that there was a principle against this [meeting] seemed to me then (and seems now) absurd. Lord Bingham had been to Number 10 and met the Prime Minister for a lengthy discussion some while before. It seemed to me extraordinary that if we met and I raised something he thought it wrong to discuss, that he did not have the mental strength to refuse to discuss it.
>
> Email from Clarke to author, 9 January 2011

Lord Bingham, who died in 2010, declined a request for an interview for this research. But in 2005, in an interview with the *Daily Telegraph*, he gave his own version of a suggested meeting between Home Secretary and Law Lord, which he described as without precedent:

> I said: 'what is the purpose of this meeting?' because it is quite clear that there are some matters it would be quite inappropriate for the law lords to discuss. I said: 'I cannot believe that it is intended to be a purely social gathering.' The answer I was given was that it was to be a purely social meeting. One was perhaps a little sceptical. Whether sceptical or not, I took the view, having discussed it with at least one of my colleagues, that it was very unwise for such a meeting to take place, for the first time ever, at that juncture.
>
> Rozenberg 2005

Clarke was all the more puzzled by the rebuff because he had had a meeting with the Swiss President of the European Court of Human Rights, Luzius Wildhaber, 'to discuss these issues in principle' (Email from Clarke to author, 9 January 2011) and could not see why a similar meeting with Bingham would breach constitutional convention. (Perhaps this is confirmation of Simon Jenkins's theory that Continental jurisprudence is regarded through a technical rather than an emotional prism.) Clarke may also have believed that, as a Home Secretary who 'would never criticize a judge for a sentence' (Interview with author, 16 September 2010) he had earned the right to a measure of trust from the senior judiciary in return. But the true sticking point was his argument that the Human Rights Act 'qualitatively changes the relationship between the executive and the judiciary, particularly around many interpretations of the European Convention on Human Rights' (Email from Clarke to author, 9 January 2011).

Lord Bingham did not agree and nor did the House of Lords Select Committee on the Constitution (2007: 33):

> While we have sympathy with the difficulties outlined by Charles Clarke in relation to the Human Rights Act, his call for meetings between the Law Lords and the Home Secretary risks an unacceptable breach of the principle of judicial independence. It is essential that the Law Lords, as the court of last resort, should not even be perceived to have prejudged an issue as a result of communications with the executive.

Conclusion

Charles Clarke and David Blunkett were not the first, nor the last, Home Secretaries to wonder how they could be rid of 'meddlesome' judges and Law Lords. Perhaps the most serious attack by ministers on senior judges came in 2010 during Alan Johnson's stewardship of the Home Office when Binyam Mohammed, an Ethiopian-born resident of the UK, alleged in a court case that he had been tortured before being sent to Guantanamo Bay and that MI5 had colluded in his mistreatment. The government was defeated at the Court of Appeal and Johnson was furious that the Master of the Rolls, Lord Neuberger, drafted severe criticism of MI5 (though he was persuaded to redact it from the published judgment). In interview, Johnson framed his anger in terms similar to those used by his predecessor as Home Secretary, Jack Straw, when he was attacked over civil liberties:

> It is such a Hampstead dinner party argument that, because now we are such a transparent society, we do not seem to be able to live with a security service that, by definition, must do their work under cover. [Defending this in court] saps the morale of the security service and it ties up hundreds of officers doing the court work, whereas they should be out there defending the public.
> Interview with author, 7 July 2010

This case reinforces the general point that issues reach a pitch on the public and/or policy agenda in tune with the context of the times. The need to reconcile the

Human Rights Act with the security implications of 9/11 put Home Secretaries from 2001 onwards in a different position from that of their predecessors. The commentator Peter Oborne argues that New Labour's assiduous courting of the media also paid dividends:

> The anti-judiciary line did not start with New Labour. Michael Howard attacked judges and tried to get the media onside but he got very little traction for that. He was painted by the media as a bungling Home Secretary who kept getting the law wrong. So, very few people defended Howard when he was slapped down by the courts, as happened repeatedly. But because New Labour had such a good relationship with the media and had a lot of papers on their side, Blunkett got a lot of media support when he was in confrontation with the judges. Papers like the *Sun*, *Mail*, *Telegraph*, and *Times* all took the government's side in their war with the judges.
>
> Interview with author, 14 December 2010

Though Peter Oborne and Charles Clarke are not natural political bedfellows, they would share common ground in their analysis of the influence of the media. After he had been sacked as Home Secretary, Clarke gave a speech about his government's relationship with the media in which he said:

> the media are not simply chroniclers of events, they are themselves actors, and indeed, often very important actors … I have no doubt that media attitudes and threats have been decisive in influencing British attitudes to the European Union, in inhibiting reform of the criminal justice system … Some in the media attempt to escape the power which they hold. They argue that they only reflect society without influencing it, that they just observe and record. But I reject that case and believe that the media should behave in a way which takes account of the influence that it has on the society in which it exists.
>
> Clarke 2007

The commentator Simon Jenkins is sceptical about the 'influence' he wields but acknowledges that his role is not merely to hold up a mirror to society:

> It would be strange, if, as a columnist, you did not hope to influence policy. And it is true that the turbulence of public discourse about topics is infinitely greater than 20 years ago. No doubt about it. The blogosphere is churning stuff out all the time – usually just garbage … I regard the media as the weather, and politicians just have to deal with it.
>
> Interview with author, 21 June 2010

But sometimes, the weather can be so unremittingly hostile that it claims casualties. The media storms over failures in public protection, to be considered in the next chapter, inflicted damage not just on judges, probation chiefs, and the Parole Board – but on Home Secretaries themselves.

4 Protecting the public or protecting the politicians?

Dancing to the tabloid tune

In June 2006, the Chief Constable of Dyfed Powys, Terry Grange, accused the government of forming policy at the behest of tabloid newspaper agendas: 'This government has accepted the principle that they are prepared to be blackmailed', he told the BBC (*BBC News Online* 2006). As spokesman for the Association of Chief Police Officers on child protection, he was enraged at a decision by the Home Secretary, John Reid, to send a minister to the United States to look at the application of Megan's Law, requiring notification of sex offenders living in the community, to see if there were lessons for the UK.[1] Reid's announcement was made in the *News of the World*, which had been running a campaign to have sex offenders removed from bail hostels (or 'approved premises' as they were officially known) close to schools (*News of the World*, 18 June 2006).

Reid also pledged that, forthwith, the eligibility regulations for accommodation in bail hostels would be changed to exclude convicted sex offenders. This decision was taken on a Friday afternoon (16 June), following a meeting with representatives of the *News of the World* at the Home Office, and trumpeted on the front page of the newspaper two days later. Despite the proximity of timing, the Home Office rejected Grange's allegation, although Reid did not object – at least, not publicly – to being reported by the newspaper as saying: 'I have [also] asked the minister to study specifically the *News of the World*'s "Sarah's Law" proposals on controlled access to information' (ibid.).[2] Thus, at the very least, the Home Secretary was allowing the impression to be given to the country's largest newspaper readership that policy on a significant and emotive issue of public protection was in lockstep with that of a tabloid campaign. A highly placed official at the National Probation Directorate who, for reasons explained later in this chapter, wishes to remain anonymous, says of this episode:

> The *News of the World* told the Home Secretary that it had obtained details of the locations of bail hostels and was prepared to publish them unless he took action to remove sex offenders. The NPD view was: 'let them go ahead and publish'. It might result in a few bricks through windows but that happens anyway in the normal course of events. We were sure we could handle the fallout. But there was no appetite on the political side to stand up to the paper.

Of course, John Reid dressed this up by saying 'we've taken a principled stand on this' – but you can draw your own conclusions.

Interview with author, 4 September 2008

Terry Grange's conclusion was stark: that Home Office collusion had been obtained by tabloid bullying: 'The reality, as I perceive it, is that the only people with any real strategic intent and understanding on where they want to go, and the will to be ruthless in getting there, is the *News of the World*' (*Guardian*, 21 June 2006).

That John Reid, newly installed at a Home Office which had presided over spectacular failures in public protection (to be analysed later in this chapter) should seize on the issue of sex offenders to project an image of granite reliability, is an illustration of Hajer's argument that:

we have only limited creativity in thinking critically about how to handle situations in which the soft underbelly of governance is exposed, that is in which emotions run high, people strongly claim a superior right to speak over others (for example, as victims) or even claim a right to take things into their own hands.

Hajer 2009: 10

Even if banning child sex offenders from approved premises was a retrograde step in terms of rehabilitation and caused logistical difficulties for the probation service, the announcement gave the Home Secretary some breathing space in a climate of intensely mediatized criticism of the government. As the director of Liberty, Shami Chakrabarti, commented:

There is a very important but complicated relationship between the government and the mass readership newspapers. People spend a few pence on those newspapers but their votes are rather more expensive. It is right that the government listen to a range of views but ultimately, when they come to making policy, it must be done in a more rational way.

Guardian, 21 June 2006

In a dissection of that relationship between media and politicians over thirty years ago, Hall *et al.* used the term 'signification spiral' to describe the complex process by which a moral panic (Cohen 2002 onwards) is mediated and is then fed back to policymakers, so-called 'primary definers', who then devise policy on the strength of it (Hall *et al.* 1978: 15). In 2005/6, that process can be seen at work in the adumbration of policy on violent crime. The British Crime Survey (BCS) for the twelve months to December 2005 showed violent crime to be 'stable', although the police recorded a 1 per cent rise in the last quarter of 2005, which would not be regarded as statistically significant (Home Office 2006a). There had been other periods when, statistically, the increase in violent crime should have placed it higher on the policy agenda,[3] but perhaps few where the 'signification spiral' was as acute.

Human rights – shield or fig leaf?

It is a characteristic of the popular media that it likes to construct an ongoing narrative which its core readership can slip on like a favourite coat. Sometimes, it is a harmless, if risible, obsession with one seminal event. For the *Daily Express*, post-1997, it was, for many years, the strange certitude that Princess Diana was murdered as the result of a conspiracy. But sometimes the narrative is subtler and has a more malign influence on public discourse, with, as Meyer and Hinchman put it, 'the media's inexorable logic strongly influencing the way the political classes conduct themselves' (Meyer and Hinchman 2002: 66). In the last two decades, one can pick out both 'political correctness' and 'health and safety' as recurring media tropes which have been adopted almost unthinkingly by right-of-centre critics of deficiencies in public policy. And since 2000, one can add to these examples 'human rights'.

In the field of public protection, a potent addition to this reductive analysis was the report into the murder of Naomi Bryant in August 2005 by a serial sex attacker, Anthony Rice, who had been freed from prison under licence, only nine months earlier. The report, by the Chief Inspector of Probation, Andrew Bridges, was published in May 2006 and included the conclusion that 'in our view, the people managing this case started to allow its public protection considerations to be undermined by its human rights considerations' (HM Inspectorate of Probation 2006: 5). For the *Sun*, this was a vindication of its campaign to scrap the Human Rights Act 1998 (HRA), and two days after the Bryant report was published, the tabloid carried a front-page splash with the strapline: 'Murdered by human rights – Beast murdered woman after being freed to protect HIS human rights' (*Sun*, 12 May 2006).

It is no surprise that, in his annual report for 2007/8, an exasperated Bridges attacked the media for 'increasingly values-opinionated "position-taking"... making it increasingly difficult to conduct a rational debate on the criminal justice system' (Bridges 2008).

His view that the media should focus on 'mundane truths' rather than 'exciting fallacies' might have applied equally to government ministers. As soon as the tabloids had waved the red flag of the HRA in front of the public in the spring and summer of 2006, both Number 10 and the Lord Chancellor, Lord Falconer, who, in other circumstances, had hailed the Act as one of New Labour's landmark achievements, were swift to demonstrate their concern by indicating that it could be amended. In this way, a media fixation about human rights became one of the dominant policy themes of the decade. When the leader of the Liberal Democrats, Nick Clegg, accused the Justice Secretary, Jack Straw, of 'sly populism' in criticizing the HRA in 2008 as a 'villain's charter' his accusation could have been applied equally to the Conservatives under David Cameron (*Guardian*, 10 December 2008).

Indeed, once he had become Prime Minister, Cameron allowed controversy about two human rights rulings – one on votes for prisoners and the other relating to the Sex Offenders Register – to slip seamlessly into an 'assault' on Britain's sovereignty when, in reality, both cases were about effective rehabilitation of convicted criminals. Once again, the 'culprit', as far as large sections of the media and many backbench MPs were concerned, was the European Court of Human Rights in Strasbourg, although the ruling that convicted sex offenders had the right to some form of review to challenge indefinite inclusion on the Sex Offenders Register was made by the UK Supreme Court in April 2010 and did not go anywhere near Strasbourg.[4]

But the newspaper headlines and straplines set the terms of the debate: 'Paedophiles and rapists win right to wipe their names from register – because it could breach THEIR human rights' (*Daily Mail*, 22 April 2010).

So that, by the time that the coalition administration came to grapple with the consequences of the ruling, the issue had become a full-blown mediated controversy about the UK's continued membership of the European Convention on Human Rights: 'Should the UK leave the ECHR?' (*Mail Online* debate, 2 March 2011).

When the Home Secretary, Theresa May, stated that: 'Public protection must come first' (*Guardian*, 17 February 2011), she was signalling to her 'core support' that government policy would not be dictated to by European judges. But you don't need to be a semiotician to uncover another (no doubt, unintended) interpretation, exemplifying Hajer's theory of the 'politics of multiplicities':

> What is crucially new nowadays is that political actors must constantly reckon with the fact that what they say at one stage, to one particular public, will often, almost instantaneously, reach another public that might 'read' what has been said in a radically different way and mobilize because of what it heard.
>
> Hajer 2009: 9

In this case, both 'publics' could agree that the real issue was about minimizing harm. But one – decidedly not the coalition's 'core support' – would read that as an acknowledgement that, if the Sex Offenders Register is to retain its effectiveness as a safeguarding mechanism, the number of people who need to be on it has to be kept to manageable proportions. Otherwise, 'this higher volume of registrants simply silts up the system and little meaningful work is carried out' (Thomas 2009: 261). Thus, one audience sees human rights as the main event; the other, as a confected sideshow.

Managing risk

The Naomi Bryant case also, rather than being about human rights, was essentially about the management of risk. As were, to a greater or lesser degree, other high profile murders such as that of the Nottingham jeweller, Marian Bates in September 2003; the Chelsea banker, John Monkton, in November 2004; and the torture, rape and murder of 16-year-old Mary-Ann Leneghan in Reading in May 2005. Quite properly, all these cases received exhaustive media attention, not merely for the nature of the crimes themselves but for the flaws they had exposed in the supervision of dangerous offenders by the probation service and the competence of decisions taken on release by the Parole Board.

The significance for the government of these cases was that, with the highly publicized passage of the Criminal Justice Act 2003, and the creation of the National Offender Management Service (NOMS) in 2004, public protection had assumed a prominence on the policy agenda which increasingly made it a target for hostile media scrutiny, with attendant dangers for justice. The senior law lord, Lord Bingham, drew attention to the implications of the public 'hue and cry' about high profile crimes, as early as July 2003, when he gave the annual Ditchley Foundation Lecture:

> The media clamour which now surrounds the administration of justice is regrettable ... It puts greater pressure on the police to find a culprit. No police force in the country wants to be publicly portrayed as having failed in its duty. But excessive pressure to produce results brings its own dangers, as the bitter experience of a series of notorious miscarriage of justice cases has shown ... I think it regrettable that criminal justice issues should have become so highly politicized.
>
> Bingham 2003

But a decade on from the Royal Commission on Criminal Justice, wrongful convictions were no longer the chief concern of the media–political nexus. If, as Tessa Boyd-Caine argues, 'the state's legitimacy turns upon how effective the government can be in showing its receptiveness' to public sentiment (Boyd-Caine 2010: 22), then, as each failure was laid bare, another thread in the mandate claimed by the Home Office and its agencies unravelled. That, in turn, led ministers and media to strike out wildly against those they would have the public believe were jeopardizing its safety – probation officers, defence lawyers and judges.

For sections of the media, the embodiment of judicial liberalism was the Lord Chief Justice, Lord Woolf, who had been labelled 'the burglar's friend' by the *Daily Mail*, in October 1993, when he, rather unwisely, suggested that people who failed to protect their property from crime, should be fined. Woolf had been sporadically at odds with the Home Secretary, David Blunkett, since the summer of 2003, over sentencing reforms. The Criminal Justice Act 2003 created an Independent Sentencing Guidelines Council, which was handed sole responsibility for issuing guidance to courts in England and Wales. In September 2004, the council, chaired by Lord Woolf, issued draft guidelines on sentences for murder which indicated that murderers who pleaded guilty could earn a discount of up to one-third from their sentence. This proposal called down a tabloid firestorm on the Lord Chief Justice's head:

> Lord Woolf is mightily out of step with mainstream public opinion, putting at risk respect for the law. He is also arrogantly overturning the policies of a government, which was elected on the specific promise it would get tough on crime.
>
> *Sun*, 22 September 2004

To underline its contempt for the Lord Chief Justice, the *Sun* urged its readers to fill in a coupon calling on Woolf to quit, which two *Sun* staffers, dressed as brown-coated removal men, attempted to hand in to the Royal Courts of Justice. Lord Woolf has no doubts that, in this instance, media criticism had a direct influence on policy:

> The media did not like our guidelines and certainly did not treat them fairly. David Blunkett reacted by, first of all, disowning the Sentencing Guidelines Council, and then was positively hostile towards it ... It is fair to say that, at that time, there were some very nasty crimes, the public was frightened by what was happening, and the media saw soft sentencing as playing into the hands of serious criminals. So, I could understand politicians, like Blunkett, trying to reassure the public. But that influenced the media and there was a kind of circle in which the politicians also acted in response to the media.
>
> Interview with author, 11 May 2009

The media attacks on Woolf were so sustained and, in some cases, so personal, that the Attorney-General, Lord Goldsmith, took the extraordinary step of calling on newspapers to drop their 'campaign of vilification'. Although it was not his job to defend one particular judge, he believed that:

> when press campaigns against individuals in the justice system go too far, especially if it involves inaccurate reporting of the facts, they run the risk of causing unfair damage to public confidence in our essentially effective and fair system of justice.[5]

Since leaving office, Lord Goldsmith has reflected on this period, in which the Home Office and sections of the media were locked in a rhetorical embrace, and that had such a profound impact on sentences:

> I was getting a lot of comment from ministerial colleagues about sentencing. But we know that the research demonstrates two things. First, that judges actually sentence more severely than the public thinks; and second, that Home Office, and other, research shows that sentences have risen over these years and this is a direct response to the 'get tough' messages coming from various quarters. It is true that sentencing does lag a little behind [the rhetoric] but it does reflect it. This is probably one reason why our sentences are higher than those in other [European] countries.
>
> Interview with author, 14 November 2008[6]

It is also telling that when the Commons Home Affairs Committee examined the bitter argument over sentencing discounts, it found that none of the parties to it had an untarnished record. In a rebuke to the Home Secretary, it concluded that he did not realize the full implications of his own legislation, the Criminal Justice Act 2003, as it went through parliament, because the provisions relating to murder tariffs were introduced at report stage (in other words, comparatively late in the passage of the bill): 'This prevented effective parliamentary scrutiny, either by select or standing committee. It is a classic illustration of the truth of the maxim, "legislate in haste and repent at leisure"' (Commons Home Affairs Committee 2004: 12–13). But it did not spare the media from criticism: 'We believe that media coverage which suggested that reductions in murder tariffs would be widespread and commonplace under the new guidelines was irresponsible and misleading' (ibid.: 14). Nor did the Sentencing Guidelines Council escape unscathed:

> we believe that the draft in its present form does not fully reflect the wishes of Parliament ... Nor does it fully reflect public disquiet about the extent to which reductions for a guilty plea ... may reduce sentences for murder significantly below the 'starting points' set out in the Act.
>
> ibid.: 3

As a coda to this section, it is instructive to contrast the febrile environment surrounding public protection in the first decade of the twenty-first century with the late 1980s, when fear of crime first began to be recognized as a consideration of policy. Between 1987 and 1991, Philippa Drew was head of the division in the Home Office responsible for the probation service and continued in a number of senior roles into the New Labour era:

> There must have been cases [in the late 1980s] where someone released from prison committed a serious crime but I do not remember a single case given a high profile by the media. There was much more recognition of the fact that not every prisoner was a saint and that the whole business of freeing prisoners on licence involved an element of risk. Although we did not talk about risk and we barely did risk assessments. It is true that there were far fewer offenders under probation supervision. There were lifers and then people on long determinate sentences released on parole – and that was it. Now, every Tom, Dick and Harry has got some form of supervision when they come out of prison.
>
> Interview with author, 23 December 2008

The development of an offender management practice based upon classification of risk is one of the striking developments of the past decade. Probation and police officers now have databases such as OASys and ViSOR to help them make an actuarial assessment of a person's risk factors.[7] Much effort has been expended by NOMS and other agencies to explain to the media that processes are in place to make us all safer and yet, as we have seen, every example where the process has been shown not to work has been magnified by the media into a crisis which often demands someone's head on a plate. And this at a time of prolonged and consistent falls in most categories of recorded crime. It is a paradox which says far more about the exploitation of public fears by politicians than it does about real changes in the pattern of crime.

The Indeterminate Sentence for Public Protection

Of the criminal justice levers at the disposal of Home Secretaries (at least, before the Home Office was split up and the Ministry of Justice was born) perhaps the most appealing is the introduction of a new sentencing regime. When it comes to message sending, this is invariably treated by the media as a clarion call worthy of in-depth reportage and analysis. In 1996, Michael Howard responded to rising crime levels with his 'three strikes and you're out' provisions in the Crime Sentences Bill. And in 2002, David Blunkett attempted to match the heightened mood of public fearfulness about violent crime with a suitably draconian penalty, the Indeterminate Sentence for Public Protection (IPP).

In May 2001, the Halliday Report *Making Punishments Work* (Halliday 2001) had highlighted a lack of disposals for people who had committed serious offences, who the courts felt presented a risk of causing further harm. In other words, these were offenders who were to be treated on the basis of potential and/or predicted future behaviour rather than a past crime (unless that crime was so serious as to warrant a life term) thus significantly modifying the 'just deserts' philosophy of punishment.

The government's response was to formulate the IPP sentence and include it in the Criminal Justice Act 2003. When it became law in April 2005, it was a radical departure in sentencing practice and led Lord Justice Judge to comment in 2006: 'Although punitive in its effect, with far-reaching consequences for the offender on whom it is imposed, it [the IPP] does not represent punishment for past offending ... the decision is directed not to the past but to the future.'[8]

Sir David Latham was a fellow member of the Court of Appeal:

> It is interesting to look at why New Labour made the philosophical change from the 'just deserts' principle to the IPP. Some people have said that the idea did not come from Blunkett himself but from one of the Home Office sentencing boys and was then picked up by the Home Secretary. It may have been a reaction to the fact that judges had been reluctant to use [Michael Howard's] 'three strikes' principle. Indeed, it was rarely used. So, it may have been that inside the Home Office, they were looking for another way to tackle the same issue – and came up eventually with the IPP.
>
> Interview with author, 17 November 2010

And one should not lose sight of the major undercurrents of this period, such as the privileging of victims as increasingly influential interest groups in the criminal justice process, alongside new constructions of the 'public', who might potentially be put at risk. These were determining the flow of sentencing policy and detaching it from traditional paradigms. Where the 'just deserts' principle assigns the 'dominant' role to the courts to pass sentences intended to deter and therefore safeguard the public, preventive detention implies that 'the bureaucracies of the criminal justice system have had to become more responsive, more attuned to the interests of individual consumers and stakeholders, and less assured in their definition of what constitutes the public interest' (Garland 2001: 117).

In this sense, the IPP sentence was never going to be popular with the judiciary and the government almost certainly realized this. Thus, it is revealing to consider how extensively ministers thought that it would be used by the courts. During the committee stage of the Criminal Justice Bill, the prisons minister, Hilary Benn, said:

> we have assumed in our modeling that over time … there would be an additional 900 in the prison population. That is only modeling, of course, and the honest answer is that it is difficult to assess the effect because it depends on the courts' interpretation of the provision.[9]

Perhaps an even more honest answer would have been that it also depended on the level of political rhetoric about violent crime, because during this period, described above, of such febrile discourse about public protection, the use of IPP sentences rocketed. Thus, in April 2007, according to the Ministry of Justice, the total adult prison population serving an IPP sentence was 2,547.[10] But, quoting statistics from the Ministry of Justice, the chair of the Parole Board, Sir Duncan Nichol, warned that, if left unchecked, the number of IPP prisoners could reach 12,500 by 2012.[11]

So, yet again, the application of sentencing provisions in an Act passed by parliament placed a strain on relations between the executive and judiciary. This is David Blunkett's position:

> There was certainly media concern about violent criminals, high profile murders, rapes and so on. But I am absolutely amazed at how widely the sentence was used. On one occasion, a court handed down a 28-day sentence and it was accompanied by an IPP. That is why I say that the judiciary has to be held to account publicly. You have to ask the judges: 'are you doing this deliberately to make a monkey out of it?' When Lord Justice Rose [Vice-President of the Criminal Division of the Court of Appeal] said that it was too complex and it could not be understood, that was ridiculous. If I am a working class lad without a law degree, why cannot the judges understand it?
> Interview with author, 8 October 2008

But seen from the bench, the issue was not how could they thwart the wishes of the Home Secretary but how could they best interpret a piece of legislation which parliament itself seems not to have fully grasped. Sir David Latham was one of the judges handling IPP appeals:

> Christopher [LJ] Rose laid down the test we should be applying on dangerousness. He felt he had watered it down as much as possible in the light of the way the statute was worded. But the key problem was that there was a presumption of dangerousness and that created quite significant difficulties for judges, who felt they had to apply it. In the Court of Appeal, we tried to 'cool down' its use as often as we could. Having said that, there may have been an over-use of it.
> Interview with author, 17 November 2010

With hindsight, David Blunkett acknowledges that: 'If I had my time again, I would have ensured that the legislation stipulated that an IPP could not be used with any sentence of less than five years' (Interview with author, 8 October 2008).

Perhaps the last word on the IPP sentence, for now, should go to Lord Justice Rose, who commented acerbically, but with some justification, during a Court of Appeal judgment: 'If a history of criminal legislation ever comes to be written, it is unlikely that 2003 will be identified as a year of exemplary skill in the annals of Parliamentary drafting.'[12]

Instant recall – the politics of fear

On 22 May 2006, John Reid became the first serving Home Secretary to give the annual Parole Board lecture. It was sixteen days since he had been appointed to the Home Office, on whose perceived incompetence on public safety the media had feasted for months. The *Sun* had run a series of powerful articles in March and April blaming the early release rules for a series of avoidable killings and demanding an urgent revision of the life licence system. Displaying the true strength of a tabloid to marry words and pictures and achieve a visceral impact, the opening line of one of the first pieces read: 'Look at this gallery of grief and weep for British justice' (*Sun*, 22 March 2006).

It was small wonder then that Reid saw the lecture as an ideal platform from which to regain the initiative and it is worth quoting from his remarks at some length because they stand as an exemplar of the extent to which public protection had taken over the policy discourse around criminal justice.

> I want to say a word about human rights ... I am not suggesting that offenders have no human rights. But I am suggesting – and rather more than that – that the community has a right to be protected from dangerous criminals ... This rebalancing of the system back in favour of victims ... ensuring that victims or their representatives get a greater say about the release of offenders back into the community. Their voice must be heard more clearly.
>
> Home Office 2006b

There was also a warning – delivered in classic intimidatory manner by a master of the art – that the Parole Board was now inescapably in the spotlight and failure to perform would be unacceptable:

> Nowadays, there is much greater independent scrutiny, through the Internet, 24-hour news cycles and greater interactivity with the news agenda, decisions are profoundly more transparent and, as result, those that take decisions much more accountable. To use a reference from my previous job [as Secretary of State for Defence], that relatively junior official has now become a 'Strategic Corporal' whose actions can have far-reaching ramifications for public confidence.
>
> ibid.

Demonstrating his own ability to manipulate the 24-hour news cycle, Reid authorized his special adviser to brief the media the day before his lecture that he was about to give victims a guaranteed place on parole boards and thus a direct say over the release of prisoners. This duly got prominent news coverage although what he actually proposed in the lecture – to consider the appointment of special advocates to put over the public's point of view – was far less dramatic (and had already been thought of by the Parole Board itself). Indeed, a survey by the Parole Board showed that of the 73 members who responded to questions, 95 per cent had been direct victims of crime.[13]

Those who argued that a balanced justice system was about more than appeasing sectional interests, however deserving, were on weak ground following the case of Anthony Rice, who murdered Naomi Bryant as a consequence of a flawed Parole Board decision to release him on life licence; and Parole Board and probation deficiencies in the case of Damien Hanson, who murdered the Chelsea banker, John Monkton, in 2004. But was it reasonable to build a policy response largely on those two high profile cases? Sir David Latham, later chair of the Parole Board, read Reid's lecture:

> I felt that Reid's ticking-off of the Parole Board on the basis of those two cases, which had gone wrong, was just ridiculous, that this was a man who did not understand what the full background was. Two cases out of how many? If I had been Reid, I would have been more circumspect and said: 'OK, there have been two bad recent cases but whether that shows a trend is something we are going to have to look at'. That is what I would have expected from a responsible politician. But to take the line he took didn't help us nor did it make for good decision-making, which is not about soundbites. We have to look carefully to make sure that the 24-hour, seven-days-a-week coverage is not distorting our decision-making.
>
> Interview with author, 17 November 2010

But again, we encounter a gap between a judicial and an executive view of what constitutes 'good decision-making'. From the Home Secretary's standpoint, his admonishment had its desired effect. At the time of the lecture, the release rate by the Parole Board of life sentence prisoners was 23 per cent and it began immediately to drop. By 2010, it was 11 per cent, with a matching sharp increase in the recall of prisoners released on licence, as probation staff became increasingly nervous of public and political reaction to another 'error'.

Sir David Latham contrasts the strongly interventionist stance of John Reid as Home Secretary with that of Jack Straw, as Justice Secretary: 'From our point of view, Straw was excellent in not criticizing or interfering. He hardly ever said anything about the Parole Board – not just in public but even privately' (ibid.).

However, as Justice Secretary, Straw became deeply embroiled in the recriminations provoked by another shocking murder – indeed, a double murder – which exposed yet again the government's unwillingness to slow the 'runaway train of public protection ... sufficiently to allow for mature reflection and informed debate' (Scott 2010: 293). The case was the murder of two French bio-chemistry students working in London, Laurent Bonomo and Gabriel Ferez, in June 2008 by Nigel Farmer and Dano Sonnex. The latter was a violent drug addict who was under probation supervision at the time of the crime and who should have been back in prison for breaching bail conditions had the police not failed to act on a recall to prison notice issued by a magistrate.

The prison service, police and probation area all bore varying degrees of responsibility for the tragedy but the most high profile casualty was the Chief Officer of Probation for London, David Scott, who resigned in February 2009 after Jack Straw made it clear that he wanted his scalp. For that reason, the case has parallels with the treatment of Sharon Shoesmith as Head of Children's Services in the London borough of Haringey, who was sacked by the Secretary of State for Children, Schools and Families, Ed Balls, in December 2008, in the wake of the Baby Peter killing. The former Chief Inspector of Probation, Professor Rod Morgan, referred to the Sonnex case as the 'probation equivalent of Baby P' (*Guardian*, 5 June 2009) and David Scott sees no reason to demur:

> I have no doubt that Straw was in a kind of bidding war with Ed Balls [over how quickly he could be rid of me]. He was posturing and sabre rattling. And the thing which caused me the greatest offence – and still does – was that there was no attempt to balance or mediate a number of complex issues which played a part in the case.
>
> Interview with author, 26 October 2010

It is these issues and how they were presented to the public which have made this case such a touchstone, both for those who argue that New Labour shamelessly 'primed' the media so that underlying factors of finance and governance were ignored or marginalized, and those who believe that it was about a failure of leadership which threatened to undermine the foundations of effective offender management if left unchecked. In some respects, there were echoes of the disputed handling of the sacking of the governor of Parkhurst prison, John Marriott, in 1995, after lapses in security at the jail (described in the following chapter). But there was one crucial difference. In that instance, the survival of the Home Secretary, Michael Howard, depended on his putting distance between his office and the fate of Marriott, thus maintaining the 'principle' that operational decisions, such as hiring and firing, were a matter for the Director General of the Prison Service, Derek Lewis.

In the Sonnex case, illustrating how, in the intervening years, a relentless media focus had made matters of public protection a vital litmus test for the perceived competence of government, it was just as important for the Secretary of State for Justice to show that he, and he alone, was at the controls. This is Jack Straw's own account:

> I came across the Sonnex case by chance. In November, I think, 2008, I was having a routine meeting with a junior minister and officials about things which might be coming up and Sonnex was mentioned. One of the reasons I have survived as a minister is that I have a very good alert system and alarm

bells rang. I said: 'hang on a second, what is going on here?' Was I aware that I needed to get on top of this because there would be a media storm if I didn't? Well, yes I was. So, I took over the issue myself, held a series of meetings to find out exactly what had happened. And what had happened had been a lamentable failure by probation officers in Greenwich and Lewisham, part of the London probation service. Then I drilled down and found out about the general performance of the service in London, massive sickness levels and so on, and that David Scott had had notice that he needed to sort things out and, in fact, that he had failed to do so.

> Interview with author, 21 September 2010

Not surprisingly, Scott's version is somewhat different:

Only two months before the murders, I had been assured by the Probation Inspectorate, at a very high level, that I had 'nothing to fear', as it was put – and in 2007, a full inspection had found the London probation service to be well led, that there was a good relationship between the chief officer and the board, that it had a clear strategy and was moving in the right direction. And that what it needed, above all else, was to nurture the quality of the casework done by probation staff with offenders. The fact is that the London service was improving and to hang all this on sickness rates was pathetic.

> Interview with author, 26 October 2010

It was not only sickness rates, though. The issue which many sections of the media picked up on, was whether the London probation service had been starved of money. It is common ground between the Justice Secretary and the probation service that the London area had an under-spend on its £154 million budget for 2008–9 of £3.5 million. David Scott and other senior probation figures maintain the reason was that the National Offender Management Service (NOMS) had taken a decision in October 2008 to encourage all probation boards to maximize under-spends to help them through a tougher financial settlement in the year 2009–10. Jack Straw is contemptuous of this explanation:

I am completely intolerant of people who fall back on the money as a crutch. At that point, the funding had not been significantly cut for the London probation service, as I recall it. The fact is that close to a billion pounds is spent on the probation service and parts of it were slack. And David Scott was paid a lot of money. He had also made himself chairman, or been made chairman, of the Association of Chief Probation Officers and it meant that his eye was off the ball. He had not got a grip.

> Interview with author, 21 September 2010

Whether this was the full picture is debatable. There were two other factors which accounted for Straw's readiness to take an unyielding line over an 'underperforming' probation area. One was the government's determination to re-brand community sentences as a rigorous alternative to custody in order to relieve pressure on prison places. Its chosen means, Community Payback, with offenders doing unpaid work wearing fluorescent orange tabards, was disapproved of by many probation officers as gesture politics designed to appeal to the tabloid agenda. In London, some staff were resistant on the grounds that putting offenders into highly visible uniforms might place them at risk in areas where there had been a spate of drive-by shootings. When two members of staff raised this objection in a memo to Phil Wheatley, then Director-General of NOMS, Straw was furious because, according to David Scott:

> He believed that London was just taking the piss. After getting a call from Phil Wheatley on a Friday night, I dealt with the matter over the weekend and got apologies from the staff concerned. I said to Phil 'let me go and see Straw to reassure him in person that I am dead serious about the work we are doing'. But he said 'not yet, he is too angry'.
>
> Interview with author, 26 October 2010

Underlying this tension was the running sore of NOMS itself, which, in 2004, pitchforked the national probation service into one over-centralized organization, alongside the prison service, on the strength of recommendations made by New Labour's all-purpose troubleshooter, Lord Carter.[14] As Professor Rod Morgan commented:

> The government has been sending mixed messages to penal decision-makers, and the integration of criminal justice has been characterized more by rhetoric than achievement. IT systems have been initiated and aborted. The creation of NOMS has been blighted by U-turns, consultancy profligacy and operational uncertainty, damaging the morale of the probation service.
>
> *Guardian*, 5 June 2009

There is much that could be written here about the morale of the probation service, which, more than any other criminal justice agency, had been at the mercy of changing political priorities for a decade, during which both its localized structure and its overall mission had been eviscerated. Now, as part of NOMS, it saw itself treated very much as a junior partner, with the managing board heavily dominated by prisons personnel. In David Scott's words:

> Far from having a national voice, the organization [i.e. the probation service] which, at any one time, supervises 200,000-plus offenders in the community, is not even represented in its own right in key national decision-making fora but subsumed within a vast Prison Service-dominated bureaucracy. A national asset is being squandered.
>
> Scott 2010: 291

Phil Wheatley, a former head of the prison service, admits that, in execution, it was not a marriage made in heaven:

The original attack on NOMS for creating a bureaucracy, and nobody being clear about what it was delivering, was probably fair comment. It was very difficult to refute that. But the idea of integrating separate services and making sure they did not trip each other up is as sane to me as making sure that the trains which use the same rail network are integrated and do not run into each other. When we turned NOMS into an agency [2008] and stopped saying that the answer to everything was the market we saw it begin to turn around.

> Interview with author, 18 June 2010

But the birth pains of the new agency, attacked, as Phil Wheatley says, 'by a combination of the *Daily Mail* and the Right for not being tough enough, and by the penal reform tendency for being too tough' (ibid.), left their mark on the Justice Secretary. Although, as Straw points out, his determination to be seen to be on top of the case meant that his own survival as a minister was never seriously in doubt, even some of the tabloids added to his discomfort by putting the contested issue of resourcing high up in their coverage of the story. For example, reporting on his parliamentary statement on the affair in June 2009, the *Sun*'s second strapline was: 'Justice Secretary insisted that the failures were NOT caused by a lack of money' (*Sun*, 9 June 2009). David Scott sees this as a limited vindication of his position:

A number of the tabloids picked up on the fact that Straw's attitude was an avoidance of responsibility by the Ministry of Justice and that it was letting politicians off the hook. When Straw said he could not abide people who used money as an excuse, that was not the issue. If he had had the wit to reflect, he would have realized that what London needed was longer-term support to plan its service and to get away from the uncertainty of 'now you have money, now you do not have it'.

> Interview with author, 26 October 2010

But that is to under-estimate the mediated pressure felt by ministers in a Gordon Brown-led administration, struggling to stem the haemorrhage of support which had sustained Tony Blair through most of his premiership. Phil Wheatley agrees that it gave Home and Justice Secretaries every incentive to appear tough on public protection:

Yes, it certainly pushed them towards that end of the spectrum. And the probation service is risky from that point of view. That is why, in the two years I was responsible for NOMS, I consistently gave out the message, to anyone who would listen, that we can make you safer but not absolutely safe. And I would say, 'let's not over-promise, because if you over-promise and it goes wrong, they will say, "but you promised!"'.

> Interview with author, 18 June 2010

Stifling probation's voice

The Sonnex case is a vivid illustration of the fact that, in general, the media has less real understanding of the work of the probation service than it does of the other key criminal justice agencies; and, being characterized, or perhaps stereotyped, as 'soft' and on the side of the offender (though that misconception should have been laid to rest in the mid-1990s), 'it has no natural allies when a crisis breaks' (David Scott, interview with author, 26 October 2010). Scott says he 'has evidence that the Met was briefing against us over Sonnex, or at least, they were certainly ensuring that their interests were protected' (ibid.).

And the police had good reason to be anxious. The Independent Police Complaints Commission examined the failings in the Sonnex case and found that they were 'a result of confusion, poor communication and weak procedures' and recommended disciplinary action against a Metropolitan Police sergeant for a breach of the Police Code of Conduct (IPCC 2009: 6). Yet, this formed only a minor part of the media narrative of the Sonnex case. As David Scott remarks:

> You have the power and media influence of the police. You have the Prison Governors Association made up of seconded governors, paid for and accommodated by the prison service. And alongside them, you had a probation service, which had no national leadership. The irony is that I had only just been appointed chair of the Probation Chiefs Association to be that public voice of the service when the Sonnex crisis broke. At the time, I was vice-chair of the London Criminal Justice Board and the Met police's attitude was 'we are all in this together, this was a bad case and nobody comes out of it well'. But when you look back at the wreckage, you see the smoking ruins of the probation service and not the police.
>
> Interview with author, 26 October 2010

The Sonnex case pointed up the handicaps under which the probation service has laboured as it struggles to be heard in the national debate about crime and punishment. When there were fifty-five probation areas, there was no national service to be represented in public fora. And once the service had become absorbed into NOMS and then placed under the political aegis of the Ministry of Justice, Chief Probation Officers were left in no doubt that it was not their role to criticize the direction of public protection policy. This left a vacuum filled by Harry Fletcher, the ubiquitous Assistant General Secretary of the National Union of Probation Officers who, de facto, was regarded by the media, not just as the 'voice' of probation but as a commentator and supplier of useful confidential intelligence about the criminal justice process as a whole. It was as if the chair of the Police Federation had staked a credible claim to be treated as spokesperson for the entire police service rather than just as the figurehead of a sectional labour interest, albeit an influential one.

It is true that between 2001 and 2004, there was a National Probation Service, theoretically independent but, in fact, operating under a directorate (NPD) which was accountable to the Home Office. Members of Probation Boards were appointed and paid by the Home Secretary. The public, and indeed the media, were allowed few glimpses of probation's distinctive contribution to public protection, as the senior official – quoted earlier and who prefers to remain anonymous for some of the reasons outlined above – explains:

> Take the release from custody of Jon Venables and Robert Thomson [the killers of James Bulger] in 2001. This was obviously a major media story but the Home Office advised the Director General of the Probation Service, Eithne Wallis, not to comment. We decided that was a mistake and that it would allow those people who needed to 'name-check' their organizations, such as Harry Fletcher and Frances Crook [Director of the Howard League for Penal Reform] to fill the vacuum. So, Eithne disregarded the advice and did an interview with the BBC. We had to fight the same battle with the Home Office over another high profile case, the conviction of Roy Whiting [for murdering Sarah Payne in 2000]. But this was the high point of working with the media. After that, the NPD became invisible as the Home Office took over.
>
> Interview with author, 4 September 2008

Thus, when the full scandal of the Naomi Bryant murder in Winchester was exposed in October 2005, the Hampshire probation service 'was not allowed to make any media comment about it' (ibid.). Even more tellingly, the Home Office connived at a calculated 'sin' of omission in the case of the Nottingham jeweller, Marian Bates, who was killed during a robbery by three men in September 2003. One of the attackers was under the supervision of a Youth Offending Team at the time, although some press outlets reported that it was probation supervision:

> We were furious because it was being reported as a failure of the probation service and I phoned up the Home Office press office and said 'you must put out a statement correcting this'. I was told 'look, as long as someone is seen to take the blame, that's OK'. And they did nothing. The Home Office press office is there to protect the political interest and not the operational interest of the department.
>
> ibid.

This raises a number of larger questions than the role of the press office. What exactly is the Home Office itself there for? How has that role changed during a 21-year period in which media scrutiny has steadily ramped up? And what part have Home Secretaries played in that transformation? The next chapter seeks to answer these questions.

5 Home Secretaries against the Home Office

The retreat of the liberals

In 1993, at the beginning of the era of 'populist punitiveness', the former Home Office minister and chair of the Parole Board, Lord Windlesham, published the second of his four-volume magnum opus, *Responses to Crime*. In it he wrote that, after the Conservatives had won their third successive election in 1987, the Home Secretary Douglas Hurd 'sensed that the time was right to draw together several strands of policy, weaving them into a coherent pattern and projecting them as a whole' (Windlesham 1993: 209).

Over a three-year period, this 'coherent pattern' found expression in a Green Paper, 'Punishment, Custody and the Community' (1988); a White Paper, 'Crime, Justice and Protecting the Public' (1990); and finally, the Criminal Justice Act 1991. It was the apotheosis of the 'platonic guardians' whose role was 'to constrain the temptations of the rulers and keep on a tight leash the untutored passions of the ruled' (Loader 2006: 563–4). This vision of criminal justice is still to be found – in academic writing, in some think tanks and penal reform groups – but not in government. Twenty years ago, it was the received opinion in the Home Office. Those who thought otherwise were the barbarians at the (Queen Anne's) gate.[1]

It is barely imaginable nowadays that a Home Secretary's greatest concern should be not rising crime or lapses in public protection but prison overcrowding. Yet, for Douglas Hurd:

> This was one of the few areas where I got into major problems and I felt pressure. When I was obliged to authorize the early release of some prisoners, I remember my PPS [parliamentary private secretary] saying 'this will be the most difficult parliamentary statement you will have to make in your career'.
> Interview with author, 21 July 2008

Michael Howard, too, encountered his most difficult, and potentially career-defining, parliamentary moment over a prisons crisis, which explains why, in the period until 1995, prison security played such a dominant role in Home Office thinking. For both media and politicians, it was a signifier of the Home Secretary's competence, as Charles Clarke was to discover in 2006, after a decade during which prisons had been of only sporadic interest to the media. Whether this was a cause of New Labour's marginalization of prison issues (and its indifference to rising numbers in prison), or an effect of it, is impossible to establish. But what is certain is that for Douglas Hurd and the 'penal elitists' (Ryan 1999) in the Home Office, prison numbers and prison conditions were central to a vision of penal policy which encompassed both humane containment and effective punishment in the community. Even Hurd's hard-line successor, David Waddington, was happy to put his name to a White Paper which emphasized alternatives to custody and contained this declaration:

> Prison is a society which requires virtually no sense of personal responsibility. The opportunity to learn from other criminals is pervasive. Imprisonment has to be justified in terms of public protection, denunciation and retribution. Otherwise, it can be a very expensive way of making bad people worse.
>
> Home Office 1990: Section 1.16

Contrast this with Michael Howard's bald assertion, only three years later, that 'prison works'. As has already been discussed, much happened between 1990 and 1993 to tilt the trajectory of criminal justice policy in a radically different direction but, for another useful insight, it is worth returning to Lord Windlesham's description of Hurd's thinking on penal matters as a 'coherent pattern'. Philippa Drew, then a senior Home Office official, believes that the mindset of a Home Secretary has a crucial influence on policy:

> The contrast between Hurd and Howard was huge. Howard was a typical lawyer. I've always taken the view that you should never make a lawyer Home Secretary. They are the worst people because they think they know the law and are frightfully good at picking up a brief and arguing to it but tomorrow it's forgotten and they've moved on. They think in terms of quick fixes. What the Home Office needs is someone who understands policy and can see the breadth of the criminal justice system and its place historically. You sentence a prisoner to 20 years. How many Home Secretaries will he see out during that time? So, the Home Secretary's job requires a mind which has the capacity to think beyond tomorrow's headlines and to see the larger picture.
>
> Interview with author, 23 December 2008

For Philippa Drew, the 'larger picture' was the landmark Criminal Justice Act 1991, which was 'an attempt to create an intellectually coherent framework within which fewer prisoners would be sentenced to shorter terms' (ibid.). Indeed, it contained a provision, unthinkable now, that courts were not to take previous convictions into account when sentencing, except in the case of persistent violent and sexual offenders. The pendulum swung fully back the other way with Howard's 1997 Crime Sentences Act – the so-called 'three strikes and you're out' measure – which covered the single issue of public protection and 'viewed increasing use of prison with enthusiasm' (Dunbar and Langdon 1998: 139).

Announced at the 1995 Conservative conference with the declaration 'if you don't want the time, don't do the crime', this legislation always seemed like an insubstantial media soundbite over-extended into a policy, with all the frailties that implies. It was a sharp contrast to the methodical gestation of the 1991 Act and its all-embracing reach across criminal justice.

And, remarkably, this Act was a response to the Woolf Report into the worst prison riot in the country's history at Strangeways, which had featured on most newspaper front pages daily for 25 days in April 1990.[2] Much has been written, of course, about the events at Strangeways but for the purposes of this study it is noteworthy for being the first 24-hour news event of the post-1989 period and for some luridly inaccurate press reporting.[3] In the first few days of the riot, which began on 1 April 1990, newspapers reported up to thirty deaths at Strangeways. In the event, nobody died in the prison, although one inmate and one prison officer died of their injuries in hospital. As the authorities eventually regained control, it is notable that much newspaper commentary emphasized the extraordinary mediatized impact of the riot. Examples include:

> A degrading public spectacle has been allowed to develop in a way clearly damaging to the good name of the country ... People all over the world have seen television and news pictures showing scenes from Manchester and elsewhere [there were riots at more than twenty prisons] often portrayed as representing 'life in Britain' today. At home, we have been subjected to the appearance of authority set at nought.
>
> *Daily Telegraph*, 26 April 1990

> The prolonged and bizarre nature of this very public siege had two unfortunate side effects. It encouraged copycat riots and it made the forces of law and order look ridiculous.
>
> *Independent*, 26 April 1990

Yet, despite the body blow to the authority of the prison service and, by extension, the government's competence, a judge with known liberal inclinations was appointed to head the inquiry and the majority of his subsequent recommendations were absorbed into a piece of legislation which, although it had a greater emphasis on prison security than in the Woolf Report, bore little or no trace of the retributive impulses which have driven most criminal justice acts since. It is impossible to escape the conclusion that, as Jameson and Allison have commented: 'By 1991, when the Woolf report was published, prison conditions had been exposed so thoroughly that no politician or journalist dared defend them or extol the virtues of imprisonment' (1995: 11).

Thus even the fangs of the tabloid media had, effectively, been drawn – at least for a while. But there is another interpretation of 'penal elitism' (Ryan 1999) which casts it in a different light, one which explains why Michael Howard found a useful ally in sections of the media in challenging some of the liberal nostrums which ruled in Queen Anne's Gate when David Windlesham, Douglas Hurd and above all, David Faulkner, the 'architect' of the 1991 Criminal Justice Act, held sway.[4] In this respect, as will be made clear, it is also helpful to examine Jack Straw's and David Blunkett's approach to the Home Office when they arrived in post.

Nothing works? Prison works!

It is a curious fact that during the late 1980s and early 1990s when recorded crime rose faster than at any time since the Second World War, there was less intense media pressure on the government over criminal justice than in more recent years when most categories of notifiable crime have demonstrably fallen. This says something about the changing nature of media coverage, alluded to in an earlier chapter; the fact that the Prime Minister was not exercised about crime in the way that successors such as Tony Blair were; and the potency of the prevailing philosophy in the Home Office that when it came to reducing re-offending 'nothing works'.[5]

Although it would be false to suggest that every senior official in the Home Office during the early 1990s was of like mind, many of the key figures were cast from the same mould – Oxbridge, liberally inclined and clubbable in the sense recognized by viewers of the TV comedy *Yes, Minister*. In other words, they represented the constant of Home Office policymaking while ministers came and went at the whim of the Prime Minister. Julian Walker, who became Michael Howard's speechwriter (the first full-time speechwriter in the Home Office), admits that she was a member of that gilded fraternity:

> Yes, I was part of that liberal establishment. There were a lot of us, particularly in the criminal justice area, who had an Oxbridge, liberal, paternalistic, left-wing sense of compassion and understanding about crime. And Michael Howard was absolutely having none of that. You know, it was 'sod your liberal, elitist compassion' – he did not put it that way but he was the precursor of the view that anti-social behaviour affects the poor much more than the rich, paving the way for a more robust approach to crime, which Labour was able to put into practice.
>
> Interview with author, 12 September 2008

Martin Narey, who subsequently became Director-General of the Prison Service and first chief executive of the National Offender Management Service (NOMS), was moving up the Home Office ladder at the time Michael Howard arrived. Born in Middlesborough and educated at Sheffield City Polytechnic (later to become Sheffield Hallam University), he was emphatically not part of the liberal elite:

> I felt like a terrible outsider when I came into the Home Office. It was almost entirely Oxbridge dominated. I remember being at an away-day event early in Howard's time (David Cameron, one of his special advisers, was there) and Chris Nuttall, then head of research, told Howard 'Home Secretary, there is nothing you can do to stop crime going up – all you can do is to manage expectations'. Howard was furious and said 'well, we will change that'. Howard also became angry when he heard the expression 'Home Office policy'. To him, it smacked of the liberal establishment inside the department seeing itself as a separate entity. His view was that there was only the Home Secretary's policy.
>
> Interview with author, 10 September 2008

Yet, even after four years under the smack of Michael Howard's tenure, and a Whitehall review which, according to Howard's head of communications from 1995, Mike Granatt, identified 'Home Office policy and ministers' policy' (Interview with author, 12 October 2010), it seems that some departments of the Home Office retained this sense of policy ownership, according to Howard's successor, Jack Straw:

> The sentencing unit, which has since been transferred to the Ministry of Justice, had some strong officials who had been there a long time and they had developed a 'departmental' policy. I explained that departments do not have policies. Ministers do. They had blithely put forward recommendations on a particular policy which they expected to be adopted. I said 'no, sorry, we're stopping and we are going to pull back'. It took a bit of a tussle until they got the point that I was not having this.
>
> Interview with author, 21 September 2010

But Home Office custom and practice tends to be more durable than the will of even the most determined and self-confident Home Secretaries (at least, until the splitting of the department in 2006 after the departure of Charles Clarke). Unlike Jack Straw, David Blunkett entered Queen Anne's Gate with front-line experience, at the Department of Education, behind him. He used it to remind the troops who was in charge:

> I had cottoned on to the fact that the Home Office was not functioning terribly well. It exuded, not so much amateurism but an image of hovering above the problems. I had seen departments where nobody was on top of what was going on. It was as though the Secretary of State was floating above the morass. I wanted to demonstrate to the department that what we did touched people outside. We were not mere policy wonks who developed legislation and saw it through parliament.
>
> Interview with author, 8 October 2008

Michael Howard says that because he had never expected to become Home Secretary, he entered the Home Office in May 1993 'with no agenda of any kind' (Interview with author, 9 July 2008). This is not borne out by the evidence. As a demonstration of his political standpoint on crime, he appointed as a minister of state David Maclean, who once wrote a speech in which he described criminals as 'vermin who should be driven from the streets' (Cohen 2003: 10). And, as a political adviser dealing with the media, he chose Patrick Rock, whose views, according to the former Director-General of the Prison Service, Derek Lewis, were 'somewhere to the right of Attila the Hun's' (Lewis 1997: 122). Nor was it long before Howard made it clear that he regarded the permanent secretary he had inherited, Sir Clive Whitmore, as part of the despised Home Office establishment which he was determined to shake up. Whitmore took the hint by retiring several months early.

For Howard, the overt justification for these manoeuvres was to make the Home Office a more effective force for fighting crime. But the sub-text was that he should be in a better position to launch a challenge for the party leadership. During this period, Phil Wheatley was moving up through the ranks of the prison service:

> With Michael Howard, lots of decisions were taken through the spectrum of 'how will that best enable me to become the next leader of the party'. That does not make the existing government work better and it may involve briefing against somebody or saying that I inherited a mess from them – Ken or Douglas or whoever – and I am now sorting it out … You would not put up with it if you were a business, say, like Tesco, trying to make a profit.
>
> Interview with author, 18 June 2010

Regarding the media, Howard insists that he was 'relaxed' unlike, he says, 'Tony Blair, who pandered to the media – his whole method of operating was to build up the media and presentation of his policies' (Interview with author, 9 July 2008). Those close to Howard's office disagree. His speechwriter, Julian Walker, said: 'I certainly would never use the word "relaxed" about him', while Mike Granatt commented:

> Howard wanted to win the battle both in policy/operational terms and political terms, which meant winning the battle in the media. As a minister, nobody was faster on his feet in my experience, than Michael Howard. He would ring me up at 6.30am and say he had already been on the *Today* programme. If he heard something in the news briefing at 6.10am that he disagreed with, he would ring up the programme and get himself on air to rebut.
>
> Interview with author, 12 October 2010

Evidence of this lawyer's resolve to have the last word (literally) can be found in correspondence with the Director-General of the BBC, John Birt, in February 1996, in the wake of the controversy over the sacking of the prisons chief, Derek Lewis. Howard had complained that he had been badly misled by the Radio 4 current affairs programme, *The World Tonight*, which had run a series of features on prisons and given a commitment that he would have a right of reply to issues and criticisms raised by other contributors. In the event, both Derek Lewis and the former Chief Inspector of Prisons, Stephen Tumim, appeared in the final programme – after Howard's interview.

Following an FOI request by the author, the BBC released the letters, in the first of which, sent on 7 February, Howard writes: 'This was outrageous behaviour by *The World Tonight*. It is the most blatant example of completely dishonest behaviour I have ever come across at the BBC. I would be grateful for your views' (Howard 1996a).

Infuriated by the, then, Director-General, John Birt's response, Howard writes again on 22 February to say that 'It dismays me, and frankly, demeans you'. The correspondence is still going on, with the complaint unresolved, on 9 April, when Howard tells Birt: 'I am appalled that you cannot offer me an apology for the worst breach of faith that I have ever suffered at the hands of the BBC' (Howard 1996b).

Eventually, on 24 April, Birt blinks first and refers the matter to the BBC's Head of Programme Complaints for a full internal inquiry. And on 28 June, the Director-General offers an apology for 'any misunderstanding'. The complaint had taken nearly five months to bring to a conclusion – and this over a broadcast heard by a few hundred thousand people at most!

In the introduction to this work, there was some discussion of Jones and Wolfe's model of 'information processing' and of journalists and politicians acting as 'interpretative communities, with each part having an impact in the formation of policy' (Koch-Baumgarten and Voltmer 2010: 4). Since Michael Howard 'felt he was entering hostile territory' at the Home Office (Crick 2005: 271), it was natural to look for allies elsewhere. For example, sections of the media:

> When you are sitting in that tower at Queen Anne's Gate [in other words, the Home Office], you rely on your officials but sometimes, you do not get much from them. And from time to time, the media would come up with stories – especially about what was going on in prison – which I would not otherwise have known about because my officials did not tell me. And some officials would not tell me things because they had their own agenda.
>
> Interview with author, 9 July 2008

Perhaps unsurprisingly, one of those officials, Philippa Drew, has a different interpretation from her former boss:

> I absolutely refute the idea that there was a conspiracy to keep things from him. Every politically experienced civil servant knows that what ministers want is no surprises, so you tell them the bad news before they read it in the press. You know that if you have not told the Home Secretary, he will come down on you like a ton of bricks. Howard might well have learned things from the media first but it was probably because junior officials were not bringing them before more senior officials, who, in turn, could have put them before Howard.
>
> Interview with author, 23 December 2008

One of the things that Howard learned about from the media was the case of 'Safari Boy'. The sobriquet had been given by a *Daily Mail* sub-editor to a 17-year-old offender, Mark Hook, who, under the supervision of Gloucestershire social services, was sent for four months to the Bryn Melyn therapy centre in North Wales in 1993. When the paper reported that, as part of his rehabilitation programme, he had been on an 80-day African safari, at a cost of £7000, a political storm broke (January 1994), with the Prime Minister, John Major, denouncing 'airy fairy theories' which appeared to reward criminal behaviour (*Guardian*, 8 January 1994). Given that the story appeared when the cheering had barely died down from Michael Howard's barnstorming Conservative conference performance, at which he had outlined a 27-point plan to make prisons and punishment more demanding, the convergence of media outrage and political opportunity were irresistible.

Howard ordered an end to all foreign trips for young offenders and outlined tougher regimes for young people given community punishments. The announcement was made in a speech given to the Central Probation Council (17 May 1994), thus helping to cement the view amongst the public that the indulgence shown to Safari Boy was yet another sign of probation laxness, whereas it had been a social services responsibility. Yet, like John Reid and the case of the Nottingham jeweller, Marian Bates, referred to in the previous chapter, Michael Howard was not to be deflected from his wider political objective, which was to transform the probation service into an effective instrument of public protection and to eradicate all traces of its historic statutory mission to 'advise, assist and befriend' the offender.

In September 2008, Jack Straw showed himself just as adept at making capital out of a perceived lapse by a criminal justice agency when the *Sun* carried a story about a Halloween party being planned at Holloway prison. Under the headline, 'Monsters' Ball', the *Sun*'s political editor, George Pascoe-Watson, wrote:

> Justice Secretary Jack Straw, this morning outlawed ALL jail parties after the *Sun*'s revelations that convicted women killers enjoyed a sickening knees-up … We reveal today how lifers at London's Holloway Prison enjoyed a sick fancy-dress party funded by taxpayers last Halloween. Another bash is being lined up for next month.
>
> *Sun*, 12 September 2008

Since the Prison Officers Association was quoted as applauding the ban, there must be a strong suspicion, based on past behaviour, that the tip-off to the tabloid came from a member of the prison staff. Philippa Drew declares an interest as a member of the Pimlico Players, a company which takes opera into prisons and was thus caught by the ban:

> In my time at the Home Office, the tabloids were blatantly offering prison staff money for bad stories about the prison service. The idea that your own staff were betraying you for money, not for conscience, is just about as bad as it gets. And, of course, media coverage is important. I remember being asked during the Learmont Inquiry [into prison security following the escapes from Whitemoor and Parkhurst prisons] 'what is your indicator for the success of the prison service?' And without thinking, I said 'it is the size of the press cuts on my desk each morning. If it is a large number, we are doing badly. If it is thin, we are doing OK'.
>
> Interview with author, 23 December 2008

Evidence that prison 'entertainment' – no matter how useful for boosting morale amongst inmates – is still a toxic political issue when stoked by the media, came in July 2010 when the prisons minister in the coalition government, Crispin Blunt, supported by the Justice Secretary, Kenneth Clarke, announced that the Straw ban would be overturned. Blunt was quoted as saying that the 'deleterious' ban was 'typical of the last administration's flakiness under pressure': 'At the slightest whiff of criticism from the popular press, policy tended to get changed and the consequences of an absurd over-reaction to offenders being exposed to comedy in prison was this damaging and daft instruction' (*Daily Mirror*, 24 July 2010).

But the headline on the story, 'David Cameron humiliates two of his top team by banning jail parties', demonstrates how badly Blunt had under-estimated the continuing mediated potency of the issue. His announcement followed a barrage of hostile tabloid stories, with the *Sun* focusing on the angle of convicted female-killers dressed up as ghouls and the *Daily Mail* raising the blood pressure of the Middle England taxpayer with the front-page headline 'Now you pay for prison parties' (*Daily Mail*, 23 July 2010). Predictably, within 48 hours, Cameron had disowned Blunt's proposal and made it clear that the ban remained in force.

The bracketing together of responses over a period of more than 15 years by three different Home Secretaries to media reporting, might lead one to the conclusion that these were all examples of a politics which, in the words of Newburn and Jones, 'downplays the complexities and long-term character of effective crime control in favour of immediate gratification of a more expressive alternative' (Newburn and Jones 2005: 73). But though Straw's prison ban undoubtedly falls into that category – it served no useful purpose other than to project an image of toughness – the actions of Howard and Reid can be seen in a different light: that of Home Secretaries with an over-arching policy objective and willing to use and be used by the media to achieve it.

In Reid's case, the objective was to restore confidence in the Home Office after the 'foreign prisoners' crisis, which will be discussed in the next chapter. To a certain extent, the objective, though limited in scope, was achieved. Howard's record is rather more nuanced. On the prisons side, there were no more high profile escapes after 1995 and the imposition of austerity measures fulfilled pledges made at Conservative conferences from 1993 onwards. The Criminal Justice and Public Order Act 1994 was a significant piece of legislation which began the process of marginalization – whether of New Age Travellers, squatters, or juvenile offenders – which New Labour was to develop into a wholesale redefinition of civil liberties.

However, Howard's claim that 'prison works' because, from 1995, the recorded crime rate began to fall steadily, is a polemical flourish with no real substance.[6] Even more noteworthy is the fact that his key stated objective, to transform the culture of the Home Office itself, did not make as much headway as he wished, according to Philippa Drew:

> In 1997, when Jack Straw became Home Secretary, there was a stunned silence from officials when he said that henceforth, a key Home Office indicator would be to reduce crime. They said 'you have got to be mad, crime is a result of societal factors and so on'. Despite four years of Michael Howard, they really had not seen that the Home Office was anything to do with cutting crime.
>
> Interview with author, 23 December 2008

This may have been because, even if he was able to articulate a policy vision, Michael Howard was not temperamentally suited to getting the best out of the officials who worked for him, says Julian Walker:

> I did think he was a bully. He seemed to relish crushing people in arguments which is a really dangerous thing to do because civil servants are fairly weak at times, a bit cerebral and a bit weedy. You know, you do not choose to go into the civil service if you are an SAS type. And if you have someone who slaps you over the head in an argument, then the next time he is wrong, you do not tell him. Michael Howard was always at risk of not being told when he was wrong because officials were too scared of his temper.
>
> Interview with author, 12 September 2008

Mike Grannatt believes, like Philippa Drew, that Howard's pre-government background as a barrister handicapped his performance as an effective minister:

> Howard was not a manager (unlike Jack Straw). He was a barrister, used to working on his own. He was also a political animal. So, when things went wrong, he was quick to blame others ... He was terrifying and officials were scared of him. I told him this and he said he did not believe it. But I think he really knew it. He was intolerant of his own vulnerability to those around him, who did not have his political antennae or drive.
>
> Interview with author, 12 October 2010

It is arguable that this failure of empathy made the task of attacking crime more difficult because it maintained the isolation of the Home Office from other agencies and government departments, as Philippa Drew points out:

> Howard stopped all consultation with outside bodies. We were not even allowed to consult the Magistrate's Association about issues. The Home Office had traditionally talked to organizations like NACRO [the National Association for the Care and Resettlement of Offenders] about policies but Howard cut their grant. When Labour came in with exactly the opposite policy – consult, consult, consult and make other government departments commit to crime issues – there was rejoicing in the corridors. At last, a sane and rational policy.
>
> Interview with author, 23 September 2008

Symbolic responses

According to Martin Narey, a few days after the 2001 election and a cabinet reshuffle, Jack Straw returned to the Home Office with a debt to repay: 'He gave me a signed £20 note because I had not embarrassed him by letting any high profile prisoners escape' (Interview with author, 10 September 2008).

It has already been observed that historically, a prisons crisis makes Home Secretaries more fearful for their jobs than any other failure of criminal justice. Straw's gesture was a nod in the direction of his predecessor, Michael Howard, who, for a few weeks in October 1995, must have wondered whether he would survive as Home Secretary in the aftermath of the escapes from Parkhurst, which had precipitated the removal of the governor, John Marriott in January of that year. As director for the prison service area, which included Parkhurst, Philippa Drew was deputed by the Director-General of the Prison Service, Derek Lewis, to go to Parkhurst and tell Marriott that he was to be transferred to prisons HQ in London:

> Marriott was very upset and angry when I gave him the bad news. But I said that the Home Secretary was going to make clear in his statement to parliament that this was an administrative move and not to be seen as a punishment. And that Marriott would have time to clear his desk and say his goodbyes. I made various phone calls from the Isle of Wight to London to agree the wording of the statement. When the final text was read over to me, I went ape and Marriott went absolutely spare. Howard was determined that the move should be that same day. It would not have made a halfpenny worth of difference which day he went but this was a sign of Howard's petty-minded punitiveness. It was an example of a small-minded, nasty man I am afraid.
>
> Interview with author, 23 December 2008

But this was rather more than a case of gratuitous vindictiveness on Howard's part. As Derek Lewis makes clear in his memoir, the Home Secretary was fighting for his survival: 'I went down to the Commons to listen to Howard's statement. He faced a noisy House ... The smell of blood was in the air, and the vultures were hovering on the benches opposite' (Lewis 1997: 171).

As Lewis points out, this was the first occasion on which Howard deployed his soon-to-be famous disclaimer that, as Home Secretary, he was responsible for policy, while the Director-General was in operational charge. The removal of a prison governor was plainly an operational decision and therefore, it was imperative that it should not be laid at Howard's door. It was equally important that an embattled minister should be portrayed as robust in the facing of waning confidence in penal policy. The answer was to use the presentational armoury at his disposal to make sure that the right 'message' was put out by the media:

> Someone, presumably Howard's special advisers, had been briefing the lobby correspondents. The result was a rash of headlines which talked of 'dismissal', 'sacking', 'firing' and 'axing', No mention was made of suspension, still less of his [Marriott] being moved to other duties. It was an outrageous misrepresentation which had staff in the prison service up in arms.
>
> ibid. 172

In the vernacular, this was a case of a Home Secretary, in Philippa Drew's words, 'wanting to have his cake and eat it' (Interview with author, 23 December

2008). But looked at evaluatively, it comes from the same mould as the sacking of Sharon Shoesmith by Ed Balls over the Baby P killing and the treatment of David Scott, the London probation chief, in the Dano Sonnex case (see Chapter 4). Superficially, we appear to be in the realm of the index of mediated policy response developed by Walgrave and Van Aelst, who classify political actions as either 'symbolic' or 'substantial', with gradations of each (Walgrave and Van Aelst 2006: 101).

Jack Straw's swift repudiation of David Scott can, arguably, be classed as 'fast symbolic', serving very little purpose other than to appear tough. Can Michael Howard's treatment of John Marriott be viewed through the same prism? There is no doubt that spectacular failures in prison security had undermined his credibility as Home Secretary.

In the week after the escape of a number of IRA inmates from Whitemoor prison on 9 September 1994, according to a senior civil servant, he was 'running about like a headless chicken, apparently making policy on the basis of what-ever was in that afternoon's *Evening Standard* editorial' (Crick 2005: 297). The Parkhurst escapes not only compounded his embarrassment but cast a shadow over his declared intention to make prison the centrepiece of his crime strategy. Seen in that light, his handling of Marriott is more 'substantive' than might, at first, appear.

For Derek Lewis, Howard's approach to many prison issues, such as home leave, 'was all about public perception, suggesting that he cared much less about prison as a way of reducing crime' (ibid.: 296). But David Blunkett, who concedes that he had much in common with Howard in his approach to the Home Office, argues that addressing public perception is a vital part of a Home Secretary's job:

> You cannot just ignore what people out there are seeing and what they are reading because they are our task masters … In a liberal democracy, the sending of signals is important and reassurance is necessary. If you do not send out signals that you have heard and understood, it leads to people getting disillusioned – and that is when you end up with far right governments getting elected.
>
> Interview with author, 8 October 2008

This view was most strongly apparent in Blunkett's robust approach to immigration and asylum issues, which – except for its impact on policies to address the growth of Islamist extremism – largely falls outside the scope of this inquiry. The commentator Peter Oborne has some sympathy with Blunkett's justification for sending signals – but only up to a point:

> In many ways, I admire Blunkett. Politics is about responding to voters and you have to be able to articulate their anxieties about illiberal issues such as race, immigration and law and order. But we operate within a rule of law and the emotive comments on certain issues by Blunkett as Home Secretary – and later, by John Reid – were irresponsible and inflammatory. If you talk about being 'swamped' by immigrants [as Blunkett did] you are licensing a certain

type of language elsewhere. It was just designed to give them a rattling good press in the *Sun* and the *Mail*.

Interview with author, 14 December 2010

After losing his job, Blunkett went on to write a column for the *Sun* so Oborne's charge appears to have some validity. But the former Home Secretary, as ever, has an answer:

I plead guilty to writing my *Sun* columns in *Sun*-ese, just as people who are writing in the *Guardian* use pompous, long, overbearing sentences. But I do not ever use language to whip up hate. I use language to reinforce a sense of identity and belonging.

Guardian Weekend, 14 February 2009

6   In the shadow of Number 10

During the period covered by this research, the influence of the office of the Prime Minister over the policies pursued by the Home Office, and latterly the Ministry of Justice, has grown enormously. In the pre-New Labour period, examples of significant pieces of legislation being actively developed by the Home Office that were stymied, or even radically re-shaped, as a result of intervention by Number 10 are scarce on the ground. But since 2001, it is equally hard to find crime-related or justice policies which do not bear some evidence of Downing Street's midwifery.

As we have seen, this came about partly because Tony Blair, unlike most previous post-war Prime Ministers, had an instinctual feel for home affairs and regarded it as at, or close to, the very core of the New Labour project. But a Prime Minister alone, even one as activist as Blair, could not hope to wield such influence without the levers of a powerful and well-resourced communications and delivery machinery at his disposal. This Blair had to an unprecedented degree and used it, at some cost to harmonious governance. Giving evidence to a House of Lords committee in 2009, the former Cabinet Secretary, Lord Armstrong of Ilminster, said:

> Some of those methods which he [Blair] would have chosen conflicted with what I see as the fundamental position of the relationship between the Prime Minister and departmental ministers. Those frictions actually created bad relations among ministers and were setbacks to the efficient and proper conduct of government.
>
> House of Lords Select Committee on the Constitution 2010: 57

But this was a triangular relationship and the third side was the media. It is indisputable that New Labour came into office with a more clearly-defined communications and presentation strategy than any previous administration. And since 1995, Blair had worked assiduously to neutralize the hostility of News Corporation's stable of newspapers which had tarnished the credentials of previous would-be Labour Prime Ministers. The result of this, according to Lance Price, who became deputy Director of Communications in 1998, working at Number 10, was that:

> [Rupert Murdoch's] presence was almost tangible in the building and it was almost as if he was the 24th member of the Cabinet. And in fact, more than

that. In some areas of policy [he was] more influential on the PM and on the direction of the government's policy, than most of the other 23.

BBC Four 2008

On the basis of this assessment, it can be inferred that where Number 10 intervened in Home Office policy formulation, it did so taking into account the line being promoted by a powerful section of the press. This chapter examines three instances where this alliance of interests took command and left the Home Office struggling to catch up.

Rehabilitation bites the dust

In June 2000, Tony Blair made a widely-reported speech at Tübingen in Germany in which he expressed his frustration with the inadequacies of the criminal justice system by suggesting that 'drunken louts' could be marched to the nearest cashpoint by a police officer to pay an on-the-spot fine.[1] Senior police ranks had not been consulted in advance of the speech and the following week, at a crime 'summit' held at Number 10, they made it clear that the idea was a non-starter. Predictably, the speech made headlines but 'cashpoint justice' was dismissed by most commentators as a flaky musing not a thought-through policy proposal.

There is one fleeting reference to this episode in Blair's memoirs (Blair 2010: 279) but, in retrospect, it can be seen as marking the point at which Number 10 became significantly more interventionist in the area of crime policy, with profound consequences. With the economy buoyant and departmental spending reins loosened after a three-year period in which Gordon Brown had held to budgetary limits set by the Conservatives, this could have been the impetus for a programme to make good on Blair's promise to be 'tough on the causes of crime'. Instead, it was the signal to ramp up the use of summary justice and skew the focus towards issues of public confidence and away from longer-term strategies to reduce re-offending. In short, it was the period in which the rehabilitation agenda, being patiently developed by the Social Exclusion Unit and inside the Home Office, evaporated in a welter of media headlines about criminal justice favouring the offender rather than the victim.

Julian Corner worked on plans to update the Rehabilitation of Offenders Act 1974, both in the Social Exclusion Unit (SEU) during 2000–2 and thereafter in the Home Office. In April 2001, Jack Straw announced a review into the working of the 1974 Act, which was felt to be impeding the employment prospects of ex-offenders. But within a month, Straw had been moved to the Foreign Office and a new team took his place at the Home Office. Corner says that the minister of state for criminal justice, Charles Falconer, had little time for the rehabilitation agenda being developed:

Falconer was far more concerned about public confidence in the system than rehabilitation. He was very sensitive to any policy which ran contrary to the notion of 'victim-centred' justice and the idea [that the government was keen to promote] that the system is 'on your side'. I recall Falconer debating the

SEU report on rehabilitation with Oliver Letwin [the Opposition spokesman] on *Newsnight* and Letwin was far to the 'left' of Falconer's view. Meanwhile, Blunkett was hardly sending out warm signals about rehabilitation either. In fact, he was not even aware that the Home Office was formulating a new rehabilitation strategy. The problem was that tackling the very high re-offending rate did not deliver any short-term gains – in terms of favourable media coverage – for ministers. Unlike the various crime 'crackdowns' which were periodically announced.

Interview with author, 6 August 2008

This was apparent from the moment that Jack Straw announced the review of the 1974 Act. In a piece of archetypal news framing, the top line of the *Daily Mail* story read: 'Criminals may be able to bury their past under a radical review of the law on disclosing previous convictions, it was announced last night' (*Daily Mail*, 26 April 2001). And showing once again the potency of the 'zero-sum' paradigm that a gain for one party in the criminal justice process must mean a loss for another, Norman Brennan, self-appointed spokesman for the Victims of Crime Trust, is quoted as saying: 'Jack Straw seems more concerned about what he can do for criminals than what he can do for victims' (ibid.).

Officials continued to work doggedly on plans for fresh legislation on cutting re-offending, while their political masters were turning their attention towards 're-balancing' the criminal justice system. Thus an SEU proposal in July 2002[2] for a so-called 'Going Straight' contract, to be signed by prisoners aged 18–20 years at the start of their sentence, seemed, even at the time, little more than a somewhat hopeful kite flying exercise, and attracted little heavyweight ministerial endorsement. And although a pledge to implement a national cross-government rehabilitation strategy made it into the White Paper 'Justice for All' also published in July 2002, (Home Office 2002a), and draft legislation was produced, it was no great surprise that it had disappeared by the time the Criminal Justice Bill was published in November 2002. David Blunkett argues that it fell by default rather than design:

The Criminal Justice Bill was a very big bill and the question was: what was going to be dropped from it? It was not a conscious decision to drop this element of the bill, although there was some confusion around how we tackled prolific offenders and how we monitor/rehabilitate them, plus how well had we sold the concept of restorative justice. I would plead guilty to not having got all the ducks in a row in order to sell it coherently.

Interview with author, 8 October 2008

The abandonment of the rehabilitation plans at a time when the prison population was considerably lower and resources far more abundant was a serious lost opportunity. As the 2002 SEU report pointed out:

No-one is ultimately responsible for the rehabilitation process at any level – from national policy to the level of the individual prisoner. Responsibility and accountability for outcomes can be very unclear. The problems in prisoners' lives are often highly complicated and inter-related. They require a co-ordinated multi-agency response, within prison, across the crucial transitions between community and custody, and sustained long after release. Without this, they are likely to fall into the gaps between services.

Social Exclusion Unit 2002: 9

Charles Clarke, who succeeded Blunkett as Home Secretary, was more instinctively favourable to a rehabilitation agenda but felt hemmed in by a media on the warpath:

The media did play a highly significant role. It is not obvious – to put it at its most generous – that locking people up is the best way to deal with re-offending. Many people would say that community sentences and unpaid work schemes are more effective (though this is controversial) in making people face up to the consequences of what they have done, than hanging around all day in a prison cell. But the media made it very difficult to develop alternatives to prison because they were presented as not the 'tough' option.

Interview with author, 16 September 2010

His view was endorsed in 2011 by Sadiq Khan, Labour's Justice spokesman. He told a Fabian Society/Prison Reform Trust event:

I feel it was a mistake to not focus more on the issue of reducing offending. We became hesitant in talking about rehabilitation. … it was seen as being soft on crime, when in fact, it is effective in reducing crime.

cited in the *Guardian*, 7 March 2011

As to why Labour was so timid on this issue, he was even blunter when interviewed: 'I think one of the things that a Labour Home Secretary and a Labour Lord Chancellor found difficult was to get out of a *Daily Mail* headlock. We allowed that tail to wag the dog' (*New Statesman*, 14 February 2011).

Sadiq Khan did not specify which Lord Chancellor he was thinking of. If he meant Lord Falconer, there were strong suspicions that, before he was elevated to the Woolsack, his ministerial role in the Home Office was to be the 'eyes and ears' of his great friend, the Prime Minister.[3] If Falconer tried his best to scupper the rehabilitation plans, ergo, he was doing so at the behest of Tony Blair, so the argument went. Martin Narey was Director-General of the Prison Service at this time and an influential figure within the Home Office:

Charlie Falconer was dismissive about the rehabilitation agenda. He used to say 'we should just concentrate on locking people up'. But talking to Charlie about prisons was like having a chat in a pub. It was no more serious than that. However, Charlie did not speak for Blair on this. Blair was fairly sound on the rehabilitation, prisoner resettlement issue, in which he was encouraged by Cherie Blair. In fact, I gave the second of a lecture series which Cherie organized at Number 10 and she made Tony sit in a room for 45 minutes while I talked about corrections policy.

Interview with author, 10 September 2008

Whatever the Prime Minister's own views on rehabilitation, there is no doubt that, in various ways, Number 10's long reach was being felt on the collar of the Home Office in new and more intrusive ways. Following the 2001 election, three new units were created: the PM's Delivery Unit, under the energetic Michael Barber; the Office of Public Sector Reform; and the PM's Forward Strategy Unit. All were based in the Cabinet Office but their influence spread throughout Whitehall. In addition, the 'blue skies' thinking of Blair's adviser, John Birt, found its way into papers on crime which Home Office ministers were expected to acknowledge, if not actually to read, let alone implement.[4]

All of this had consequences for the Home Office, which expended a great deal of energy trying to prevent the PM's Delivery Unit and Strategy Unit micro-managing its work. Sue Jago, who worked on youth justice under Straw and was a senior official in the Criminal Policy Directorate under Blunkett, noticed the difference after 2001:

By this time, you could not move within the Home Office without clearing things with Number 10. This was especially true of media announcements. We had far more freedom of movement between 1997 and 2001. That was also because, in my view, Jack Straw was the last Home Secretary who did what he thought was right and was not looking over his shoulder all of the time.

Interview with author, 7 July 2008

It is also true that Straw had been a special adviser (to Barbara Castle); he knew the civil service mind intimately – his wife, Alice Perkins, was a senior Treasury official – and he was thoroughly at home with the detail of administration:

I always made it clear to whoever was Prime Minister, Tony or Gordon, that thanks very much, I could run a department of state, I could agree a broad agenda with the PM, and if he did not mind, I would get on with it. I cannot speak particularly for David [Blunkett] but, yes, I think Number 10 was more interventionist in his time.

Interview with author, 21 September 2010

Blunkett's characteristically self-effacing view is this:

Number 10 was certainly taking a greater interest in crime and thus in the Home Office post-2001. But there is the rub. Whatever department I was in, the PM would take a greater interest – for example, education or later, pensions and welfare reform. It was almost as if I carried kerosene with me to make the department's work flammable! The point is that anything which

Tony considered had a real political and public salience, he would place me in post there because he believed I shared his political antennae. And generally, I did.

Interview with author, 8 October 2008

Blunkett's special adviser, Huw Evans, believes there were other reasons for Blair's interventionism in home affairs:

The Home Office was always the department which he was most interested in, which got his juices flowing. He regarded it as New Labour's compact with middle Britain to sort out crime and anti-social behaviour and so on. There was also an element of displacement activity after 2001 because the PM and some of his advisers were frustrated at how little involvement they could have with economic policy as a result of the well-documented relationship difficulties with Number 11. So they piled in even more on the Home Office brief.

Interview with author, 10 February 2010

The street crime panic

Standing back for a moment, it is possible to observe a number of different but convergent themes emerging from 2001 onwards. After a first term in which the Prime Minister's domestic focus had been chiefly on education, other policy strands around crime and insecurity began to surge to the fore. The issues to do with security and asylum/immigration will be dealt with fully in Chapter 11. Here, the relevant concern is with Blair's determination to address the kind of crime which was coming to dominate the news agenda – above all, street robbery. So, on the one hand, there is a governmental emphasis on sharpening delivery of policies. And on the other, a media focusing fairly unremittingly from 2001 onwards on street crime and a concomitant lack of public confidence in the process of justice.

Put simply, which was cause and which effect? Was the media performing an agenda-setting role, on the seminal McCombs and Shaw model? (McCombs and Shaw 1972). On this postulation, the prominence and newsworthiness of stories in the media feeds into the public agenda, so-called 'salience transfer', making it difficult in a democracy for a politician to ignore the groundswell. Or was this an example of 'indexing hypothesis' (Bennett 1990), in which the official discourse and priorities of government set the terms of the media coverage?

The answer, fence-sitting as it may sound, is that the policy field is rarely susceptible to ironclad communications theorizing – or, as David Blunkett puts it: 'The froth and the reality get terribly mixed up because, as a politician, you are responding to public fears' (Interview with author, 8 October 2008).

Thus neither model of the media–public agenda relationship wholly accounts for the new priorities post-2001. However, others take a different and less nuanced view. Citing a series of governmental initiatives on crime, adopted between 2001 and 2003, Michael Tonry comments:

A few of those initiatives are important. Some are worthy. Many are 'noise on the stairs'. Serious policy processes are evidence-based, measured and cumulative. Serious media strategies are attention-grabbing and sensational. Looked at as a whole, the items in Table 2.2 [i.e. the government initiatives] appear much more to evidence a media than a criminal justice policy strategy.

Tonry 2004: 47

But to present the one strategy in opposition to the other is to miss the political point. A criminal justice process in which the public is fast losing confidence is a big problem for government and needs to be addressed by a clutch of means – including through the media. Identifying when that had become a priority was one of the talents which Tony Blair had as Prime Minister, as Huw Evans acknowledges:

There were areas where Blair's intervention and instincts were entirely correct and he got things in the right place. The street crime initiative is one example of that. David was aware of the problem and thought he should do something about it but the Prime Minister was one step ahead in terms of having a plan and a strategy that he wanted implemented in 2002.

Interview with author, 10 February 2010

And as the former chief executive of the National Offender Management Service, Phil Wheatley, points out, the media had picked up on a genuine problem which had slipped under the policy radar:

Street robbery had gone through the roof. The police were not gripping it. It just was not being dealt with as a serious issue. None of us in the law and order business had appeared to notice how bad it was in the big conurbations – London, Birmingham and so on. And knowing the rising rate of street crime, I thought 'this cannot go on for ever'. It did eventually become a scandal, Blair moved in on it and personally took charge of an action plan campaign, which forced people to pay attention and deploy resources to tackle it.

Interview with author, 18 June 2010

The scale of the problem, aggravated by the stealing of mobile phones, was pointed up in Home Office research. One study showed that although robbery overall declined by 3 per cent between 1999/2000 and 2000/2001, the taking of mobiles increased by a whopping 96 per cent (Harrington and Mayhew 2001: 269). Another Home Office report showed that 43 per cent of all robberies from the person in the police force areas studied involved mobile phones (Smith 2003: 540).

The cold statistics were given potency by some graphic media reporting, such as this story in the *Daily Mail*: 'A 12-year-old girl was stabbed twice when she refused to give her mobile phone to muggers. The youngster, who suffered a punctured lung in the attack, is the latest victim of Britain's rising tide of violent street crime' (*Daily Mail*, 24 February 2002).

Albeit belatedly, the Metropolitan Police was the first force to divert resources and manpower to tackling street crime, with an initiative launched at Christmas 2001, called Operation Safer Streets. According to the Commissioner, Sir John Stevens, this led to a massive fall in robberies in the first month. Nevertheless, in February 2002, the Home Secretary, David Blunkett, was telling the *Evening Standard* that Stevens 'had until August to get the matter in hand or else I would be replaced' (Stevens 2006: 297).[5]

Blunkett was reported as saying that the media focus on violent street crime was 'affecting the psyche of the nation' (*Guardian*, 5 February 2002) and he has since admitted that he was under some pressure from what was, not merely a crime story, but a mediated sociological phenomenon:

> My perception was that the media had hit on something, even if it was exaggerated. Street crime suddenly took off in London in 2002. It went up by 25 per cent in six months and the media was carrying quotes from high profile stars who said they were going to leave the UK because their mobile or their palm-top had been stolen. So, instead of working class communities bearing the brunt, the better off were crying foul. Editors of newspapers knew someone or had a relative who had had their mobile stolen, so it was certainly written about much more in 2002.
>
> Interview with author, 8 October 2008

And there is solid statistical evidence to demonstrate that these stories were having an impact on public perceptions. The 2002 British Crime Survey found that 43 per cent of tabloid readers believed that crime had increased 'a lot' (compared to 26 per cent of broadsheet readers) (Simmons and Dodd 2003: 6) while 17 per cent of tabloid readers admitted to being 'very worried' about being assaulted (the figure for broadsheet readers was 6 per cent). And this at a time when, statistically, the risk of becoming a victim of crime was said to be 'at an all-time low' (ibid.: 134).

The Prime Minister's response was to set up a street crime committee and that was followed by the first so-called 'summit', involving a range of different agencies, at Downing Street in March 2002. On the spectrum of 'sending signals', Number 10 summits have a special 'frequency' all of their own and are often derided by commentators. Yes, they garner headlines but beyond that? Blunkett has an answer:

> The summits did more than I expected because we brought together not just government department but other agencies and we got them to 'walk through' the system or process, as Blair used to put it. So, where we identified blockages we began to unravel them. In other words, one part of the criminal justice system might be doing quite a good job but another would be completely off-beam. For example, the Met police were improving their detection and arrest levels but the London probation service was dysfunctional, so between them, they were not presenting cases in court which should have gone to trial. And it led to re-offending while people were waiting to be tried. Summits

were also useful in determining whether we could implement initiatives via ministerial orders rather than primary legislation.

Interview with author, 8 October 2008

This period of the first few months of 2002 was notable for the flowering in the media of another crime phenomenon called car-jacking, which also had an impact on policy. The former presenter of the BBC *Crimewatch* programme, Nick Ross, has raised this as an example of the symbiosis between media and police, which serves often to distort the true picture of crime rather than illuminate it. It is worth quoting his thoughts at some length to make the point:

> A chap in south London was murdered, apparently for the theft of his car. So every newspaper dispatched reporters to find out about car-jacking. And very soon, we heard that there was an epidemic. There had been 112 cases in the last few months in London. It was not quite clear, reading the *Evening Standard*, which few months, but the figure of 112 stuck in my mind. And I was quite intrigued because there is no offence of car-jacking ... so who was defining what car-jacking was, and where did the figures come from?[6]

The *Standard* said the figures had come from the police. So, he rang Scotland Yard's Vehicle Crime Unit, which said the figures had originated with the press office. The press office admitted that they had supplied the stats – but on what evidence? They were an estimate, he was told: 'It was a guess. There was no evidence to it whatsoever and yet that has really gone down into national consciousness as an epidemic.'[7]

It should not come as a great surprise to learn that the 'epidemic' of an offence which did not officially exist became conflated in policy responses (and, indeed, media coverage) with street robbery. As in:

> David Blunkett yesterday promised a crackdown on carjackers and mobile phone muggers. The Home Secretary warned the thugs behind a recent spate of violent vehicle thefts that they would be 'banged away for a very long time' ... Mr Blunkett said he would press judges to impose the toughest possible sentences on such criminals.
>
> *Daily Mail*, 5 February 2002

In fact, the Home Secretary had already been overtaken by events. The week before, on 30 January 2002, the Lord Chief Justice, Lord Woolf, sitting in the Court of Appeal, caused a surprise by issuing a guideline ruling on mobile phone theft when he increased the sentences on two teenage phone thieves. Henceforth, he announced, offenders could expect a minimum prison sentence of 18 months, up to three years if they used a weapon and five years or more if they inflicted serious violence. Lord Woolf does not seek to hide the fact that this was a response to media stories:

> Yes it was. Rightly or wrongly, I was convinced that people were frightened of leaving their houses, and frightened of their children taking a mobile phone with them to school. I have never been particularly convinced by the

effectiveness of deterrent sentences but that was a deliberate attempt to deter mobile phone robbery. ... And as a result, that particular offence went off the radar as a special problem.

Interview with author, 11 May 2009

Indeed it did. Whether as a result of draconian penalties or the impact of the government's Street Crime Initiative launched in the Spring, the fact is that by September 2002, the recorded figures for street robberies were on a downward trend. This was just as well because the Prime Minister had given a deadline of September for measurable progress when he addressed the issue in parliament. As David Blunkett points out, that pledge ran as a fairly prominent media story for three days – notwithstanding the fact that Blunkett himself had set the same dead-line in an earlier interview with the *Evening Standard*. He observes at the time: 'It seems that the lobby journalists do not know anything. The corporate amnesia is just unbelievable' (Blunkett 2006: 372).

Number 10 calls the tune, the Home Office pays the price

In June 2003, David Blunkett made a speech at a conference organized by the Coalition for the Removal of Pimping (CROP) in Leeds. He told his audience:

> Prostitution and the issues surrounding it are difficult to talk about openly and are not talked about enough. I want to open up the debate. We need to address the problems that contribute to the chaotic lives that victims of prostitution often lead, in order to create safer neighbourhoods and an escape route for those trapped by vice.
>
> Home Office 2003[8]

The CROP speech was a routine engagement and thus far, Blunkett had stuck to his speaking brief. But his final line caught some of his own officials completely off guard: 'I intend to publish a paper to launch a sensible debate on this issue as soon as the groundwork has been completed' (ibid.).

Sue Jago was working in the Sex Offences Unit of the Criminal Policy Directorate:

> Blunkett's announcement of a review – and that it would report by the end of the year – took everyone by complete surprise. But he was piloting through the sex offences and domestic violence legislation and he regarded this, too, as a prior-ity. He used to say 'there are things which a Home Secretary has to do and things which he is remembered for – and this is what I want to be remembered for'.
>
> Interview with author, 7 July 2008

Perhaps more than any other recent Home Secretary, Blunkett's administra-tive pragmatism was tempered by a strong dose of emotional commitment to a cause, and this was one. Through the Crime Reduction Programme, the Home Office funded the 'What Works: Tackling Prostitution' scheme, in which eleven projects around the country were demonstrating the part effective intervention could play in providing exit routes from prostitution. They included so-called 'tolerance zones', increased police action against pimps, and the provision of housing and drug treatment for sex workers. However, it is a truism that, just as there are no votes in prisons (though that may change as a result of an ECHR ruling in 2010), there is precious little electoral gain for a government that wishes to reform laws on prostitution. The paper on prostitution, which canvassed the idea of 'managed areas', similar to those in some continental European states, had first to be approved by Number 10. Sue Jago headed the Prostitution Review team and it was her job to write the paper promised by Blunkett:

> The response [from Number 10] was: 'you will publish this over our dead body'. They took the view that if you tried to move the debate forward on prostitution, the media would ask: 'are you intending to legalize brothels?' Tony Blair did not want that. But interestingly, Blunkett was prepared to push this, despite Number 10's hostility.
>
> ibid.

The Home Secretary was already battle-hardened in this respect. In July 2001, he had had a spat with Number 10 over a speech on sentencing in which he intended to float the idea of 'custody minus' (a custodial sentence which, in practice, becomes a community punishment unless the terms are breached). Officials from the Strategy Unit wanted to take the reference out. Blunkett describes this intervention as symptomatic of 'people in Number 10 trying to use TB's [Tony Blair's] name to preclude senior cabinet ministers from contributing their own thoughts and ideas' (Blunkett 2006: 278–9).

The finessing of a consultation paper when there is such a strongly declared difference of view between a Home Secretary and Prime Minister throws a fascinating light on how policy discussion was conducted under New Labour. One of Blunkett's special advisers, Katherine Raymond, emerged as a pivotal figure in the policy dance over prostitution, brokering the relationship between the Home Office unit working on the strategy and Blunkett, and between Blunkett and Number 10. It is clear from Home Office sources that Blunkett would tell Raymond that he had squared the paper with the Prime Minister, while she would be given an entirely different message from Number 10, from where the command went out to re-draft so as to exclude any mention of legalizing brothels.

Katherine Raymond gave her account in 2006 when she had left the Home Office. She confirmed the deep divisions over the paper:

> In Whitehall, only a handful of politicians and officials wanted the report to see the light of day. At the Home Office, we were divided between those eager to publish – and be damned if necessary – and those wanting the whole issue to go away. In the end, and despite opposition from a Number 10 terrified of a hostile media response, the 'damned' won, not least because David Blunkett wanted what he called a 'grown-up debate'.
>
> *Observer*, 17 December 2006

But it was something of a pyrrhic victory because the consultation paper, published under the title 'Paying the Price', in July 2004, was, in Katherine Raymond's own words 'a watered-down series of proposals that took a small step in the right direction' (ibid.).[9] The licensing of brothels was mentioned – but on page 86, two pages from the end of the substantive section of the document (paragraph 9.14 onwards). Otherwise, the verdict of Teela Sanders, who has studied this subject, is probably fair:

> there are some praiseworthy efforts in the consultation paper to address serious protection issues for certain groups ... However, the language ... is one of enforcement, which echoes the policing practices witnessed across the country in recent years ... I suggest that the combination of a political doctrine of anti-social behaviour, Victorian morality and the continual scapegoating of sex workers forms the backbone of the Home Office document's content.
>
> Sanders 2005: 9–12

Number 10 was correct in predicting the media response, which tended to reflect the police view about the risks, rather than opportunities, in reforming the law. Typical were these headlines: 'Tread warily on vice reform, say police' (*Guardian*, 18 July 2004); 'Met vice chief attacks plans to legalise the sex industry' (*Evening Standard*, 20 August 2004).

'Paying the Price' led to what Teela Sanders has called 'four months of mild media interest' (Sanders 2005) which, no doubt, suited the Prime Minister's purpose because he was able to shelve any action until January 2006 when the government finally announced its strategy for reducing street prostitution. Ruling out 'managed zones', the Home Office minister, Fiona Mactaggart, said:

> I cannot accept that we should turn a blind eye to a problem that causes misery for people living in or near red-light areas. There is no evidence that decriminalization or licensing prostitution would achieve our objectives of reducing exploitation, improving the safety of those involved, and making local communities safer.
>
> Home Office 2006c

Invoking the interest of 'communities' over the safety of individual women, whose lives were put at risk on the street every day, neatly illustrates the pre-eminence of that New Labour nostrum as Tony Blair's premiership neared its end.

The press operation

It has been said often that one of New Labour's faults was to behave, for the first few years in government, as though it was still in opposition.[10] The party's well-practised facility for presentation had got it into office but both Alastair Campbell and Peter Mandelson were worried about what would happen in government if newly empowered ministers went 'off-message'. Campbell's first act was to orchestrate a purge of departmental communications directors. Mike Grannatt, by now head of the Government Information Service, was one of only two to survive:

> Campbell and Mandelson both feared that instead of shadow ministers being tied to their pagers, we would have ministers with huge staffs and their own little empires. Just after the election, they summoned the heads of communication of every department to a drinks do at Number 10 and the two of them did a double act in front of us, more or less reading out a speech, alternating, line by line. The burden was 'these guys – i.e. ministers – will turn into robber barons, so your job is to be our shock troops in controlling them'. And we thought, do they understand the constitutional niceties here? None of us work for them, we work for our Secretaries of State and the idea that we could keep them in line with the message from Number 10 was absurd.
>
> Interview with author, 12 October 2010

But it did not stop Number 10 from trying. To lend more muscle to Downing Street's operation, a strategic communications unit was set up alongside the press office, squeezing the room for manoeuvre of individual departments. As stated earlier, Jack Straw made it abundantly clear that he could run the Home Office without interference. Yet there were open channels of communication with the PM's Policy Unit, and Downing Street advisers were not reticent about commenting on Home Office legislative proposals. When Straw was drafting his White Paper on Youth Justice, one of those advisers, David Miliband, sent him a two-page note with a number of suggestions for improvement: 'I have four relatively small points, where I think clarification would ensure that the case is stronger, or that you are not attacked for things you are not saying' (David Miliband personal communication to Home Secretary, 17 November 1997, Restricted circulation, not published).

This was the normal intercourse of administration and, according to Julian Walker, the Home Office official, there was little friction with Miliband: 'You expect Number 10 not to be happy with you at times and to say that what you are doing is rubbish ... but David Miliband was not like that. I was completely smitten by him. I thought he was delightful' (Interview with author, 12 September 2008).

Straw's special adviser, Ed Owen, recalls that between 1997 and 1999, the relationship with the PM's Policy Unit was generally cordial, mainly because dealings usually went through Liz Lloyd, who had had responsibility for Home Affairs policy in the leader's office since 1994 and was regarded almost as part of the 'family'. But from 1999, the Home Office began to be subject to more intervention from Number 10:

> I suspect that what happened was that Labour was probably riding high on law and order for the first two years in government and then, as the shine wore off and difficult decisions had to be made, and as the election loomed

nearer, Number 10 began to get a bit jittery. There was increasing concern about asylum and immigration so, yes, it did get more interventionist in that period.

Interview with author, 1 October 2008

This jitteriness erupted a month before the 2001 election when Number 10 fed an exclusive story to the *Sun* that Jack Straw was to be moved and replaced by David Blunkett, who was quoted as declaring provocatively, 'I will make Jack Straw look like a liberal' (*Sun*, 30 April 2001). Ed Owen describes it as 'a Number 10 wind-up', while Straw says:

I did not think it was particularly comradely and David has been generous enough to concede that it was not. I had been shadow Home Secretary for four years and Home Secretary for four years. I had enjoyed it but it had been tough and ... I did not particularly appreciate learning that from the *Sun*.

Interview with author, 21 September 2010

In the first few months of New Labour's second term, the dynamic which governed relations between the press operation at the Home Office and Number 10 was badly disturbed. Many officials in the Home Office did not quickly forgive Blunkett for denigrating Jack Straw's time as Home Secretary. In his diary (later published as *The Blunkett Tapes*), written at the time, he quotes Straw as complaining in a phone call: 'You have drawn a line. It is year zero from June 7. You are overturning everything' (Blunkett 2006: 285). With hindsight, Blunkett makes a half-apology:

I was harsher on my colleagues than I should have been when I became Home Secretary. In retrospect, I was unfair about what had been achieved between 1997 and 2001 and what it had been possible to achieve. But I had cottoned on to the fact that the Home Office was not functioning terribly well. The obvious shambles which was immigration is the best example of that.

Interview with author, 8 October 2008

A bigger problem was that, although Tony Blair had appointed probably his closest ally in government to replace Jack Straw, Alastair Campbell's instinct at Number 10 was to keep a tight control over the Home Office media operation. It did not help that the two key figures, Julia Simpson, head of communications, and Huw Evans, were both new in post and struggling to find their feet, as Evans explains:

When David became Home Secretary, our in-tray was enormous. The asylum situation was at breaking point, there were major issues about crime, which had come up during the election campaign, and the Bradford and Oldham riots, so there were a lot of pressing issues which needed to be gripped. ... We had some spats in those first few months with Number 10 press officers, who were issuing comments on the Home Office view of things, which did not accord with David's view at all. He got very irate at that and there was a bust-up when David, Julia and I basically told Number 10 to get lost.

Interview with author, 10 February 2010

Relationships improved with personnel changes in Number 10 but Blair was not averse to demonstrating that, as well as appointing ministers, he could choose the time at which to apply pressure to them to do his bidding. One of these occasions was a television interview in February 2003:

> It was on *Newsnight* and the Prime Minister announced that the government would halve the number of asylum claims in a year. It was a sort of arbitrary target and it was a deliberate ambush on the Home Office, even though he claimed it was a mistake. So that was difficult for us.

ibid.

In July 2004, Blair struck again as the Home Office was about to launch its five-year crime plan:

> Tony gave a speech in which he said crime was all the fault of the 1960s, which was nothing to do with the sort of crime plan we had been developing and it was not what we had agreed in terms of messaging. But that was an example of the Prime Minister deciding he was going to do it because it was what he wanted to say. And you know, if he overrides what you want, that is his prerogative at the end of the day.

ibid.

The foreign prisoners scandal

The most obvious fault line which ran through the New Labour years was the Blair–Brown split. This study does not seek to bring fresh insights to that much discussed rupture, unparalleled in government in modern times. But insofar as it had consequences for the downfall of a Home Secretary under the most intense mediated scrutiny, it is relevant to weigh in evidence. The Home Secretary was Charles Clarke and he was brought low by the unfolding scandal that up to 1,000 foreign-born prisoners, who should have been deported after completing their sentence, had, unaccountably, slipped through holes in the system and been allowed to remain in the country, some going on to commit further serious crimes.

In their study of media and policy, Koch-Baumgarten and Voltmer write:

> Information obtained from the media provides them [politicians] with clues which help them to monitor the movements of their opponents and to gauge their own standing within an ever-shifting constellation of policy coalitions. They can then adjust their own strategies, which may include re-framing an issue or policy proposal, distracting attention from unfavourable issues to safer ones, or using the media to attack the position of their own opponents.

Koch-Baumgarten and Voltmer 2010: 3

Under New Labour administrations, this internecine sniping was invariably linked to the ongoing struggle for supremacy between Blairites and Brownites. Mike Grannatt, the former head of the Government Information Service, observed much of it at close quarters:

> It was part of the DNA of New Labour to see everything in terms of power politics and that is how you bring people down, by mounting a campaign against them through the media. As soon as this organism was placed into the petri dish of Whitehall, it went mad. People like Brown, a child of Glasgow politics, and Blunkett, who'd also been involved in it for a long time, just carried on in that vein.
>
> Interview with author, 12 October 2010

The chief 'seconds' in Blair's corner were Peter Mandelson and Alastair Campbell, both adept at feeding off and instigating media stories designed to paint Brown in an unflattering light.[11] On Brown's behalf, Ed Balls and Brown's former special adviser, Charlie Whelan, were the most active proponents.

The revelations about the 'missing' foreign prisoners broke in the media in the last week of April 2006, coinciding with a period of mounting tension within the upper reaches of government. The local elections were imminent and Labour was expected to do badly; and Brown's simmering frustration over Blair's refusal to set a date for handing over power had led to what many, both inside and outside government, interpreted as an attempted coup against the Prime Minister.

Looking at media coverage of the foreign prisoner issue, what is most striking is the consistently aggressive tone taken by the *Daily Mirror*, a Labour-supporting newspaper and, in other circumstances, to be found offering a corrective view to the consistently anti-government stance taken by competitors such as the *Mail* and *Express*. On this issue, however, the *Mirror* maintained an unforgiving pursuit of the Home Secretary and only 24 hours after the first admission of the blunder, it was reporting:

> Charles Clarke was last night fighting for his political survival, with the backing of Tony Blair and at least three Cabinet ministers ... a Westminster insider said: 'His position is extremely precarious. It is a feeling that it is one more thing and he is out'.
>
> *Daily Mirror*, 27 April 2006

The following day, the *Mirror* kept up the pressure with a story on the crime figures, which, in fact, showed that total recorded crime was stable, but which was framed in such a way as 'dealing another body blow to reeling Home Secretary Charles Clarke' (*Daily Mirror*, 28 April 2006). And it continued in this vein until the evening of the local elections on 6 May 2006, when Clarke was sacked by the Prime Minister. Of course, the rest of the daily press and indeed, broadcasters, could smell blood, too, but the *Mirror*'s coverage stands out.

Charles Clarke was a Blairite through and through and had never hidden his hostility to Brown. Neither Clarke himself nor the author has definitive evidence that the *Mirror* deputy political editor, Bob Roberts, who wrote the series of stories, had been deliberately reflecting Brown's perspective on the issue which, put bluntly, was that the removal of a heavyweight Blairite (in more senses than one!) could only be to Brown's benefit. But it would not take a huge leap of the imagination to infer it, because, as Clarke says:

> The *Mirror* was always very close to Brown [mainly because of the close links between Charlie Whelan and the paper's former labour editor, now associate editor (politics), Kevin Maguire]. And Gordon was always about the business of eliminating enemies. Although I do not blame the media for my demise, I believe I could have survived had it not been for the disastrous local election results and the attempted Brown putsch against Blair.
>
> Interview with author, 16 September 2010

It is only right to report that others regard Clarke's view that he could have survived such a calamitous Home Office error as fanciful, although if he had used the media more skilfully, he might just have rescued a desperate situation, even though he lost some parliamentary backing right at the beginning of the crisis:

> My big mistake was to make a written statement [on April 25 2006] and hold a press conference rather than address the House. It made me appear evasive and put me on the back foot and then the media started to get going ... I was not very good at dealing with the modern media political world. I did not like all that and it was one of my weaknesses. Both Blunkett and Tony Blair saw that as much more part of the job than I did – and they were probably right.
>
> ibid.

7   Addicted to distortion: the media and UK drugs policy

Introduction

This and the following chapter were written shortly after the publication of the UK coalition government's first drugs strategy (Home Office 2010). It provides a useful vantage point from which to look back over a 20-year period during which the relationship between drugs and crime, drugs and health and, as will be argued, drugs and morality, have been amongst the most heavily mediated of policy areas in the UK, with the result that politicians and other 'primary definers' (Hall *et al.* 1978: 57) absorbed media comment and responses, producing what theorists of moral panic have called a 'signification spiral' (Critcher 2003:15), in which, like some auto-immune disease, the panic feeds off itself, with consequent implications for policy.

The concluding line of the foreword to the strategy document reads:

> The UK is, of course, not unique in having to confront drug misuse. So, as we build upon this strategy, we are committed to continuing to review new evidence on what works in other countries and what we can learn from it.
>
> Home Office 2010: 4

It may be premature to write off this commitment to frame policy around evidence as a rhetorical one only, but, as we shall see, the early auguries were not good.

Despite the mainstream media's abiding pre-occupation with the social consequences of drug use – which will form the focus of this chapter – it paid remarkably little attention to the launch of the strategy, sceptical perhaps of the claim that it represented a 'fundamental difference ... from those that have gone before it'. But within days, jaundiced journalistic palates were unexpectedly stimulated by a declaration from a former Home Office drugs minister, which reinforced the time-honoured adage that, while 'dog bites man' is not news, 'man bites dog' assuredly is.[1]

The ex-minister in question, Bob Ainsworth, MP for Coventry North East, announced himself in favour of legalizing substances, including heroin and cocaine, under a system of strict regulation, as an alternative to what he called 'the failed war on drugs' – a war which he had prosecuted without any overt demur while in office between 2001 and 2003 (his comments were reported widely in newspapers, radio and TV on 16 December 2010 and repeated by Ainsworth during a debate in Westminster Hall on the same day). It is a familiar media trope to, as it were, put the cart before the horse and accord the response to an event, initiative, policy announcement or legal judgment primacy over the thing being responded to, thus 'framing' the issue 'in such a way as to promote a particular problem definition, causal interpretation, moral evaluation, and/or treatment recommendation for the item described' (Entman 1993: 52).

In this vein, the *Daily Mail* headline over the Ainsworth story was: 'Ex-minister condemned as "irresponsible" by party for drugs u-turn' (*Daily Mail,* 16 December 2010). Indeed, the Labour Party leader, Ed Miliband, moved swiftly to distance himself from Ainsworth's comments and, despite the coalition government's promise to examine 'what works in other countries', the crime prevention minister, James Brokenshire, wasted no time in denouncing decriminalization as a 'simplistic solution' (BBC News Online 2010).

Thus, at time of writing, there is little expectation that, although some liberal media outlets – notably, the *Observer,* in a number of features and authored opinion articles during 2010 and a series of three documentaries in the Channel 4 *Dispatches* strand by the film-maker, Angus Macqueen, called 'Our Drugs Wars'[2] – have sought to expand the boundaries of public discourse on drugs policy, government, of whatever stripe, remains immutably committed to what the 2010 strategy terms two 'over-arching' aims: to reduce illicit and other harmful drug use and to increase the numbers recovering from their dependence. Beyond that limited ambition, in the parlance of medieval cartographers, 'there be dragons'!

There is a considerable body of research on the relationship between drug policy and crime, both in the UK and the United States (see, for example, Reuter and Stevens 2008; Warburton *et al.* 2005; and MacKenzie and Uchida 1994). Useful work has been done on the media and representation of drugs (see, Taylor 2008; Forsyth 2001; Coomber *et al.* 2000; and Gossop 1996). Mark Monaghan (2008) has explored the role that 'evidence' has played in the making of recent policy on cannabis.

Less well covered is the link between the media and drugs policy. Simon Cross (2007) has dissected the argument around cannabis reclassification between 2000 and 2004 as refracted through newspapers such as the *Independent on Sunday,* the *Daily Mail, The Times* and the *Telegraph.* Paul Manning (2007: 150–64) reaches into the previous decade to untangle the media's reporting on the drug ecstasy and its relationship to public policy debates of the time, and finds that coverage was disproportionate, compared to that of volatile substance abuse (the sniffing of glue, aerosols and lighter fuel, etc.) and that the reason was chiefly to be found in newspapers' symbolic framing of the substances according to the class and social grouping of users.

This research is an attempt to bring all of these strands together and, by taking a heavily policy-centric approach, examines how certain newspapers have circumscribed the responses of government to the impact of drugs on society in the first decade of the twenty-first century, with the outcome that drug classification has become observably detached from drug harm; how the transition from Tony Blair to Gordon Brown extinguished a brief flowering of realism about cannabis;

and tests the assertion made by the sacked chair of the Advisory Council on the Misuse of Drugs (ACMD), Professor David Nutt, in the *Guardian* that, amidst the moral tumult around drugs policy, it was the behaviour of the New Labour administration that was 'immoral' for claiming that science 'directed policy-making' (Aitkenhead 2010). Most of the direct quotations which follow are from interviews conducted by the author with former members of the ACMD, former Home Secretaries, Charles Clarke and Alan Johnson and other policy and media actors.

The mephedrone scare

'The "death" drug we can't police' *(Daily Mail*, 18 March 2010); 'Police reveal 180 pupils at one school off sick after taking legal "Meow Meow" party drug' *(Daily Mail,* 8 March 2010); 'Sex-tear injury on "cat" drug' *(Sun,* 27 November 2009): all of these headlines refer to the drug mephedrone, a short-acting stimulant with effects similar to those of amphetamines.[3] Also known colloquially as plant food, meow meow (hence the reference to 'cat' drug in the *Sun* headline), m-cat or bubbles, mephedrone was legal in the UK and freely available for purchase over the Internet, until a government prohibition took effect on 16 April 2010, following a recommendation from the ACMD at the end of March. The banning order came a year after the ACMD launched an investigation, at the government's request, into the 'legal high', Spice, a synthetic cannabinoid mixed with aromatic herbs and available both online and through backstreet 'head shops'. For much of that year, a number of newspapers maintained a steady focus on the potentially deleterious impact on the predominantly young users of 'legal highs', exerting considerable pressure on the Home Office to classify named substances under the 1971 Misuse of Drugs Act (MDA).

In relation to mephedrone, that pressure was ratcheted up after the widely reported deaths of two teenage men, Louis Wainwright, aged 18, and Nicholas Smith, 19, in Scunthorpe in March 2010. The *Daily Mail* story of 17 March, headlined 'Action pledged on "meow meow" drug after two teen friends die within hours of taking "legal high"', quoted the Business Secretary, Peter Mandelson, as promising: 'We will take any action that is needed, any action that is justified, to deal with this and to avert such tragic consequences occurring in the future'. A robust pledge, this was perhaps weakened by Mandelson's admission that he had never previously heard of mephedrone until approached for a comment from the *Mail*!

In the same report, the shadow Home Secretary, Chris Grayling, is quoted as saying that there was 'a very strong case' for the drug to be banned and that his party would carry out an urgent review of 'legal highs' if elected. With a general election imminent – it took place on 6 May 2010 – the Home Secretary, Alan Johnson, was clearly under some pressure to act, as he acknowledged after his government had been defeated at the polls:

> The reason we hurried up banning mephedrone was firstly, a lot of newspaper stories after the deaths of the two boys in Scunthorpe but also an election was coming and we wanted to get it through parliament before the dissolution.
>
> Interview with author, 7 July 2010

Asked whether there was also a desire to show the media, ahead of the election, that the government was being 'tough' on drugs, Mr Johnson said:

> Well, you never know whether, at the back of your mind, there are other considerations but I like to think it was the importance of getting the ban on the statute book before the election. We honestly didn't do it [i.e. ban it] to grandstand in that way. We were being led by the ACMD ... legal highs had become a big issue.
>
> ibid.

The term 'issue' is problematic and deserves some consideration. A political 'issue' frequently has a symbiotic relationship with what Galtung and Ruge refer to as 'continuity' in their celebrated analysis of news values. As they put it, 'once something has hit the headlines and been defined as "news", then it will continue to be defined as news for some time, even if the amplitude is drastically reduced' (Galtung and Ruge 1973: 65). Even at lower amplitude, the drumbeat of a running story which threatens to destabilize or, at the very least, embarrass government, if left unaddressed, can appear insistently loud to ministerial ears. The weight of headlines about mephedrone was certainly perceived to carry that risk for the Home Secretary.[4]

In truth though, the mainstream media arrived fairly late on the scene in recognizing the growing allure of mephedrone. It was being mentioned with increasing regularity on websites, both general and drugs-oriented, for well over a year before it emerged as a political 'issue'. Harry Shapiro is director of communications for DrugScope, a leading drug information and policy charity:

> Mephedrone is an interesting phenomenon. It's the first time I can think of where you have a drug becoming apparently that popular while it was legal – unlike cocaine, ecstasy, amphetamines, which became popular *after* they were banned. We were picking up reports of use from rural Scotland, mid-Wales, as well as the big urban areas and this was because of the influence of the Internet. Indeed, we were ahead of the game and carried an article on mephedrone in our publication, *Druglink,* in March 2009. After the mainstream media started splashing on mephedrone in autumn 2009, we did some 'mystery shopping' and found that interest in the drug spiked, probably as a result of the media publicity.
>
> Interview with author, 22 June 2010

When the prohibition on mephedrone came into force by statutory instrument on 16 April 2010,[5] the *Sun* headline on that day was: 'Meow banned from midnight – drug illegal in victory for the *Sun*'. Allowing for the habitual solipsism of News International's market leader (who can forget the triumphalist headline on John Major's surprise victory in the 1992 general election: 'It's *The Sun* Wot Won It'?), it is true that the *Sun* had launched a campaign to outlaw mephedrone in the middle of March under the slogan 'Ban Meow Now'. It is impossible to assess the impact of this campaign on ministers but it was reported elsewhere, in the *Guardian* (17 March 2009), that the Home Secretary had intervened person-ally in March to hasten the conclusion of the ACMD inquiry on which he was statutorily obliged to base any policy decision. So, the *Sun*'s boast casts a reflec-tive light on Alan Johnson's assertion that his government 'was being led by the ACMD' (ibid.). It also prompts the question: was it science or realpolitik which was leading the ACMD?[6]

The ACMD published its long-awaited report on mephedrone at a meeting on 31 March 2010, a fortnight after the deaths of the two Scunthorpe teenagers, referred to above, had made news headlines. Because of the level of media interest, the first part of the meeting was opened to the media. Under the section 'Cases of death where cathinones have been implicated', the report refers to 'at least 18 deaths in England' and 'at least seven deaths in Scotland', with another case 'probable' (ACMD 2010: 19). The chair of the ACMD, Professor Les Iversen, who had replaced the sacked David Nutt, made it clear that the two Scunthorpe deaths were included in the calculation; this, despite the fact that no inquests had been held nor toxicology results released to determine cause of death.[7]

Eric Carlin was a member of the ACMD at the time of the mephedrone report but resigned four days later. In his letter of resignation to the Home Secretary, he protested at what he said was a rushed recommendation, 'unduly based on media and political pressure' (Carlin 2010). He elaborated on that view in an interview with the author:

> The meeting to discuss mephedrone was unique. We didn't even have the papers before the meeting. They were actually tabled as we sat down. This had never happened before. The chair controlled the morning part of the meeting very tightly and we were told we had to make our recommendations before the afternoon because the chair had to attend a joint press conference with the Home Secretary to announce the decision.
>
> Interview with author, 13 May 2010

Professor Les King would have been at the meeting but he had resigned from the ACMD following the sacking of David Nutt in October 2009:

> The ACMD report on mephedrone was the most blatant example of the committee being used to rubber stamp government policy. That was the lowest point to which the ACMD had sunk. The report itself was very thin and I wouldn't have wanted to be associated with it. Les Iversen was told to leave the meeting early in order to attend a press conference at which Alan Johnson was going to announce the banning of mephedrone. That was disgraceful. He seems to be unrepentant and doesn't appear to recognize that he has been a tool of politicians in the Home Office. He'll be remembered for not standing up to the Home Secretary.
>
> Interview with author, 22 June 2010

Few would argue with the proposition that the issue of drugs is as ferociously contested and heavily mediated as any area of public policy. Partly for that reason, it produces opinions which are often one-sided and judgments about the role of evidence in policymaking, which Mark Monaghan has called 'zero sum statements' (Monaghan 2008: 228). Professor David Nutt argues that the New Labour administration played fast and loose with science, using it merely as a prop to support its own policy agenda on drug classification and ignoring it when politics dictated. However, it should be remembered that it was the ACMD itself which chose to launch an inquiry into mephedrone, in December 2009, and that, independently of government, it had concluded that it should be classified under the MDA. The issue is: how far did the committee depart from accepted norms of evidence-gathering and the accumulation of solid pharmacological data in producing a report which was to be the basis for a policy decision by government?

Jeremy Sare was Secretary of the ACMD from May 2003 until December 2004 and then became head of Drug Legislation at the Home Office until January 2006:

> The [ACMD] report has serious gaps in basic information. For example, it admits there is 'no purity available' so we don't know how strong the drug is. The epidemiology was based, in part, on an article for *The New Musical Express*. Data on prevalence was derived from a survey conducted by dance culture magazine, *Mixmag*, and is also based on bare numbers of hits on the 'Talk to Frank' website [run by the Home Office]. That is no measure of its use. It is quite astonishing that there are no studies on dependency, treatment or prevention.
>
> Sare 2010

Sare continued the theme in an interview for this research:

> The mephedrone report is absolutely shocking. It includes the press story about 180 children at a Leicestershire school becoming ill after taking mephedrone, which is simply not true. That's astonishing. And from speaking to members of the ACMD, who were at the meeting when it was launched, the picture is one of utter chaos.
>
> Interview with author, 15 June 2010

The agony and the ecstasy

Professor Nutt's demise as chair of the ACMD in October 2009 was a downfall in two parts. First, in January, there was the 'notorious' paper which he wrote for the *Journal of Psychopharmacology* (Nutt 2009a) comparing the number of deaths from horse-riding to deaths from ecstasy. In the words of former Home Secretary, Alan Johnson 'that earned him a yellow card from Jacqui Smith' (Interview with author, 7 July 2010). Then, to continue the football analogy, Johnson himself brandished the red card after publication of Nutt's Eve Saville lecture at the Centre for Crime and Justice Studies at King's College London, which was widely reported (Nutt 2009b).[8] The circumstances by which his comments blew up into a media storm offer an illuminating insight into the, often collusive, relationship between press and politicians. This is Nutt's account:

I first made the comparison between deaths from horse-riding and from ecstasy after discovering that head injuries from falling off horses is the commonest cause of Parkinson's disease in the shire counties. My point was: so why are we so hung up on ecstasy? I introduced the concept at a meeting at the Beckley Foundation in December 2008. People there found it interesting so I wrote a paper for the *Journal of Psychopharmacology* in which I expanded on the idea of threshold of harm, and ran it by the Chief Scientist at the Home Office, Professor Paul Wiles. He said it was valuable and interesting and helped broaden the debate, asked me to moderate one or two things – for example, don't say this should be the basis for law – but he had no objections to it being published. As often happens these days, the paper's first publication was online. I didn't even know that it had appeared until a reporter from the *Daily Telegraph* rang me on a Friday morning and asked me: 'do you stand by this article?'.

Interview with author, 13 May 2010

All credit then to an alert journalist for spotting it? Well, not quite, it seems.

The reporter said he had just found the journal paper online but I think I'm being 'searched'. There are a group of people out there, an anti-drugs cabal, scanning the literature. That's how the *Telegraph* learned of it. The reporter asked me: 'who paid you to write it?' I said: 'what do you mean, paid me?' Once the *Telegraph* had run it, it took off in all the other papers, the BBC and so on. On the Monday morning, the Home Secretary, Jacqui Smith, rang me at my clinic and I said: 'Am I being sacked?' It was a coincidence of timing that she was in the middle of a media storm of her own over her parliamentary expenses and it was a useful distraction to have a go at me. She was able to say she'd told me off, that I'd apologized because I'd upset families of those who had died and that I had promised not to stray into this territory again. The whole thing was bizarre.

ibid.

It has not been possible to verify Professor Nutt's supposition that anti-drugs groups routinely track his writings on the Internet nor that this was how the *Telegraph* learned of his ecstasy paper but, if true – and there is certainly nothing discreditable about such methodology – it merely indicates that, while new media is, in many respects, a threat to printed newspapers, it is also sometimes an ally (a theme explored in more detail in Chapter 10). It also points up the fact that Professor Nutt's comments in an 'obscure' journal would have been of little concern to the Home Office had they not received wider dissemination. The same observation holds true of the Eve Saville lecture which was delivered in July at King's College London, to a small invited audience, and ruffled few government feathers. But upon publication of the lecture in October, Professor Nutt's fate was sealed.

This issue of mediated controversy will be picked up again later but it is worth dwelling here on Nutt's question: why are we so hung up on ecstasy? What buttons does the drug press amongst politicians and pundits alike which ensures that irrational prejudice and logical *non sequiturs* are substituted for rational appraisal, as in this response from the *Daily Mail* columnist, Melanie Philips, to Nutt's *Journal of Psychopharmacology* paper:

> The comparison [between horse riding and ecstasy] is simply ridiculous. Horse riding is not inherently harmful. Drug taking is. Horse riding is not addictive. Drug taking is. Most people who ride horses do not come to any harm. The only reason there are not many more deaths from ecstasy is that unlike horse riding, it is illegal.
>
> *Daily Mail*, 9 February 2009

In his paper, 'Crime as a Signal, Crime as a Memory', Martin Innes explores why certain serious offences function as social signifiers and explains that the mediated representation of these crimes is 'interpreted by audiences as an index of the state of society and social order' (Innes 2004: 17). According to Critcher (2003: 59), ecstasy is regarded as problematic by the powerful 'because the symbolic meanings associated with it transgress norms of risk avoidance and bodily discipline'. Thus, when Nutt decided to evaluate the comparative risk of taking ecstasy in his journal paper, he was wading into deep political waters. By his own admission, he should have expected trouble:

> The ACMD had been looking at ecstasy and was going to recommend it be downgraded from Class A to Class B. But the Home Office had told the Commons Science and Technology Committee that whatever we recommended, they were not going to downgrade. It was all about messages. They knew an election was coming and wanted to appear tough.
>
> Interview with author, 13 May 2010

It is instructive to compare the political reaction to this episode with an occasion, seventeen years earlier, when the Conservatives were in power and a supposedly 'maverick' view of ecstasy demonstrated that media representation can be as powerful a stimulant as some drugs. In 1992, when raves and rave music had popularized ecstasy as the substance of choice among young clubbers, the Mersey Regional Health Authority asked the regional Drug Training and Information Centre to produce a leaflet offering advice on harm reduction to ecstasy users. Professor Pat O'Hare, a drugs consultant, was then director of the centre:

> By 1992, ecstasy was enormous on Merseyside and had completely taken over the drug scene. The leaflet was approved by the press people from the health authority and the head of the Merseyside drug squad probably saw it too. Under the heading: 'Chill Out: A Raver's Guide', the first sentence read: 'It's not a good idea to use ecstasy, however if you do…'. And that was followed by sensible precautions to take to reduce harm. Then about a fortnight after the leaflet appeared, the local paper, the *Liverpool Echo*, got hold of it and I thought 'f—k me!'.
>
> Interview with author, 4 June 2010.

The *Echo* headlined its front-page story 'Raving Mad' and described the 'glossy drugs leaflet that every Merseyside parent will view with outrage' (*Liverpool Echo*, 28 January 1992). Local MP, and minister for Overseas Development, Lynda Chalker, complained that the leaflet told readers 'how to take drugs safely' instead of 'hammering home the message that drugs are wrong and drugs kill'. But worse was to come when the national press picked up the story the following day.

The main leader column in the *Daily Star*, 'Star says', was headed: 'Menace on the Mersey' and, describing the Mersey Regional Drug Training Centre as 'mutton-heads', and the leaflet as 'evil twaddle', urged readers to discover the location of the centre. 'Then they should storm the place and dump all 20,000 copies of this pernicious pamphlet deep in the Mersey. Followed by Mr O'Hare' (*Daily Star*, 29 January 1992). Other national papers, especially the *Sun* and the *Daily Mail*, also did their bit to stoke up the controversy.

Prof. O'Hare recalls that the press furore even led to a call in parliament for the training centre's funding to be removed. Given that this drama, like the one involving Professor Nutt in 2009, was played out only months before a general election, it would have been quite understandable if the Conservative chair of the Merseyside Regional Health Authority, Sir Donald Wilson – a personal friend of the recently resigned Conservative leader, Mrs Thatcher – had withdrawn his support from the beleaguered Pat O'Hare. He did not, as O'Hare explains:

> Sir Donald asked the official in charge of health promotion at the authority: 'Has the leaflet gone over the edge, or is it on the edge?' The reply was: 'It's on the edge'. Sir Donald then said: 'Tell Pat O'Hare to go out and defend it with his life.' That was fantastic because he could have withdrawn our funding just like that. So, I appeared everywhere in the media defending the leaflet. In fact, the *Echo* gave me a double-page spread to put my case. No similar offer was made by the national press. With them, I believe it's best to say nothing and eventually they move on to something/someone else.
>
> Interview with author, 4 June 2010

So, unlike David Nutt, who found himself living on borrowed time after his journal article on ecstasy, Pat O'Hare, in his own words, was 'bulletproof' once he had secured the backing of Tory grandee, Sir Donald Wilson:

> In fact, I would say that we won the argument, to the extent that we never had any further criticism about future leaflets, which were far more hard-hitting. One about cocaine even had a mirror on the front with a line of coke. To my mind, the ecstasy leaflet marked a sea-change and the harm reduction approach became, or was confirmed as, government policy.
>
> ibid.

Fast forward to New Labour and a moral certainty about ecstasy and the dangers it represented was noticeably hardening the policy arteries. Well-argued recommendations from both the Runciman Inquiry (Runciman 2000) and the Home Affairs Select Committee's *Third Report* (2002) that ecstasy should be downgraded from Class A to B left the government unmoved. Indeed, so urgent was the apparent need to reassure people that policy would not change that the Home Secretary, David Blunkett, responded the same day as the publication of the Home Affairs Committee report by saying 'reclassification of ecstasy is not on the government's agenda' (*Mail Online,* 22 May 2002). A member of the committee, the Labour MP, Chris Mullin – later to become a minister – commented: 'The government is always saying … that we follow the science … all we are saying to them is to follow the science in relation to drugs because it is … overwhelmingly clear' (ibid.).

Advise – and consent?

Despite such pleas, the policy process in relation to ecstasy was to remain sclerotic throughout New Labour's second and third terms in office. Thus, inside the Westminster 'village' and amongst the drugs agencies and think tanks, Jacqui Smith's reprimand of her chief drugs adviser, Professor Nutt, in February 2009[9] for straying beyond his advisory brief in comparing the dangers of ecstasy to those of horse-riding, came as little surprise, even if it was a brief media sensation. However, within the scientific community, it caused a collective shudder because it was by no means the first occasion that empirical research lost out to realpolitik under both New Labour and Conservative administrations. To promote a more mature reportage of science issues and give the scientific community a voice in the national news media, the Science Media Centre was established, following a report in 2000 by the Lords Select Committee on Science and Technology.[10] The director of the centre, Fiona Fox, believes the public deserves better than an enforced purdah on government 'experts':

> Sometimes I am shouting in the office in frustration when scientists say they're not allowed to speak because I know deep down that if they were, it would not do the government any harm. Look at all the surveys which show that government scientists are not trusted – on issues like swine flu, BSE and so on. Whereas, independent scientists tend to be trusted more. The members of the committee set up to deal with swine flu, SAGE, had to sign confidentiality clauses banning them from speaking to the media. One scientist was reminded by a civil servant that he had signed the Official Secrets Act!
> Interview with author, 11 June 2010

David Nutt's bruising encounter with the Home Secretary thus spurred Ms Fox into action:

> I was so disturbed by what I saw as chairs of independent scientific advisory committees being silenced or managed that I called a private dinner with the then science minister, Lord Drayson. It included about seven chairs of advisory committees who, one way or another, had been treated badly. We agreed that there should be a principled defence of the right of

scientists to speak out in public independently, and one of the issues was: who is their press office? (An issue we have raised many times.) When Jacqui Smith attacked Nutt, he phoned me and said that his press office was the Home Office. Now, if you're a 25-year-old Home Office press officer, are you going to stand against the Home Secretary and represent Nutt? Of course not.

ibid.

There are, of course, two separate and equally important issues at stake here. One is the role of expert scientific advice and knowledge in public debates about policy. The other is the right of the government to ignore such advice if it chooses. Though the ACMD has a statutory function to deliver expert advice and recommendations, the Home Secretary is not obliged to adopt them. Fiona Fox does not take issue with that:

All of the scientific experts on the ACMD – bar David Nutt – went out of their way to stress that science should not trump drugs policy. And I agree that a drugs strategy is not only a question of scientific evidence. What the police think is important. What voters think matters. All that scientists are asking for is honesty, for government to say 'we are banning this substance against the weight of evidence because we would rather go with the police opinion than yours'. That's what the dispute was about – honesty.

ibid.

This reflection raises another area of interest for those researching the interaction of media and policy. Should bodies like the ACMD, which advise government on the basis of scientifically reputable evidence-gathering, be allowed to share their expertise directly with the media in order to inform understanding of public policy issues and thus inject some 'honesty' into debate? After all, the Home Office has allowed other 'backroom boys' to emerge blinking into the media spotlight to help illuminate contentious areas – similarly to on-the-record briefings by the Director of Research, Development and Statistics, (the process began in the late 1990s under Professor Paul Wiles, later to become Chief Scientist and now retired) when the quarterly crime figures are published. Jeremy Sare recalls only one occasion when there was direct contact between the ACMD and media during his time:

That was when Michael Rawlins (then chair of the ACMD) did an interview with the *Daily Telegraph* in autumn 2004. It was based on the 'table of harms' drawn up by David Nutt [then chair of the ACMD technical committee], and Rawlins expressed the opinion that, if adopted, it could lead to a complete shake-up of the whole classification system. This caused some alarm among ministers, and the head of the drugs strategy directorate, Vic Hogg, almost certainly 'had words' with Rawlins. On reflection, it would have helped a more mature public debate on drugs if there had been media briefings with the ACMD.

Interview with author, 15 June 2010

Nutt's 'table of harms' article (Nutt *et al.* 2007) was not published until March 2007 (in *The Lancet)*. Professor Les King was one of the co-authors of the review:

> It started life back in 2000 and we looked at about 20 substances and tried to rate them in terms of harm. Initially the Home Office drugs policy branch was quite enthusiastic about our work and there seemed to be a window of opportunity to influence classification policy. But when they saw what was coming out of our review, they started to get cold feet and they said: 'we don't think it would be in the public interest for you to publish'. Why did they do that? Because they were a very cautious, conservative bunch of officials who were anticipating what the Home Secretary would say if our conclusions were to be publicly aired.
>
> Interview with author, 22 June 2010

There is general agreement from 'insiders' that Michael Rawlins managed to navigate the often turbulent currents of drugs policymaking with less distress than his successor, David Nutt. Indeed, Nutt, certainly more forthright, has been accused of naïvety:

> Was I naïve? Well, perhaps you could say 'innocent'. I always took the view that the only way you could change things was to tell the truth. But the politicians were only completely comfortable if you told them what they wanted to hear. Bring a drug into the Drugs Act? Fine. Move a drug up the classification table? Fine. But move something down the table – oh my God, you can't do that. It will send the wrong message, society will collapse. The fact is that they lack the courage to confront the realities of relative harm. I don't have any regrets about what I did. I don't think I could have done it any better because their minds were made up.
>
> Interview with author, 13 May 2010

David Nutt's sacking as chair of the ACMD on 30 October 2009, the day after his Eve Saville lecture, could certainly have been handled with more finesse. After all, he was given the news by email late on a Friday afternoon. Not even a face-to-face dismissal, as he explains:

> My secretary told me I had an email from the Home Secretary. I opened it and it asked me to resign. I replied that I would not. So, I was sacked – by return email. I never saw the Home Secretary (Alan Johnson) again after that. The remarkable thing was that only three days earlier, I'd met him to discuss things like spice, GBL, synthetic cannabinoids and I thought we were getting on really well. No hint of what was to come.
>
> ibid.

For Alan Johnson, it was simply a case of abuse of trust.

> The media reported the context as though there was a problem with every scientific committee which reports to government, and with the ACMD, in

particular. There was no problem with the ACMD. It had done a brilliant job on policy recommendations on synthetic cannabinoids, for example. The problem was with David Nutt. He didn't take notice of the yellow card issued by Jacqui Smith and went on and committed another offence. The trust which you need in that kind of relationship had just disappeared.

Interview with author, 7 July 2010

But the Home Secretary's letter of dismissal released to the press later the same day, 30 October 2009, makes it clear that it was 'going public' with comments critical of policy, which was the real sacking offence.

Dear Professor Nutt,

... I have concerns regarding your recent comments, that have received so much media attention ... When you wrote previously around the relative harms of drugs, comparing ecstasy with the risks of horse-riding, my predecessor made clear that it is not the job of the chair of the government's advisory committee to comment or initiate a public debate on the policy framework for drugs. Given this, I was surprised and disappointed by your further comments to the press this week. I cannot have public confusion between scientific advice and policy and have therefore lost confidence in your ability to advise me as chair of the Advisory Council on the Misuse of Drugs. I would therefore ask you to step down from the council with immediate effect.

Johnson 2009

Experts in semantics could spend a profitable time interrogating Mr Johnson's use of the word 'advise'. After which, they might well conclude that what he really means is 'tell me what I want to hear and have already decided to do'. But what the Home Secretary does not say in the letter is as revealing as what he does. Ten days after it was sent, he admitted in another letter, to the Liberal Democrat science spokesman, Evan Harris MP, and reported in the *Guardian* (9 November 2009), that the Home Office had been forewarned both of the journal paper on ecstasy in January 2009 and the Eve Saville lecture in July. But, said Johnson, the Home Office was unaware that the lecture was going to be published three months later by the Centre for Crime and Justice Studies (ibid.). Publication, then, was the crime, rather than the opinions of Professor Nutt *per se*.

As Richard Garside, director of the Centre for Crime and Justice Studies, commented in the *Guardian* (31 October 2009): 'The message is that when it comes to the Home Office's relationship with the research community, honest researchers should be seen but not heard.' Which, in one sense, is the inverse of the relationship between the popular media and the Home Office in which 'he who shouts loudest' can often elicit a government response, as long as the organization is thought to reflect the views of an important 'demographic' which ministers feel they ignore at their peril.

An example is the policy response to the drug GBL, known in party-going and dance circles as 'liquid ecstasy' and, like its chemical partner GHB, implicated in a small number of deaths of young people from 2007 onwards. One was that of a young medical student called Hester Stewart in April 2009. Blonde, vivacious and from an articulate middle-class family who lived in Brighton, she embodied many of the stereotypes which have long focused press reportage on some drugs deaths rather than others. A decade and a half earlier, Leah Betts, who died after taking one ecstasy tablet on her eighteenth birthday, had attracted a similar ghoulish notoriety in the media (Manning 2007).

Hester Stewart's death was not just a personal tragedy for her family but a political embarrassment because the Home Office had promised in the summer of 2008 to ban GBL but had not yet done so, provoking headlines such as: 'Medical student dies after taking "party drug" GBL that Home Office failed to ban' (*Daily Telegraph*, 28 April 2009); 'Coma in a bottle: GBL, the 50p party drug which is easier to obtain than heroin ... and is legal' (*Daily Mail*, 1 May 2009).

Hester's mother, Maryon, a prominent writer on nutrition, described in authored articles in the press and in a *Daily Telegraph* (28 April 2009) interview that she felt 'cheated, frustrated and angry' that the Home Office had not made good on its promise. Although Jacqui Smith was Home Secretary at the time of Hester's death, within weeks she had lost her post over the expenses scandal and it fell to Alan Johnson to meet the angry and bereaved parents:

> I remember Hester's mum coming to see me and she wanted something done quickly, overnight. She was involved in the media. [*Author: Did that carry weight with you?*] Not really. She was particularly upset but we said if we ban it without proper consultation, we'll be judicially reviewed. We did try to speed things up as much as possible because a face-to-face meeting with parents who had watched their daughter die was very powerful. It had great emotional impact.
>
> Interview with author, 7 July 2010

This was an impact 'amplified' through the media. So it was no surprise that in August 2009 the Home Secretary announced that GBL would be banned, despite uncertainty about how widespread its use was – at the time of writing, none of the large UK surveys yet include GHB/GBL in their regular user surveys (Shapiro 2011) – and notwithstanding concerns that drug treatment services would struggle to cope with addicts unable to get it. Underlying those reservations is the knowledge that it would inevitably be replaced by one of a number of other 'legal highs' marketed via the Internet. Thus, on New Year's Eve, 2010, the popular students' website, The Student Room (www.thestudentroom.co.uk) published the results of an online survey of 450 people aged 16–24, which showed that one in three had experimented with 'legal highs'.

In response, the crime prevention minister, James Brokenshire, told the Press Association (31 December 2010) that the government 'wanted to send a clear message ... that just because a drug is advertised as "legal" does not mean it is or that it's safe.' However, students (and many others) might wonder why, if the government believed that clarity of messages was crucial to a credible drugs policy, it continued to stand four-square behind a classification system which purports to be about relative harm and yet brackets ecstasy and crack cocaine as equally dangerous and has no rating whatsoever for the most widely consumed substance of all, alcohol.

Drugs and morality

In his conclusion to 'Under a cloud', Simon Cross writes of the 'cloud of morality, ambivalence and uncertainty that hangs over the cannabis user' (Cross 2007: 147). The issue of morality is especially pertinent to any consideration of drugs policy generally because, in the second half of the New Labour era, any position which sought to challenge the drugs laws quickly came under attack in the media with a vehemence which seems to reek of moral indignation. Consider these two *ad hominem* salvos aimed at David Nutt:

> Professor David Nutt, that ninnybrained menace to the nation's young people … I do hope that, long before the end of his smug life, Professor Nutt wakes up one night in a cold sweat and realizes what it is that he has done.
>
> Peter Hitchens, *Mail on Sunday,* 28 March 2010

> You really do have to scrape your jaw off the floor. Not only will such trivialization of ecstasy users cause grave distress to parents whose children have died from taking the drug but it knocks the ground from under the feet of parents terrified that their children will start taking it.
>
> Melanie Phillips, *Daily Mail,* 9 February 2010

Roger Silverstone has shown how a ubiquitous and multi-platform media shapes the world view and moral outlook of its citizens (Silverstone 2007). This research argues that, by defining the contours of public discourse on drugs, influential parts of the UK media have undoubtedly circumscribed the policy options open to government; so much so that Home Secretaries can find themselves behaving like characters from *Alice in Wonderland*. David Nutt describes an exchange with the former Home Secretary, Jacqui Smith, over his paper on ecstasy:

> SMITH: You cannot compare the harms of an illegal activity with a legal one.
> NUTT: But don't we need to compare the harms, in order to see if something should be illegal?
> SMITH (AFTER A LONG PAUSE): You cannot compare the harms of an illegal activity with a legal one.
>
> Aitkenhead 2010

If scientists, who tend to believe in empirical evidence and logic rather than articles of faith, have been frustrated, so have a number of police chiefs who have had to enforce the drugs laws. Thus, few, apart from the 'maverick' Richard Brunstrom, the former chief constable of North Wales, have sought to articulate their personal support for decriminalization or legalization whilst in post. Tom

Lloyd, former chief constable of Cambridgeshire, admits to feeling inhibited when in office:

> Challenging drugs policy is what the Americans call a 'third rail' topic. In other words, it is dangerous so it is taboo. In my view, one of the reasons is that the media harmfully restricts debate on it. And the politicians, who have to win over the public to get votes, think 'we will get a kicking from the media if we stick our heads above the parapet on this and it will lose us votes'. One senior politician admitted to me 'we don't lead on drugs, we follow public opinion'.
>
> Interview with author, 2 June 2010

But 'public opinion', insofar as it has a 'view' on drugs, rather than an aggregate of different views, really has no compass reading other than the classification system to go on. *Pace* David Nutt and Jacqui Smith, it is a moribund circular argument. The consequence of a 40-year-old system which arbitrarily puts very different drugs – such as ecstasy and crack cocaine – into the same category of harm inevitably creates a disconnection between the law and people's own experiences. And this means that the entire classification system becomes less about the actual risk associated with certain drugs and rather more about society's heavily mediated moral disapproval.

Tom Lloyd believes this is why drugs policy presents unique challenges for government:

> Unlike transport, education, health and so on, drugs have attained a status of being about morals and morality. You are immoral if you take drugs and immoral if you argue against a change of policy. So, you have these overtones of undermining the nation's children if you suggest tampering with a 40-year-old system of prohibition. It's very close to a religion which you must not criticize.
>
> ibid.

8 The cannabis conundrum

Introduction

The previous chapter used the examples of the drugs mephedrone and ecstasy to examine the role of the media in policymaking and to interrogate the sending of 'messages' on drugs policy by government. This chapter continues and broadens that theme to include an examination of the role of agencies such as the police in a discursive interpretation of policy on cannabis classification. In so doing, it takes up the challenge posed by, amongst others, Michael Tonry, who writes: 'The important question ... is whether policy-making gives good faith consideration to the credible systematic evidence that is available or whether it disregards it entirely for reasons of ideology or political self-interest' (Tonry 2003: 2). The argument which will be advanced is that for the first half of the New Labour era, 1997–2003/4, the dominant motif of UK drugs strategy, as reflected through the media, was the perceived link between drugs and crime. Thereafter, and particularly during Gordon Brown's premiership, the hegemony of the unaccountable 'morality police' of the *Daily Mail et al.* made it increasingly difficult for the administration to look beyond electoral survival in its approach to drug strategy.

Stuart Taylor, in a study of media representations of drug use, has written that 'news media and governmental beliefs mirror each other and have both adopted a stance that serious or "problematic" drug use is dangerous and causes further criminality' (Taylor 2008: 369). Taylor shows how the media has reinforced notions of social exclusion by its problematic portrayal of crack and heroin users, thus developing Boland's view that 'the debate on illegal drugs is filled less with actual truths and more with misinformation which creates public fear and provides a questionable basis for public policy' (Boland 2008: 173).

New Labour's first stab at public policy on drugs in government was the document *Tackling Drugs to Build a Better Britain*, published in January 1998 (Department of Health 1998). Given the extensive work done in opposition on crime and disorder, it is no surprise that 'protecting communities from drug-related criminal and anti-social behaviour' was a key goal of the strategy. After all, Home Office research published in February 1998, and based on ethnographic sampling conducted by the Office for National Statistics in 1997, showed that in those working class communities which the new government had targeted as its route back to power, there was a strongly-held view (stronger than in better-off areas) that drugs were a prime cause of crime. For *Public Perceptions of Drug Related Crime in 1997* (Charles 1998), respondents were asked to select, from a list of possible causes of crime, the one they perceived as dominant. Of nine potential causes, including unemployment, poverty, family breakdown and alcohol, drugs was rated the second most influential. Only poor parental discipline rated higher.

The police were also emphasizing the drugs–crime link at every opportunity as one explanation for the exponential increase in property theft and burglaries which had inflated the crime figures in the early to mid-1990s, and for the rise in street crime from the late 1990s. In January 1999, the country's largest force, the Met, established a dedicated drugs directorate, headed by Commander Andy Hayman (later to rise to prominence in the counter-terrorism field). He told *Police Review* that since April 1997, arresting officers across the Met had checked arrestees against a drugs-specific database. It showed that 'shoplifting is the top drug-related offence, followed by burglary. It also reveals that 30–35 per cent of people accused of crime are connected with drug misuse' (Bratby 1999). At a Scotland Yard briefing for members of the Crime Reporters Association, attended by the author, on 31 May 2001, Commander Tim Godwin spoke of three features common to the bulk of street crime in the capital. The key one was the drugs market.

It is not the purpose of this work to attempt to unpick the correlation between drug dependency and offending, identified by a number of studies (see, for example, Seddon 2000; and Stevens *et al.* 2005). Suffice to say that the relationship is more complex than those in charge of framing policy have understood. As Mike Hough and Darian Mitchell point out: 'That there are links between some forms of illicit drug use and crime is obvious. The precise nature of these links is not' (Hough and Mitchell 2003: 27). But there is general agreement amongst researchers – and indeed the police – that so-called 'problem drug users' – defined as those dependent on substances such as heroin, crack and powder cocaine or amphetamines – are 'likely to be heavily involved in acquisitive crime' (ibid.).

A survey of people in Met custody, during the year 2000/1, indicated that 57 per cent admitted to taking heroin in the thirty days before arrest; 52 per cent to taking crack and 13 per cent powder cocaine (Fellows and Madden 2004). Even a Labour-sympathizing newspaper, such as the *Observer*, was quick to comment, only weeks before the general election of 2001, that the survey findings 'will embarrass Jack Straw', who had pledged at his party's 1996 conference, the last before coming to power, to 'curtail the rise in drug addicts and drug-related crime' (*Observer*, 20 April 2001). And, by implication, the Home Secretary had failed in that objective.

This, then, in admittedly broad brush terms, was the policy inheritance awaiting David Blunkett, who became Home Secretary following New Labour's re-election in June 2001.

It has been noted earlier in this book that Blunkett defined himself in office, largely by contrast to what he (and Tony Blair) perceived to be the laxness of the department under his predecessor, Jack Straw (Blunkett 2006: 285). 'I'll make Jack Straw look like a liberal' was the unwelcome headline on page six of the

Sun, which first informed Straw before the election that he would be moved in the event of another poll triumph (*Sun,* 30 April 2001). But, interestingly, on drugs policy, and specifically cannabis classification, it was Straw who took the more conventionally 'hard-line' position, rejecting the recommendation of the Runciman Inquiry (Runciman 2000) that cannabis (as well as LSD and ecstasy) should be reclassified, while Blunkett was determined to downgrade cannabis at the earliest opportunity, as his special adviser dealing with the media, Huw Evans, explains:

> Cannabis re-classification was something that David wanted to do from his first day in the job. He came into office with a fixed view and having done quite a lot of work on it privately, reading up on all the issues, he was very clear that he wanted to reclassify. But he wanted a strategy to work out how to do it, so, for the first few months in office, it was a very tightly guarded secret amongst his inner circle that he planned to do it.
>
> Interview with author, 10 February 2010

But why did he want it reclassified?

> I think there were two reasons. He felt that because cannabis was an arresta-ble offence as a Class B drug, it gave the police an excuse to go after minor dealers, rather than focus on the real toughies. He didn't want to give the police any excuse not to be doing the hard work and he felt it was too easy for them to go after minor druggies, spending hours booking them into the station, racking up overtime, and avoiding going out onto the streets to track down the real nasty pieces of work. The second reason, if I'm honest, is that I think he wanted some big announcements which demonstrated that he had fresh ideas, that he was decisive and a game-changer. That's very much part of his profile and self-image as a politician.
>
> ibid.

Undoubtedly, many of these unflattering perceptions about the police had been imbibed over the years as Blunkett listened to complaints at his weekly constitu-ency surgery in Sheffield Brightside, both as MP and city councillor, that too little was being done to tackle anti-social behaviour and crime on those estates where the impact of hard drugs, especially heroin, had taken a grip. More than any other Home Secretary of recent times, David Blunkett's philosophy was a patch-work of convictions stitched together from his long experience as a local politi-cian in Sheffield (see, for example, his manifesto for social and political change, *Politics and Progress: Renewing Democracy and Civil Society,* 2001). But, like all incoming Home Secretaries, he also knew that one force, above all, acted as a barometer for national police-related issues and, accordingly, he made it an early priority to get out on to the streets of the capital, absorbing the views of brass hats and beat bobbies alike. One of the boroughs he chose to visit was Lambeth, where a young Oxford-educated officer clearly destined for higher things, called Brian Paddick, had been appointed commander in the summer of 2001.

Doing the Lambeth walk – policing cannabis, watching the media

The so-called Lambeth Experiment, in which people found in possession of small amounts of cannabis were given a formal verbal warning rather than being arrested and/or cautioned, began on 2 July 2001 and was originally sanctioned as a six-month pilot scheme by the Met Commissioner, Sir John Stevens. If David Blunkett's argument that cannabis should be reclassified had a pragmatic rather than a moral foundation, Brian Paddick's idea was also born of a pragmatic desire to fight crime more effectively and to show sensitivity to the area being policed. As he wrote in the *Guardian* (2 July 2002) on the first anniversary of the experiment:

> Different communities tolerate different types and levels of criminality. If you want community support for policing, you must concentrate on the crimes at the top of the community's list. In Lambeth, crack cocaine, heroin and street robbery were at the top; cannabis was nowhere to be seen. Some even saw cannabis as an excuse for officers to stop, search and criminalise young people. Everyone saw the difference between 'hard' and 'soft' drugs in terms of policing priorities.

David Blunkett endorsed that approach in his diaries when, only ten days after his appointment as Home Secretary, he was shown around the Cowley estate in Brixton by Paddick, whom he describes as an 'interesting' man. They then went on to Brixton police station:

> It was terribly hot because the air conditioning wasn't working … In the canteen, two officers were writing up notes from an arrest at 8.10am and they were still writing them up after 11.00 – and then they were going to have to put the notes into a computer, rather than having a laptop at the point of arrest and charge so that they could just tap in all the details on a set format. What a farce. No wonder they don't want to charge people for things like cannabis.
>
> Blunkett 2006: 273

This passage of the book is also peppered with references to the chaotically dysfunctional and, in this instance, ill-informed, department of state he had inherited:

> Paddick is trying this experiment and I said to him on Tuesday that my priorities are tackling Class A drugs and violent crime. It is the traffickers and pushers we need to nail. So that fitted in extremely well but it was a good job that I had seen him. The Department hadn't told me what he was intending to do, and if I hadn't had a conversation with him, they wouldn't have known.
>
> ibid.

Neither David Blunkett nor Brian Paddick was naïve enough to think that an innovative stance on drugs, even a 'soft' drug such as cannabis, would earn them a 'free pass' with the media without some sort of planned strategy to put in place, as Huw Evans affirms:

> We were very concerned about the media handling prior to the announce-ment on re-classification. We knew it wouldn't be universally popular and David was particularly worried about the *Mail* and the *Sun*, for obvious reasons. But he felt he could at least neutralize them by focusing on the fact that it would allow a better focus on Class A drugs and that he was doing it for good crime-fighting reasons and not because he was some sort of 1960s liberal.
>
> Interview with author, 10 February 2010

Blunkett announced that he was minded to reclassify when he appeared before the Home Affairs Select Committee on 23 October 2001. The press release put out by his department is a model of 'news framing' (Entman 1993) in which the revelation about cannabis (he had asked the Advisory Council on the Misuse of Drugs to examine the case for re-classification) doesn't appear until line ten and the headline reads 'Blunkett to Focus on the Menace of Hard Drugs' (Home Office 2001a).

Brian Paddick, too, was media savvy. Though he was later to be badly burned by a hostile tabloid press, he knew well that, in the Met, the country's most 'polit-ical' force, where senior officers jostle for the Commissioner's favour like rival medieval barons, a sympathetic media could be a powerful weapon:

> My attitude towards the media was formed when I became the borough commander in Merton, more than two years before I took over in Lambeth. A neighbourhood watch co-ordinator, who used to work for a national news-paper, came to see me and gave me some sage advice. He said: 'Look, in the good old days, we journalists used to have a really good relationship with the police. It was a quid pro quo. In return for giving us exclusives, senior inves-tigating officers would get their appeals for information published and so on. You mustn't exclude the media, you must talk to them.' I realized the value of what he was saying and I decided to engage with it.
>
> Interview with author, 23 September 2010

His opportunity came when he was named commander-designate in Lambeth and visited by a canny freelancer called Ken Hyder, a longtime member of the Crime Reporters Association, the Scotland Yard-approved 'lobby' for crime and home affairs correspondents:

> Ken said to me: 'All the previous borough commanders in Lambeth have failed. So what are you going to do that's different?' I told him that I was thinking of not arresting people for cannabis and explained why. Ken hung on to that for about 12 months while we consulted local people, marshalled our arguments, with Ken acting as devil's advocate, and when we were confi-dent that that we could see off our detractors, Ken ran it on the front page of

the *Evening Standard* in March 2001 and that's the first that anyone at DPA [Directorate of Public Affairs at Scotland Yard] knew about it.

ibid.

It was a clever tactic in terms of internal Met politics because Paddick's immediate boss was Mike Todd, another aspirant for the top post, with whom Paddick had a combustible relationship:

> I knew that if I submitted a full report on my plans to Todd, it probably wouldn't go any further. In fact, I subsequently found out that he was briefing against me. I thought the only way to get approval for the idea was a direct approach via the media. That's what I did. [*Author: What was the reaction of the DPA and, especially, Sir John Stevens, the Commissioner?*] John Stephens did what he always did. He said absolutely nothing at all and waited for two to three days to see what happened, what the reaction would be. Apart from Ann Widdecombe, who said I was usurping the power of parliament by not enforcing laws which had been duly passed, the reaction was overwhelmingly positive, both from commentators and the media itself.

ibid.

Stevens was blessed with two (amongst many) qualities which made him a memorable Commissioner. One was a finely-honed instinct for self-preservation. Thus later, when media criticism of the pilot built up, he took to calling it 'The Paddick Experiment' (ibid.). But he was also the 'copper's copper' of press cliché, with an innate feel for sentiment in the ranks and he was mindful of a potential problem which had arisen in Lambeth only a month before Paddick's arrival. A police constable in Brixton, Ross Callaghan, had been charged with misfeasance in a public office, after failing an integrity test set by the Yard's Department for Professional Standards. He had thrown away some cannabis found in a car rather than 'booking it in' at the police station. Other officers in his team, outraged that he had been sent for trial for what they, and, in truth, many others elsewhere in the Met considered to be a trifling misdemeanour, and not inconsistent with a policy of 'informal disposal' (Warburton *et al.* 2005: 113) threatened that henceforth, in Brian Paddick's words 'they would no longer turn a blind eye to cannabis or put it down the drain but arrest anyone they found with it' (*Guardian*, 2 July 2002).

Paddick convinced Stevens that the effect on a community, already deeply suspicious of the police, of a massive increase in numbers of arrests for possessing even small amounts of cannabis would be near catastrophic. The so-called 'softly softly' approach was duly approved and subsequently 'endorsed' by the first detailed study of the policing of cannabis in England, commissioned to examine the potential impact of re-classification, which concluded that removing a 'significant source of friction' between mainly young people and the police should be seen 'as a benefit' (May *et al.* 2002).

But the re-classification issue had complicated the Lambeth Experiment by overlaying what had been a limited exercise in police pragmatism with a competing set of national considerations which muddied the waters. One was the secrecy with which the re-classification announcement had been plotted by Blunkett's inner circle. The news was kept from the media until Blunkett himself revealed his intention at the Home Affairs Select Committee in October 2001, prompting him to comment wryly in his memoirs that it was unprecedented that all those in the know – including the chair of the Advisory Council on the Misuse of Drugs (ACMD), Michael Rawlins, and the 'Drugs Tsar', Keith Hellawell – 'had kept mum': 'This silence was unheard of in my time in government, when everything we did was likely to be leaked, usually with malice aforethought' (Blunkett 2006: 309–10).

However, what Blunkett saw as a matter for self-congratulation, others, especially in the police, viewed as the Whitehall machine, as usual, bouncing the professionals into a change of policy for which they were ill-prepared. Andy Hayman had been the lead spokesman on drugs for the Association of Chief Police Officers (ACPO) from 1998 to 2000 and in 2001 was a Deputy Assistant Commissioner in the Met:

> The night before Blunkett's appearance at the Home Affairs Committee, the police minister, John Denham, told David Phillips, [the ACPO president] and myself what was coming. There was no negotiation, it came completely from left-field. We both sat there at 7pm and said: 'Well, ACPO is totally wrong-footed on this.' We had no choice but to give it moderate support because to do anything else would have been a bun fight.
>
> Interview with author, 20 April 2010

Brian Paddick was also discomforted:

> When Blunkett said he was going to reclassify cannabis, it all started to go wrong for the Lambeth Experiment because the pilot was then extended and it became a political issue. It went from a scheme dreamed up by a slightly 'strange' police commander in a small part of south London to something which, potentially, was going to result in a change in the law and go nationwide. And that was when Associated [Newspapers, publishers of the *Daily Mail*] started to come after me.
>
> Interview with author, 23 September 2010

Brian Paddick's more general observations on the Metropolitan Police and the media form part of Chapter 9. But Andy Hayman's comments reflect only one of a number of conflicting views within the ranks of the police about cannabis re-classification. Members of the Crime Reporters Association (including the author) recall briefings at Scotland Yard by the Met Commissioner, Sir John Stevens, and some of his senior management, at which there was general support for downgrading cannabis on the grounds that it would free up police time to concentrate on Class A drug offenders. Amongst many rank and file officers in England and Wales, however – and some more senior ones, including a number of chief constables – opinion was divided, with considerable opposition expressed to re-classification on various grounds: that it was 'political correctness gone mad'; that much useful police intelligence flowed from having the power to arrest suspected cannabis offenders; and that it was 'the thin end of the wedge' to remove the discretion of the constable on the beat to decide when to make an arrest.

Andy Hayman was constrained from publicly voicing these views at the time but, looking back, he argues that, by forcing through his policy change, the Home Secretary was making life difficult for those who had to enforce it:

> We spent 19 months after that [the re-classification announcement] trying to put the genie back in the bottle and it was impossible. Blunkett wanted to have his cake and eat it. He wanted cannabis to be downgraded but he also wanted the arrest powers to be kept. It was incompatible. In fact, we tried to kick it into the long grass, and on the street, the police carried on what they had been doing for years and ignored it.
>
> Interview with author, 20 April 2010

This, perhaps surprisingly candid observation, is supported by Jeremy Sare, who was part of the secretariat of the ACMD in 2002, and became secretary in 2003:

> I was part of a Joseph Rowntree Foundation study on police enforcement pre- and post-cannabis re-classification and we found that three out of four police forces in England and Wales had not changed their tactics and were still arresting people, contrary to the guidelines – and, as a consequence, 50 per cent of those arrested were from ethnic minorities.
>
> Interview with author, 15 June 2010

This illustrates not only the ability of the police to subtly bend official guidance and circulars (ACPO 2003) or, not so subtly, ignore them altogether, but also a wider truth about policymaking: that the time which frequently elapses between a policy announcement and its implementation opens up a gaping crevice of opportunity for those who wish to bury it. Huw Evans admits to being wrongfooted on cannabis re-classification:

> What I think we didn't anticipate at the time was just how long it would take to actually get the change done, which carried its own risks, especially media-wise. It was 2004 before the law was changed and the drug re-classified, and that time allowed all the opponents to build up a head of steam. It enabled the media critics to really pull us apart and those in the Cabinet, who didn't agree with the policy [Jack Straw being one] and who hadn't been consulted, to nobble Tony Blair and say: 'What on earth are you doing? Why are you letting this go through?'
>
> Interview with author, 10 February 2010

Blair himself, though increasingly 'nervous about the backlash' (ibid.), continued to support his Home Secretary.

> I don't think re-classification is something the PM would ever have done himself. But he went with David's judgment and, honourably, took the view

that he'd backed him at the outset and that he should, you know, let him get on with it.

ibid.

This may be an example of personal loyalty – Blair regarded Blunkett as one of his most trusted allies in government – trumping the Prime Minister's normally well-tuned antennae for political trouble.[1] After all, the police were gradually closing ranks behind the view that re-classification was a mistake, and Keith Hellawell, the Anti-Drugs Co-ordinator (so-called 'Drugs Tsar') had bludgeoned his way into the headlines on the very day of Blunkett's re-classification announcement, in July 2002, by resigning in protest because he said he had not been consulted and was against the change. Hellawell expressed his unhappiness to the press, 'I don't know where he got his advice from; it certainly wasn't from me' (*Daily Telegraph*, 11 July 2002).

Within the Home Secretary's inner sanctum, Hellawell's resignation was seen as less about a disagreement on drugs policy and more to do with a piece of leftover acrimony arising from the decision to place the Drug Tsar in the Cabinet Office, and thus directly answerable to the Prime Minister, rather than in the Home Office. In a typical Blairite fudge, Hellawell was given a princely salary – reputed to be the highest non-ministerial remuneration in Whitehall – but no budgetary powers and no power base. It was a recipe for an inter-departmental standoff, as Huw Evans explains:

> David felt very strongly that the drugs tsar should be in the Home Office, so there was tension there anyway. But frankly, he thought he'd squared Hellawell in October 2001 before he revealed his intention to reclassify at the Home Affairs Committee. So he was not only surprised but irritated that in July 2002, Hellawell claimed his advice hadn't been sought so that he could resign in a blaze of publicity. But I think at the end of the day, David didn't much care whether Hellawell agreed or not and he wasn't going to be that upset if the drugs tsar decided to go off and do something else. David was far more comfortable dealing with drugs policy on his own than having some drugs tsar floating around in the Cabinet Office working on a different strategy.
>
> Interview with author, 10 February 2010

The Dacre Effect

Until either Gordon Brown or Paul Dacre, the editor of the *Daily Mail*, publish their memoirs, the closeness of the relationship between the two men can only be guessed at. But from the comments of those around them, it is evident that their values and sense of right and wrong had a lot in common, as the media watcher James Robinson, noted: 'Dacre has been close to Brown since he was Chancellor and shares his sense of moral purpose ...' (James Robinson, *Observer*, 9 November 2008). For Dacre, the mere fact that Brown was not Tony Blair might have been part of the attraction. In 2002, in the run-up to the war against Iraq,

David Blunkett observed Blair under attack from the *Daily Mail* and noted 'a kind of hatred from Paul Dacre' (Blunkett 2006: 391). The result was that Brown enjoyed an unexpected honeymoon period from the arch Labour-hating *Mail*, when he took over the reins from Blair in the summer of 2007. That autumn, the new PM flirted with the idea of calling a snap election to benefit from the 'I'm not Tony' effect. Professor David Nutt was then chair of the ACMD Technical Committee:

> The rumour is that Brown did a deal with Paul Dacre. Dacre said there are three things you must do to get *Mail* support, one of which is to reclassify cannabis ... the government is fixated on a daily basis on whatever the *Mail*'s attitude is. What will the *Mail* think? That was the mantra. It's pathetic really.
> Interview with author, 13 May 2010[2]

Yet, revealingly, at the beginning of the decade, the same Dacre-edited *Daily Mail* and its sister paper, the *Mail on Sunday* were sending out very different signals in relation to cannabis. Five months after publication of the Runciman Inquiry report, which provoked the most extensive debate on drugs reform in England and Wales up to that point, Paul Dacre signed off this leader in the *Daily Mail*:

> This paper has consistently argued for honest adult debate. When millions of otherwise decent citizens routinely break the law and criminals grow rich because of the cannabis ban, the case for a fundamental review is persuasive. And wouldn't police make better use of their time by concentrating on hard drugs?
> *Daily Mail*, 2 July 2000

Even with a caveat pointing out the dangers of decriminalization, this blast of realism hardly sounds like the Middle England moralizing of the *Mail* of later in the decade. And the following day, the *Mail* leader writers returned to the subject: 'We must face the fact that the debate on drugs is shifting. More and more people on the Right as well as the Left are calling for the decriminalization of soft drugs' (*Daily Mail*, 3 July 2000).

In October 2000, the *Mail on Sunday* (15 October 2000) carried a leader article, prompted by a commissioned poll showing a two-to-one majority in favour of decriminalizing cannabis, and headlined 'Time for debate – but first give us the facts'. And, as has been noted elsewhere (Cross 2007), during the late 1990s and until about 2002, the *Daily Telegraph*, too, was arguing for reform of the cannabis laws.

Jeremy Sare, former secretary of the Advisory Council on the Misuse of Drugs and later head of drugs legislation at the Home Office, joined the ACMD secretariat in January 2002 during this period, which many in the drugs reform lobby refer to as a 'brief window of opportunity':

> The *Mail* did have an alternative view about drugs in that period, which was very different from now. It was concerned, in a rare moment of clarity, about

the criminalization of young people for possession of cannabis. It thought it was disproportionate for young people to be arrested at the rate of 60,000 a year, and given a criminal record which would affect their career, travel etc. It also seemed a waste of police time. Whether that influenced David Blunkett [i.e. in reclassifying cannabis as Class C] is pure speculation. But there certainly seemed to be a break in the clouds when he became Home Secretary and made his views known.

Interview with author, 15 June 2010

But it would be a mistake to imagine that the temporary epiphany of the middle market press on cannabis came about spontaneously. It required those skeins of influence which bind together the media and the policy sphere to be expertly tugged by someone wise in the ways of the English establishment. Dame Ruth Runciman, whose husband, Garry, had chaired the Royal Commission on Criminal Justice (1993), which helped salve the Conservative government's conscience after the appalling series of miscarriages of justice in the 1970s and 1980s, was the ideal person to parlay the findings of her own inquiry (Runciman 2000) into political pressure on the government.[3] The *Guardian* columnist (and former *Times* editor) Simon Jenkins was a member of the inquiry team:

> Ruth Runciman spent a lot of time with Paul Dacre and the *Telegraph* editor, pre-briefing them before the report was published and taking them carefully through all our arguments. Admittedly, our report was, to put it mildly, not very liberal – it certainly didn't advocate legalization, it was about re-classification. But as a result of the briefings, the editors were on our side. They wrote leaders which were on side. We had opinion surveys in support. It was remarkably consensual.

Interview with author, 21 June 2010

Simon Jenkins believes that Jack Straw's swift rejection of the inquiry's recommendation on cannabis (see, for example, 'Why we won't be going soft on cannabis', *News of the World*, 2 April 2000) was because the government's communications chief, Alastair Campbell, 'had rubbished the Runciman report at every opportunity unattributably and demanded that Straw reject it before it even came out' (Interview with author, ibid.). Whether it was the fact that Straw had chosen the Murdoch press to deliver his response or whether papers like the *Mail* and *Telegraph* saw genuine merits in re-classification, the window of media debate continued to stay open until 2002. But by the time that David Blunkett announced in July of that year that (hardly a surprise!) he was accepting the recommendation of the ACMD that cannabis should be re-classified, his ability to manipulate media opinion in his favour was ebbing away. In the words of Warburton *et al.* (2005: 116), 'the press was rediscovering its taste for a hard prohibitionist line'. One reason was the mistaken, some might say mischievous, perception that cannabis was going to be decriminalized or even legalized. 'Cannabis to be "legalized" within a year' (*Sunday Times*, 30 June 2002). Despite the fact that the Home Office press note announcing re-classification made it crystal clear in the opening sentence that neither legalization nor decriminalization were on the agenda (Home Office 2002b), the anti-Blunkett backlash had already begun – as this punning headline demonstrates: 'Has Blunkett made a hash of it?' (*Daily Mail* 12 July 2002). It was to get a whole lot worse.

In 2006, the Commons Science and Technology Committee provided a lucid and balanced account of the confusion, reflected in media reporting, surrounding the re-classification of cannabis. It noted that 'the weeks leading up to and following the implementation of re-classification [29 January 2004] saw a media mael-strom of reporting about cannabis' (House of Commons Science and Technology Committee 2006: 23). Different approaches were being adopted by different police forces and the Met Commissioner, Sir John Stevens, was quoted as saying that the position needed clarifying because junior officers in his force had told him they were 'muddled' about the drug's status (*Daily Telegraph*, 23 January 2004). The Home Office was forced to launch a one million pound advertising campaign targeted at young people to reinforce the message that cannabis was still an illegal drug (Home Office 2004).

The committee commented tartly:

> The timing of the second review [into the status of cannabis] against a back-drop of intense media hype, and so soon after the change in cannabis clas-sification had come into effect, gave the impression that a media outcry was sufficient to trigger a review.
>
> House of Commons Science and Technology Committee 2006: 24

Thus, even before re-classification had taken effect, the foundation on which the policy was based was crumbling. Thereafter, the media-led dismantling of the entire edifice can be summed up in one small, infelicitous word: skunk.

Skunk leaves a nasty smell

Grown hydroponically in 'cannabis factories' in the UK rather than imported mainly as resin, skunk accounted for 15 per cent of the market in 2002 and at least 70 per cent by 2008, according to an ACMD assessment in February 2008 (Hardwick and King 2008). The increase in the popularity of skunk was not in doubt. But what was a matter of fierce and unresolved dispute amongst researchers was the potency and harm factor of skunk compared to the strains of cannabis which dominated the market a decade earlier.

Some of the broadsheet press reflected these differences of opinion. Few of the tabloids and middle market papers did, even sporadically. Instead, readers were subjected to a relentless drumbeat of stories, often based around personal accounts, of the link between 'super strength' skunk, which was allegedly twenty to thirty times stronger than the cannabis of old, and psychosis in users. The 'evidence' was so compelling that the *Mail on Sunday* (18 January 2004) published an edito-rial headlined: 'What will Britain be like when there's a whole generation hearing voices in their heads?' As Lord Victor Adebowale, chief executive of the charity Turning Point, commented in 2005:

Looking at media coverage over the 16 months since re-classification, you would think that a raft of new reports had been produced showing that cannabis had caused a host of mental health problems and the problem was at epidemic proportions. Yet, the evidence of the drug's long-term effect on mental health is not clear.

Adebowale 2005: 30

By this point, 2005, Charles Clarke had replaced Blunkett as Home Secretary and was later quoted as saying he was 'very worried' about emerging evidence suggesting a possible link between cannabis use and mental illness (*The Times*, 5 January 2006). In March 2005, he asked the ACMD to revisit the classification of cannabis, also asking for advice on the extent to which the potency of cannabis products had increased:

I thought David was wrong to reclassify cannabis when he did. I asked the ACMD to review it and my expectation was that we would reverse Blunkett's decision. But I didn't try to press them in any way. My main concern was the impact of classification on use of the drug. I spoke to Tony [Blair] before we gave him the ACMD's report [December 2005], which recommended leaving it at Class C, and said I was really in two minds as to whether to accept the recommendation or not. Significantly, Tony said 'you decide, it's a tight call and I'll back you whatever you decide to do'.

Interview with author, 16 September 2010

In the event, Clarke decided to leave cannabis a Class C drug. He states: 'What convinced me was the proof that cannabis use had probably gone down since re-classification' (ibid.). Certainly, British Crime Survey data suggested that cannabis use had gradually declined amongst people in the 16–24 age bracket and that usage in older age groups had remained stable (Home Office 2005a). But it was widely reported at the time that Clarke's decision was heavily influenced by threats from members of the ACMD to resign if he rejected their recommendation (see, for example, 'Expert advisers threaten revolt against Clarke', *Guardian*, 14 January 2006; and 'No turning back on "soft" cannabis laws', *Evening Standard*, 16 January 2006).

One of the ACMD members who warned Clarke against ignoring the committee's advice was Dr Les King, formerly head of the Forensic Science Service's (FSS) drugs intelligence unit. He had also watched with interest the growing media-led concern about 'super strength' skunk and after Clarke had been sacked as Home Secretary and Gordon Brown had replaced Tony Blair, carried out a scientific assessment of what had, hitherto, been chiefly anecdotal reportage:

I did a report on cannabis potency in 2007 in conjunction with the Home Office people at Sandridge near St. Albans and the FSS. To our surprise, Gordon Brown asked to see a copy of our conclusions. He clearly read it and not long after, came out with the statement that skunk is lethal. We all laughed. It wasn't supported by our research at all and I don't know why he did that. The report acknowledged that hydroponic cultivation leads to higher strength material but not 20 times the strength. Perhaps 2–3 times stronger. True, it's the dominant product on the market. But we don't know that strength is a factor in harm. We don't make that kind of distinction with any other drugs. For example, the strength of amphetamines available on the street is more than double what it was but we don't make a song and dance about it because we assume that users will titrate [take a lesser amount] if it's too strong. I think the newspaper stories about links between skunk and schizophrenia must have had an impact on policy. Newspapers and their readers like anecdotal stories, we all do, but you don't construct a policy based on anecdote ... as time goes on, the less I am inclined to think that cannabis has any serious impact on long-term psychosis.

Interview with author, 22 June 2010

For well-documented reasons, Charles Clarke may not be the most objective judge of Gordon Brown, given his frequently voiced criticisms of Brown's leadership 'defects' and Clarke's long-standing role as a key Blairite. With that health warning, and bearing in mind that he, too, had been concerned about skunk, this is Clarke's view of Brown's early decision to reverse the downgrading of cannabis:

Gordon said, unbelievably, that he wanted to reclassify and in my view, it was an attempt to appear tougher than Blair. It was prejudging the cannabis issue and a complete distortion of government. On what basis does the PM of the day take a decision like that? If it's true that he did a deal with Dacre – and I don't know about that – well, you can't just say 'blimey, that fits the prejudices of the *Mail* editor or those of the general population, so I'll do it.' That was the big difference between Gordon and Tony. Tony had his own prejudices but he didn't exercise them irresponsibly in the way Gordon did.

Interview with author, 16 September 2010

However, Alan Johnson, who held a number of posts in both the Blair and Brown administrations – including that of Home Secretary – differs from his former colleague. In 2007, yet to take over from Jacqui Smith at the Home Office, he was Secretary of State for Health. Did he share the Prime Minister's view about cannabis?

The majority of the Cabinet felt it should be reclassified. That was because of skunk. I was in Health at the time and the effects on psychotic illness were becoming apparent. We in the Department of Health would have been cheering on Jacqui Smith in reclassifying cannabis.

Interview with author, 7 July 2010

Freedom of information? Not in this case

No government has had such a sensitive ear for presentational matters as the New Labour one. And of all the issues which passed across ministerial desks between 1997 and 2010, drugs policy was perhaps the most heavily mediated of all. This research has shown how the banning of mephedrone was pushed forward at breakneck speed because, with a forthcoming election, the government was determined not to provide any crumbs of comfort to those who wanted to paint it as 'soft' on drugs. And cannabis policy, through the twists and turns of downgrading to Class C under David Blunkett, the growing popularity of skunk and the re-classification to Class B under Gordon Brown, has consistently borne the imprint of media representation.

In the light of this, it was natural to want to discover how the Home Office prepared for the media response before the various policy decisions relating to cannabis classification discussed in this chapter were taken. Accordingly, a Freedom of Information (FOI) request was submitted on 16 June 2009 asking:

> What discussions took place with special advisers, the Home Office press office and Number 10 Policy Unit about the likely media response before:
>
> 1   David Blunkett's announcement in October 2001 that he was minded to reclassify cannabis as a Class C drug;
> 2   Charles Clarke's decision in January 2006 that cannabis should remain as a Class C drug; and
> 3   Jacqui Smith's announcement in May 2008 that cannabis would be reclassified as a Class B drug.

It is not part of this research to critique the shortcomings in FOI legislation which allow the government, any government, to block disclosure of so many matters of public interest. But the response of the Home Office to this request – an excessively tardy one which was not delivered until four months after the request was made – is worth reproducing for what it tells us about the way government does business and what it perceives as being in the 'public interest'.

Under the heading: 'General considerations favouring disclosure', Richard Mullins, of the Home Office FOI unit, acknowledges that the request has a number of merits:

> Your request concerns a high profile subject and there is therefore an argument to be made that there is a strong public interest in disclosing the information to provide greater transparency.

> Disclosure of this information would also be likely to aid an informed public debate on this subject as it would raise public awareness of the decision-making processes involved in this matter.

> It can also be argued that, in providing the advice given in the decision-making process, any poor advice put forward would be brought to light and,

as such, it would be likely that the quality of any future advice put forward would be of a higher calibre.

Mullins 2009

Such a parade of persuasive reasons in favour of disclosure had, almost inevitably, to be a prelude to refusal. And, indeed, the request was denied under section 36(2) (b) and (c) of the FOI Act, though only after it had been considered at ministerial level. This section 'exempts certain information from disclosure if its release would, or would be likely to, inhibit the free and frank provision of advice or ... exchange of views ... or would otherwise prejudice ... the effective conduct of public affairs' (ibid.). It hardly needs iteration that only the most blinkered civil servant could seriously argue that recent drugs policy is an example of the 'effective conduct of public affairs' but, be that as it may, an appeal against this decision was also turned down – after another lengthy delay of four months.

There is one brief but significant coda to this issue of release of Home Office material about drug classification, which reinforces the thesis that from 2006 onwards, a succession of New Labour Home Secretaries set their face resolutely, almost as a matter of faith, against any moves which might be interpreted as a weakening of a 'tough' policy on drugs. In March 2010, The Information Commissioner ruled against the Home Office, which, for over three years, had resisted an FOI request from the Drug Equality Alliance (DEA).[4] The subject of the request was the review of the drug classification system ordered by Charles Clarke in 2006 before he was sacked, which produced a hitherto unpublished consultation document drawn up by the Home Office Crime and Drug Strategy Directorate (2006).

The fact that this document had never seen the light of day is attributable to the new regime ushered in by Clarke's successor, John Reid, widely viewed in his numerous ministerial posts as the government's roving 'enforcer'. Reid's arrival at the Home Office led, in the words of Jeremy Sare, to 'a lockdown in which the department became much more risk-averse':

The story goes that when Reid arrived, all the new ministers were taken on a weekend away at a country hotel. Vernon Coaker had the drugs portfolio and was running down his list of projects and got to the drug classification review. Reid interrupted him, pointed out of the window to a large meadow and said 'that's where I want it to go'. As far as he was concerned, it was back to the Straw era – hold the line, there's no votes in drug reform, let's park the whole issue.

Interview with author, 15 June 2010

This study would undoubtedly have benefited from Reid's willingness to be interviewed. Two approaches were made – in August 2008 and August 2010 – but each was rebuffed on the grounds of a 'full diary'.[5] The 51-page consultation document (Home Office Crime and Drug Strategy Directorate 2006)[6] was not published in full at the time of the Information Commissioner's ruling because the Home Office – no doubt, with the pending 2010 general election in mind – appealed the decision. So, only a heavily redacted version emerged before the election. But on 9 July 2010, the Home Office lost its appeal and the unexpurgated version could at last be read.

And quite remarkable it is. Indeed, the BBC Social Affairs Editor, Mark Easton (2010), on his blog calls it 'dynamite'. Why? Consider this passage in the section (6.3) dealing with one of the key unresolved questions of the drugs debate:

> To many young people, the regulation of tobacco and alcohol and the prohibition of drugs presents a dichotomy in terms of harm. They question why substances of considerable harm, such as cigarettes and alcohol, are able to be consumed relatively easily when possessing a drug like cannabis can lead to prosecution.
>
> Home Office Crime and Drug Strategy Directorate 2006: 16

In acknowledging that, like controlled drugs, both tobacco and alcohol are 'substances that alter mental functioning' (ibid.: 11), the review appears to support the idea that they might be included in the classification system, although 'in a way which would stop short of imposing comparable controls' (ibid.: 17). Thus, more than three years before David Nutt was sacked for saying the unsayable, officials in the Home Office were thinking along the same lines and committing their thoughts to print. Ministers, too, it seems, were also prepared to be more candid than at any time under New Labour. Consider paragraph 1.2 of the ministerial foreword (presumably written by Vernon Coaker):

> the classification system, and the way in which it is operated, lacks clarity, and has led to prolonged disagreements over whether certain drugs have been classified correctly according to their relative harms. This has been particularly true in the case of cannabis, the re-classification of which from a Class B to a Class C drug in January 2004, resulted in a degree of public confusion as to the government's view of its harmfulness and illegality.
>
> ibid.: 3

Conclusion

These two chapters on the mediatization of drugs policy began with one (published) government document – the 2010 drugs strategy – and end with another, a document which remained in a Home Office filing cabinet for more than three years. During that period, in a number of countries – Mexico, the United States, Portugal, Switzerland and Germany amongst others – the scope of public discourse on drugs has been broadened and formerly taboo policies such as decriminalization have not only been discussed but, in some cases, implemented. Is it pure coincidence that, unlike the UK, none of those countries has such an influential tabloid media which feeds its readers a daily diet of binary archetypes – 'evil' drug dealers, 'innocent' victims, and so on – and thus imprisons the policymakers in a tiny legislative space bounded by a 40-year-old law, the Misuse of Drugs Act, 1971?

This research cannot answer that question because it does not encompass any comparative content/textual analysis of media in those countries named. But as the 'traditional' media, especially print newspapers, fractures in the face of social networking, user generated content, and so on, it is worth asking whether new media can break the logjam of thinking on drugs. Some of the most perceptive commentary on the FOI releases discussed above is to be found on blogs, websites and even Twitter, and Danny Kushlick, of the pro-legalization think tank, Transform, believes that the impact of viral 'messages' is changing the terms of the policy debate:

> Activists can now set up a Google news alert and collate a number of news sources and ping round 50 stories on a daily basis. I think this is significant. In 2000, we did a poll on support in the UK for legalization. It was eight per cent and that was constant across age, social class, gender. Now [2010], we are at 20 per cent. Some of this has come about because of the 'visual' media. Programmes like *The Wire* and *Shameless* have helped in this normalizing process. But the shift in the debate has also come about because of the vacuum left by the policymakers. Their narrative is that you can't take a progressive position because the right-wing media will tear you apart. But meanwhile, there's this whole progressive conversation going on out there which is feeding into the policy discourse. So, we have reached a point where only three major newspaper columnists – Peter Hitchens, Melanie Phillips and Simon Heffer – are firmly anti-legalization.
>
> Interview with author, 25 May 2010

Of course, the Internet is a repository of as much ill-informed nonsense and prejudice dressed up as argument as the mainstream media, so campaigners would be foolish to rest too many hopes on new media being the catalyst for a radical change of strategy by government. The last word on New Labour and why its drugs strategy was, in the end, more about symbolism than tangible achievement, is left to Harry Shapiro, director of communications for DrugScope:

> Drugs policy is very difficult for government to direct. Like reducing poverty, there is so much which lies outside its control. Availability, for one thing. Dissuading young people from taking drugs, despite education programmes, for another. All the evidence shows that there is very little that government can do to change behaviour. And, of course, this gives the media a stick with which to whack the politicians and to indulge in gross over-simplifications. The result is that if you look at a kind of arc of intent and aspiration at the beginning of the New Labour era, you can see that Blair's personal agenda gave a high priority to tackling the link between drugs and crime but by the end of it, the whole of this ambitious agenda had shrunk to a relatively trivial argument about classification.
>
> Interview with author, 22 June 2010

9 Police and the media

This chapter is about the relationship between the police and the media, how that relationship is changing, partly as a result of 'new media', and the consequences for both policy and operations. It will examine the mediatized scrutiny of the Metropolitan Police under the Commissionership of Sir Ian Blair and look, in particular, at public order policing, where 3G phone footage, YouTube, Twitter and Facebook have created fresh dynamics for holding to account police practices, driving society closer to a state that the radical criminologist, Thomas Mathieson (1997), has termed 'synopticon', in which the many (citizens) are able to maintain surveillance on the few (the forces of law and order).[1] As Sir Hugh Orde, president of the Association of Chief Police Officers, has said:

> It is about developments in the ability to communicate. (Fifteen years ago) nobody had a mobile phone with a camera. No-one was a video cameraman apart from (professional) video cameramen. As a police officer, the notion that you could be photographed/filmed doing a Section 44 stop [under the Terrorism Act 2000] just was not there unless someone got real lucky. Now it is routine for the news organizations to say 'send us your video clips'.
>
> Interview with author, 4 August, 2010

The wider sociological import of new media for the processes of criminal justice, including policing, and for 'journalism', will be the subject of the next chapter. A police service already nervous about the prospect of directly elected commissioners overseeing their performance may have good reason to view a potential army of citizens with cameras with some trepidation.

Order, order

Viewers of television programmes about crime detection have become familiar over the years with the phrase 'the golden hour'. It is the period immediately after a serious crime has been reported, when the gathering of evidence provides the best chance of a successful detection. Behind the scenes, in police communication teams, the same prescription has been followed in releasing information to the media, intended to shape coverage of the case. Chris Webb, deputy director of the Department of Public Affairs at Scotland Yard, put it like this: 'We have what we call a golden hour. It is an hour to get a grip, to get control of the situation or others will do it on our behalf' (*PR Week*, 25 July 2007).

On Wednesday 1 April 2009, during a demonstration against the G20 meeting in London, a newspaper seller called Ian Tomlinson collapsed and died close to a police cordon. The first press statement put out by Scotland Yard (four hours later) was six paragraphs long and selectively framed to suggest that the police had acted as Good Samaritans when a member of the public had approached an officer about the victim's plight:

> That officer sent two police medics through the cordon line and into St Michael's Alley, where they found a man who had stopped breathing. They called for London Ambulance Service support ... The officers took the decision to move him as, during this time, a number of missiles – believed to be bottles – were being thrown at them.[2]

This ordered the official narrative of Tomlinson's death, conforming to the long-established concept of 'inferential structure', in which an audience absorbs certain messages from the frame of reference selected instinctively (or 'unwittingly') by the news media (Lang and Lang 1955). With the notable exception of the *Guardian*, the mainstream press and broadcasters emphasized protester violence in their initial coverage. The *Daily Mirror* (2 April 2009) reported that the police 'were pelted with bottles by a screaming mob', and the *Daily Mail* informed its readers that the police were 'pelted with bottles as a medical team tried to revive a demonstrator' (2 April 2009). Richard Offer, who was head of media at the Independent Police Complaints Commission from its inception in 2004 until 2008, argues that the Met has 'form' in manipulating stories where someone has died amidst allegations of excessive force, so that it is absolved of blame:

> I tell you where I would criticize the Met. It was very adept at vilifying the person who had died – much more than forces outside London. Somehow, information would 'get out' that the person had been arrested for this or done that or been suspected of the other, usually to his or her detriment. So that whoever had been shot, or died in some other way, was always made out to be the villain. It was a deliberate tactic.
>
> Interview with author, 19 February 2010

Reviewing the sequence of statements and press reports, the *Guardian* later wrote:

> In the space of five days, through a combination of official guidance, strong suggestion and press releases, those responsible for examining the circumstances surrounding Mr. Tomlinson's death within the City of London police and the IPCC, appeared to be steering the story to what they thought would be its conclusion: that the newspaper vendor suffered an unprovoked heart attack as he made his way home on the night of the G20 protests.
>
> *Guardian*, 9 April 2009

But when video footage was posted on the *Guardian*'s website on the evening of 7 April, showing that, moments before his death, Tomlinson had been violently shoved to the ground by a police officer, the officially sanctioned version began to unravel at breakneck speed, with damaging consequences for the Metropolitan Police and the Home Office. A flurry of time-stamped photographs of police heavy-handedness bordering on brutality appeared in the media: print, online and broadcast; by 11 April 2009, the IPCC had received 120 complaints relating to police actions at the protest; and the independence of the IPCC itself was called into question, prompting the body to announce an unprecedented inquiry into the 'media handling' of the affair by both the Met and City of London force.

At time of writing, the full ramifications of Ian Tomlinson's death have yet to unfold (the inquest has just concluded with a verdict of unlawful killing and now the Director of Public Prosecutions must decide whether to press criminal charges). But in an excellent early analysis, Greer and McLaughlin argue that evidence supplied by protesters 'would critically destabilize this initial inferential structure and radically transform how the policing of G20 was interpreted and understood' (Greer and McLaughlin 2010a: 1050). If one accepts Lance Bennett's indexing thesis (Bennett 1990) that the parameters of media debate are often set by official and/or government discourse (though his case studies focus on foreign affairs), then an observer with a 3G phone or an unobtrusive video camera, and websites with a global reach, pose a serious challenge to the hegemony of the police. This is true in circumstances not merely of organized civil protest but also the myriad unplanned daily contacts between officers and public, where emotions are running high.

As in many issues connected to policing, the United States has led the way and the repercussions of the camcorder-filmed beating of a black suspect, Rodney King, by a group of mainly white police officers in Los Angeles in 1992 are well-known. In a test of the indexing hypothesis on such 'dramatic' news events, Regina Lawrence argues that there is a greater frequency of 'non-official' viewpoints in mass media coverage of police brutality than in many other policy areas (Lawrence 1996). No doubt, this is explained by the human interest nature of the subject matter and the asymmetric balance of power between the individual and an agency of the state. But the major development since the 1990s is the speed at which disaffection with the police response to an incident, or crime, can force a change of policy. Consider how long it took the murder of Stephen Lawrence in 1993 to mutate from a single human tragedy arising from a botched investigation into an indictment of 'institutional racism' which left no public organization in the country untouched. By contrast, within hours of the posting of the video of Tomlinson's last moments on the website of one national newspaper, the IPCC had cancelled its decision to allow the City of London force to continue to manage the inquiry and appointed independent investigators, thus signalling that the maintenance of public confidence was going to be a fundamental concern. Within another 24 hours, the officer shown in the footage pushing Tomlinson to the ground had been suspended. And thereafter, the Met's handling of the G20 protests was the subject of two parliamentary inquiries and a national review of public order policing tactics by

HM Chief Inspector of Constabulary. The HMIC report, published in February 2011, recorded just how much policy and operational change had taken place, including involving members of the National Union of Journalists in public order training exercises, ensuring that officers are clearly identified by their numbers, and exerting tighter command and control over the use of photography by Forward Intelligence Teams.[3]

There is a thread which links the gradual, slower-paced momentum of the Stephen Lawrence campaign to the rapid-fire response to the Tomlinson death and that is the role of the activist lawyer, who knows how and when to train a media spotlight on the police to achieve results. The Lawrence murder was the first high profile case where proprietary exclusivity over developments during a long-running criminal investigation passed from the police to another actor – the lawyer appointed to represent the Lawrences. Instead of being able to maintain a 'bridgehead' to the community through the family liaison officer, the police were forced to be largely reactive, as the solicitor, Imran Khan, and barrister, Michael Mansfield, took charge and successfully engaged the media in an alliance of self-interest. The result, as Simon Cottle has written, is that:

> If dominant sources and elite power ... were at work on this case, at least it was apparent that they were not completely controlling the media narrative ... [The media] purposefully propelled the story forward on the public stage and generalized the case to a wider readership or audience ... They were inside the frame and often reconfiguring it as they moved forward.
>
> Cottle 2004: 25

This phenomenon, of the media 'performing' the story rather than merely reporting it, in conjunction with lawyers well versed in presentational techniques, is one of the most noteworthy of the past two decades. It is particularly important in the public order arena because the police have not been sluggish in exploiting new technology to regain the upper hand. Head-mounted cameras, CCTV and the targeted photographing of activists by Forward Intelligence Teams have enabled forces to present the Crown Prosecution Service with seemingly 'watertight' evidence in cases of civil protest. But social media has equipped the lawyer of 2010 with the tools to fight back.

Matt Foot, of Birnberg Peirce & Partners, represented a 23-year-old journalism graduate called Jake Smith, who was arrested following two protests at the Israeli embassy in London over Israel's invasion of Gaza in January 2009. He was charged with two counts of violent disorder. The police submitted video evidence which, they said, showed Smith throwing a stick at the police, and on a different occasion, pushing barricades towards police lines. Smith was amongst a minority of those arrested to plead not guilty and was on bail for 14 months facing the prospect of a jail term (others arrested during the protests had received sentences ranging from eight to 30 months). In March 2010, shortly before the trial, footage which cast a completely different light on events was discovered on YouTube. Matt Foot says this was crucial to the collapse of the case:

It was found by chance by a friend of Jake's, who was trawling YouTube for any footage of the protests which might help his defence. It was shot by someone who obviously knew what he was doing because the camera had been placed on top of a pole so that it gave a far better perspective. It showed Jake being beaten by the police moments before he pushed the barricades and it also showed clearly that the man who threw the stick was not Jake.

Interview with author, 10 September 2010

On the strength of this discovery, one working day before the trial was due to start, Foot was invited by Kensington police to view seven and a half hours of footage which had not been disclosed to the defence and which the police said 'might be relevant'. It fully supported the partial evidence of the YouTube material and the prosecution dropped the case:

Without the YouTube footage, I doubt whether we would have got to the truth. This is part of our work now, trawling sites like YouTube looking for material. It is very time consuming and obviously we do not have the resources of the police or the state so we usually need somebody, perhaps a friend of the accused, to volunteer to do it for free. But it is transforming the way we defend in these cases of public protest.

ibid.

The way the police handle such cases has also been transformed by media technology. Whereas, in the past, their evidence would be in the form of written statements disclosed to the defence, now it is contained on videotape. Matt Foot says it is an effective means of maintaining control:

Sometimes, of course, the defendant is bang to rights and the video shows it. But often, what you get is a heavily edited version of events in which the full context is taken out. And they only give it to you on a terrible undertaking that you will not disclose it to anybody else – and only show it to the client in your office. So, it is a horrific sort of process. There is also a problem with CCTV because where the police and prosecution believe they have a strong case they usually supply CCTV footage. But CCTV is not neutral. The cameras tend to be controlled by the police and they will only disclose selective clips.

ibid.

It is an aspect of policing that is increasingly being discussed, both in Bramshill seminar rooms and ACPO media committees.[4] Not operational practice itself; that has long been regularly reviewed and updated in the light of events, but the need to defend it, and just as importantly, the manner in which it should best be defended, when media scrutiny uncovers lacunae or worse. Even so, when the killing of the Brazilian, Jean Charles de Menezes (discussed later in this chapter), revealed the existence of Operation Kratos, a new firearms strategy devised to deal with suicide bombers, such was the intensity of the debate that police chiefs floundered. Similarly, the focus by parts of the media, particularly the *Guardian*, on public order policing uncovered many disturbing encroachments on civil liberties and forced an embarrassing admission that, in some cases, tactics had run ahead of legal authority to employ them.

In March 2009, a Freedom of Information Act request revealed that a number of police forces were shooting video footage of people attending protests and holding photographs and other details on a database known as Crimint, which is routinely used to catalogue criminal intelligence. Journalists covering protests were also targeted (see the *Guardian*, 7 March 2009). Within two months, the Appeal Court had ruled that the practice was unlawful under the privacy sections of the Human Rights Act.[5] And thereafter, the Association of Chief Police Officers conceded that such use of surveillance data, overseen by ACPO, was almost certainly at the very edges of accountability and needed to be reviewed.

Ironically, the ACPO president, Sir Hugh Orde, believes that the police are also being targeted – by a voracious and expanding media:

> There is an overwhelming number of freelances these days looking for a story because they have to earn a living. And correspondingly fewer [staff] journalists who need a long-term relationship with the cops. So, you get a huge number of FOI requests, which have to be answered at great cost to the police service … You see some bizarre things unraveling which put more pressure on police chiefs as the media almost creates the crisis and then feeds off a crisis of its own making … This is a completely different dynamic from 20 years ago.
>
> Interview with author, 4 August 2010

The Met and the media

As has been shown, operational strategy and tactics in public order policing have been deeply influenced by the mediatized scrutiny of events like the G20 protest in 2009 (and, indeed, by controversy surrounding earlier mass demonstrations, such as the protest against the Chinese president in 2001). Senior officers in the Met feel they are caught on the horns of a dilemma. Not to be seen to respond by reviewing guidelines and instructions would appear insensitive, not to say intransigent, while conceding too much ground to its critics would seriously undermine morale. Mike Messenger, a former Met commander responsible for public order, believes there is a danger of 'getting carried away with media hysteria':

> I think people were dismayed at some of what they have seen [at the G20 demonstration] but we need to step back and see what has happened in the round … it needs to be looked at in a much more reflective and comprehensive way … I would be very surprised if it was not having some negative impact on officer morale … Public opinion of the majority of police officers is disproportionately affected by the minority of actions covered by the media.
>
> *Police* magazine, May 2009

Not for the first time, the police have been caught out by their relative unfamiliarity with the new media which they are being urged to embrace. Scouring messages on bulletin boards to assess whether violence is planned has yielded useful information but is not a failsafe method of spotting trouble. And there are serious potential pitfalls to engaging in viral dialogue, as former Deputy Assistant Commissioner, Brian Paddick, points out:

> The Met has already had problems with Facebook and other social networking sites where, in the run-up to the G20 protests, officers were publishing what might have been seen as inflammatory stuff – how they were up for it or whatever. So, it is going to become increasingly difficult for the Met to control information in the way they have liked to in the past.
>
> Interview with author, 23 September 2010

Paddick knows better than most the perils which the web holds for the unwary officer. In February 2002, recently appointed as borough commander in Lambeth, he contributed some thoughts to a locally-based website called urban75, self-described as an 'underground e-zine'.[6] The site hosted a variety of radical bulletin boards:

> There had been a high profile death of a man called Derek Bennett and a number of completely false allegations of police brutality. We were getting a real kicking on these bulletin boards, nobody was speaking up for the police and ... eventually, I decided that I had to take them on. So I signed on as 'Brian the Commander' and engaged in discussion ... unfortunately, or fortunately, one of the discussions was on anarchy.
>
> ibid.

Paddick's comment that 'The concept of anarchy has always appealed to me' (though he added the rider that 'it didn't work in practice') was picked up by another respondent who worked for the *Big Issue* and from there (15 June 2002), it quickly became a minor *cause célèbre* in the press, with the *Sun* labelling him 'Commander Crackpot'.[7] For the Met, Paddick's 'offence' was to subvert the normative behaviour of the hierarchy by communicating openly with the outside world, unmediated by the press office. 'Just me raw, talking to the people in the community' (ibid.). This did not prevent his promotion to Deputy Assistant Commissioner in November 2003 but neither did it quell the snide comments from within his own organization, unsubtly fed to the press. Thus, the *Sun* story on his appointment carried the comment from an unnamed police source: 'How can the squad [the territorial policing support unit, for which Paddick assumed responsibility] be bossed by a man who finds anarchy attractive?' (*Sun*, 26 November 2003).

Chapter 8 examined in some depth Brian Paddick's cannabis 'experiment' in Brixton and the beginning of a media backlash. His is an instructive case study in how the Met conducts its internal politics, and the incessant jockeying for preferment, through parts of the media. In an echo of Alastair Campbell's insinuation to the political columnist, Andrew Rawnsley, that Gordon Brown had 'psychological flaws' (see Chapter 6), Paddick was the subject of similar treatment when he was moved from Brixton after his former partner had sold details of their life together to the *Mail on Sunday* in March 2002:

> Just after I had been banished from Brixton, I got a phone call from a free-lance who had been asked by the editor of the *Evening Standard* to do a 'sympathetic' piece on me. He said 'well, we have heard that you are down, depressed and seeing a therapist'. I said 'What else have you heard?' 'That you are unpredictable and unreliable.' Now that was a very interesting phrase, 'unpredictable and unreliable', because it was exactly what Mike Todd [his immediate superior] had said to me on the phone at the weekend. Subsequently, although journalists guard their sources jealously, after lunch and a few glasses of wine, the reporter admitted that it was Mike Todd who had spoken to him.
>
> Interview with author, 23 September 2010[8]

The interaction between journalists and their police sources is an under-researched area of criminology and where it is dealt with, the focus tends to be on the mechanics of the relationship. In his landmark work, Chibnall describes the symbiosis between crime reporters and their police contacts (Chibnall 1977). While in *Reporting Crime*, Schlesinger and Tumber unpick the way journalists receive and disseminate information from the police and 'offer some insights into the agenda-building process in the crime and criminal justice field' (Schlesinger and Tumber 1994: 38). But they do not seek to explain the use made by the police (or, for that matter, the Home Office) of the media for fighting internal policy or personality battles. Before he joined the IPCC, Richard Offer was head of the press office at the Police Complaints Authority:

> The thing I noticed about the Met was that every single person who had a grievance went rushing off to the media – and each section fought its case through the press. For example, I was always teasing John Steele [the *Daily Telegraph* crime correspondent] that he was the official spokesman for the firearms unit because they trusted him and he picked up a lot of stories from the unit. Similarly, whenever a squad was threatened with cuts or disband-ment, the story would appear in the *Evening Standard* written by Justin Davenport [the crime correspondent]. You never saw this in other forces, because even the larger ones might have no more than four or five officers of ACPO rank and they tend to work together. In the Met, you have so many people of that rank, all with their own political agenda. And so of course, they spend a lot of time trying to undermine their rivals.
>
> Interview with author, 19 February 2010

In this, the corporate factionalism of the Met was not so very different from that of other large organizations. But it was self-evidently of abiding interest to the media when the 'story' coalesced around issues which can loosely be bundled together as 'political correctness'. Since the Macpherson Report into the Stephen Lawrence investigation, any signs that the Met had either failed adequately to address its 'institutional racism' or was hogtied by the label, was seized on by print and broadcast journalists. In this way, reporters looking for a story and senior officers fighting to get to the top table, forged alliances.

Assistant Commissioner Tarique Ghaffur was the most senior Asian police officer in the country when he launched a claim for racial discrimination against the force in the summer of 2008. In September, he was suspended following an extraordinary press conference in which he attacked the commissioner, Ian Blair, personally, and claimed that he had been sidelined and humiliated in his role as head of security planning for the London 2012 Olympics. But even before that, many of the grievances which had animated Ghaffur had been aired in sections of the media. Brian Paddick has analysed the cultural dynamics which made the clash inevitable:

> All of the decisions made by the top team at the Met are actually pre-determined in discussions held in wine bars, pubs and restaurants around Scotland Yard. So, when you get into the formal meeting, it is a done deal. Nobody listens to what anybody is saying because they have already made up their minds in those informal meetings. It is the way the world works. Tarique is Asian and Muslim. He was never invited to those pre-meeting discussions so he could not understand why, in the formal setting, his arguments were not being listened to. He thought it was because they did not like him. In fact, it was indirect racism in that he was not invited to the informal sessions where the decisions were actually made. Therefore, he felt that, despite the collective responsibility of the managing board, he had to talk to the media – simply because he was so frustrated that he was being excluded from the formal process.
>
> Interview with author, 23 September 2010

It can be argued, of course, that, as the country's largest and most important force, the Met has always been riven by internal divisions. Sir Robert Mark wrote in his autobiography that when he arrived as Commissioner in 1972: 'I felt rather like the representative of a leper colony attending the annual garden party of a colonial governor' (Mark 1978, cited in the *Guardian*, 13 March 2008).

The animus against Mark was centred on his drive to root out corruption but, according to the former Assistant Commissioner, Terrorism, Andy Hayman, antagonism in the upper echelons of the Met is a fairly constant phenomenon:

> I was reading recently about the tensions in the Mark period and it as if time has not moved on at all. The Met is like any major bank or other large institution. People in the top team have their own personal agenda, some are more spiteful than loyal.
>
> Interview with author, 20 April 2010

But the media has moved on and the amplification of those agendas has a far stronger resonance in 2010 than it did a generation ago.

The downfall of Ian Blair

There are only five references to Ian Blair in John Stevens's 381-page autobiography and one of those is when Stevens misheard his press chief on the phone and thought that Ian Blair had been found lying drunk in Leicester Square (in July 2000) when, in fact, it was the Prime Minister's son, Euan (Stevens 2006: 295). Given the thesis already outlined about the clash of egos and ambitions at Scotland Yard, it is not unexpected that Stevens should wish to largely airbrush his deputy from an account of his own time as commissioner. But Blair's demise as the country's 'top cop' is a cautionary example of the way the media and political expedience can meld, with far-reaching impact.

Like the earlier analysis in this chapter on the G20 protest, this section draws on recent work done by Greer and McLaughlin on what they call Ian Blair's 'trial by media'(Greer and McLaughlin 2010b). Signs that newspapers such as the *Daily Mail* were going to exploit every opportunity to 'de-legitimate' Blair (ibid.) were evident early in his commissionership. Only four months after he had taken over from Stevens in February 2005, Blair lost an employment tribunal case brought by three white Met officers, who had claimed racial discrimination. They had been disciplined after an Asian officer had accused them of making racially derogatory comments at a training day. Blair's commitment to improving the diversity of the Met was well-known and by no means universally supported by rank-and-file officers. Thus the *Mail*'s headline on the case 'The police chief who hung his officers out to dry' (*Daily Mail*, 28 June 2005) carried a toxic charge for the Commissioner, the more so because, in a force as large as the Met, where contact with the leadership is necessarily limited, opinion tends to be shaped by the press and the *Mail* is widely read. Blair admitted as much in an interview after the tribunal had issued its ruling:

> I am aware of what an enormously powerful newspaper the *Daily Mail* is. I have got to do something to repair the damage of the headline. It hurt the organization … it also hurt personally. I knew when I saw it.
>
> *Guardian*, 2 July 2005

It was Blair's misfortune that before he could do anything to repair the damage, the young Brazilian, Jean Charles de Menezes, was shot dead by firearms officers on 22 July 2005 as part of the investigation into the 7/7 bombings and this came to define his period in post. In a vivid illustration of the Met's 'golden hour' principle at work, the press bureau did little to counteract reports from eye-witnesses, which found their way into the media, that de Menezes had been shot because he had vaulted a ticket barrier and was wearing a bulky jacket, which could have concealed explosives. Neither claim was true. But more damaging was Blair's statement at a hastily arranged news conference that the shooting was 'directly linked to the ongoing and expanding anti-terrorist operation' (IPCC 2007: 6). It later emerged that, by this point, a number of his senior colleagues were already aware that an innocent man had been killed but that Blair, himself, was in ignorance until the following morning.

The dictum of the 'golden hour' largely held good at a time when the police position in the 'hierarchy of credibility' (Becker 1967) was widely accepted, enabling them to manage the flow of information without being challenged by competing versions of the facts. But the de Menezes affair shows that that is no longer the case, as Mike Grannatt, a former head of communications at Scotland Yard, points out:

> I agree with the 'golden hour' theory of news ... But it is now a double-edged sword because the official version can unravel. The first hour is always chaos – especially after events like the 7/7 bombings – and now people's expectations have changed. They used to know it was chaos during that hour but nobody questioned that. Now, we have recordings, official and unofficial, which show the chaos in gory detail and it is held up as fault. So, what was once this ability to propagate information has become [through the media] the ability to apportion fault and blame.
>
> Interview with author, 12 October 2010

The fallout from the de Menezes shooting demonstrates the truth that when an event of such dramatic significance occurs, the demand from the media for what politicians often dismissively call a 'running commentary' is hard to resist. In this case, it was an unattributable briefing given to the crime correspondents lobby, the Crime Reporters Association (CRA), by Andy Hayman, in his role as Assistant Commissioner, Terrorism, which became a principal point of issue. It turned on whether Hayman had told the journalists that the dead man was 'not believed to be one of the suspects' or whether he had omitted the words 'believed to be', thereby raising the question of why Blair himself had spoken at a news conference, less than an hour earlier, of the killing being part of 'an ongoing and expanding anti-terrorist operation' (IPCC 2007).

The investigation by the Independent Police Complaints Commission into the way that Hayman passed on the information at his disposal, concluded that:

> AC Hayman was aware of the emerging evidence and failed in his responsibility to keep the Commissioner informed ... It is apparent that he deliberately withheld the information, both that he had briefed the CRA and on the contents of that briefing ... He therefore misled the Commissioner, other senior MPS officers and representatives of the Metropolitan Police Authority and Home Office, who were present.
>
> IPCC, ibid.: 92–101

That Andy Hayman should be censured over his handling of the media is perhaps not so surprising because he had pursued what might be considered a risky media-centric approach to his various posts since the late 1990s when he became spokesman on drugs for the Association of Chief Police Officers:

> When I got to a senior rank, I realized that the culture of the police was, in general, apprehensive, nervous and defensive about the media. If anything,

it was to close the door to journalists. I thought it was a bit of a contradiction because ... as soon as some major event or crime happened, or the police needed help in finding a missing person or a witness, the first thing they would do was turn to the media. So, when I became an ACPO spokesman, I had a bit of a mission to change that culture.

Interview with author, 20 April 2010

When Hayman was appointed Chief Constable of Norfolk in 2000, among his first decisions were to increase the pay of the head of communications and to introduce regular monthly briefings for the media, along the lines of those held by the Met Commissioner for the CRA. Richard Offer says he behaved differently from most chief constables:

There was an interesting article written by the crime correspondent of the *Eastern Daily Press* which gave some interesting insights into Hayman's methods. He was always on the phone to reporters, giving them stories which they would never get from a 'normal' chief constable. So he certainly played things differently.

Interview with author, 19 February 2010

But the media–police nexus is one of mutual self-interest and carries no lifetime guarantees of loyalty on either side, as Sir Huge Orde, president of the Association of Chief Police Officers, says:

If any chief seriously thinks they can have a crime reporter as a personal friend, they are potty ... If any chief or any cop thinks they can influence what is written, in other words, get stuff either inserted or deleted, that is not a [realistic] relationship, it is a bad place to be ... The complexity of policing is very hard to sell.

Interview with author, 4 August 2010

It is equally true that the complexity, voracity and fickleness of the media are often something of a mystery to senior police officers, and although Andy Hayman and Ian Blair were very different personalities, they both suffered at the hands of a mediated culture which neither fully understood. What parts of the media saw in Blair that it did not like was a hubris which jarred with the favoured stereotypes of the 'copper's copper' (his predecessor, John Stevens) or the quietly effective managerialism of other recent highly regarded Commissioners (such as Sir Peter Imbert). When Blair mused about the middle class feeling too 'superior' to join the police service (as he did during his Dimbleby lecture in November 2005) or wondered why so much media coverage had been devoted to the Soham murders and so little to the killing of an Asian builders merchant in East London in January 2006 (as he did at a meeting of the Metropolitan Police Authority on 26 January 2006), he was merely confirming the view of the *Daily Mail* that he 'should remember that he is not a politician' (*Daily Mail* comment, 29 January 2006).[9]

Ironically, his namesake, the politician called Blair, got away with believing that he knew as much about how to tackle crime as the professionals. It was his successor, Gordon Brown, who suffered from walking in the shadow of a popular leader and gifted communicator in very much the same way that Ian Blair was handicapped by following John Stevens. Indeed, the parallel is underscored by the anti-Ian Blair briefing which went on, according to one of his inner circle, Brian Paddick:

> I remember when Ian was getting a very hard time in the press, not long after he had taken over, and I was in the senior officers' canteen with some of the press staff. I said to Dick Fedorcio [head of communications] 'Dick, how much is he paying you?' And Dick said 'What do you mean?' I said 'John Stevens, how much is he paying you to arrange all this bad publicity for Ian?' ... The thing about Stevens is that if he was tipped off that there was going to be something very negative in the press, he could probably make a phone call and get it pulled or moderated. Ian Blair went on a similar charm offensive with editors and the feedback that I got was 'could you tell him not to have any more lunches with editors because they come away with a worse opinion of him than before'.
>
> Interview with author, 23 September 2010

Paddick's words need to be considered in the context of his own falling-out with Blair and – for those who have trouble detecting irony when they see it – it should be pointed out that he was not literally suggesting that Stevens was paying to spread unflattering stories about Blair, nor that Fedorcio was doing so. But his recollection points up the fact that, in most respects, Ian Blair should have been one of the more secure Met Commissioners of recent years. In the Home Office, he was regarded as the outstanding choice to succeed Stevens. His commitment to introducing neighbourhood police teams throughout London chimed perfectly with New Labour strategy. He was intellectually better equipped to do the most challenging job in policing than virtually any of his post-war predecessors. And yet, almost from the moment he entered his eighth floor office in Scotland Yard, he was a beleaguered figure, and from as early as 2006, characterized as the 'gaffe-prone' Commissioner (Greer and McLaughlin 2010b: 37), he was little more than a lame duck.

This study has been at pains to resist the temptation to fit case studies into the conceptual frameworks of communication theory but it is hard to escape the view that, in Blair's case, the agenda-setting and framing of the news media, fuelled by what Greer and McLaughlin call 'the politics of outrage' (ibid.), bear a great responsibility for his plight. As the columnist Simon Jenkins wrote in 2006:

> London's police chief, Sir Ian Blair, is being dragged into the street by a mob of journalists and politicians, blood-stained but still twitching. He is taunted, spat at, kicked and beaten. The editor of the *Sun* is looking for a gibbet and of the *Mail* for a rope. Politicians are queuing to thwack the horse from under the gallows.
>
> *Guardian*, 14 June 2006

For David Blunkett, interviewed for this research less than a week after Blair announced his (forced) resignation in October 2008, there was no doubt about who was to blame:

> This is a case of someone being brought down by the media. You would have to be living in a cave in the middle of Derbyshire rather than a cottage [a reference to Blunkett's out-of-London accommodation at the time] not to see a juxtaposition between the *Daily Mail* attacking Blair and, on the same day, the new mayor of London, Boris Johnson, sacking him.
>
> Interview with author, 8 October 2008

But in retrospect, the question is not: why did Blair decide to quit eighteen months short of his five-year tenure? Rather, it is: how did he cling on for three and a half years under such withering fire? The answer is that he had the staunch support of the Labour mayor of London, Ken Livingstone, and of successive Labour Home Secretaries. Although this provided a bulwark against the media's hostility, it was a dangerous party politicization of policing – dangerous for democratic accountability and, as it turned out, for Blair himself when the tide turned and the Conservatives entered City Hall. As Mike Grannatt says:

> The clever cops, such as Stevens, Imbert and Mark, knew their strength came from being at arm's length from the Home Office, so they could demonstrate their independence to the troops. Blair's mistake was getting too close to Number 10.
>
> Interview with author, 12 October 2010

Blair initially agreed to be interviewed for this study and a series of seven questions were submitted to him in September 2010. Three are reproduced here:

1 The media loves to pigeonhole a Met Commissioner. John Stevens was the 'copper's copper'. You were the 'politically correct, New Labour' Commissioner. To what extent did this media label influence/affect attitudes within the higher reaches of the Met, which, as we know, is a highly political organization with, at any one time, a number of strong personalities jockeying for power/influence?
2 You clearly relished the opportunity to engage in the 'public sphere' via the media but how far is it possible in this media-centric age for a Commissioner to keep his own counsel on an issue or delay making a public response to a 'crisis' which is dominating the headlines?
3 The media (specifically *The Times*) increased the pressure on you in September 2008 by claiming that plans were afoot to force you from office. At the start of 2006, the *Mirror* reported that a coup was being planned by a 'cabal' of senior officers. With hindsight, do you think you could have devised a media strategy which made you less vulnerable to media attacks?

Blair, who was in the United States at the time, replied after nearly a month:

Jon, I am sorry not to have replied earlier. I am equally sorry to withdraw my offer to help you. The problem, which is not your fault, is that your questions are very accurate as to the concerns that surrounded my period of tenure and I need to preserve my privacy on them. I have spent the last two years refusing to comment on some of the issues you raise and that is how I intend to stay for the future. I do not think I can help. Best wishes for the future.

Ian Blair email, 4 October 2010

The numbers game

In Chapter 1, the issue of police numbers was touched on as an example of a government, New Labour, enacting a strategy which could not be wholly reconciled with its stated commitment to evidence-based policymaking. In the same way that tougher sentencing became a *sine qua non* of Home Office policy from 1993 onwards, so the boosting of the number of police officers available for patrol duties became a central pledge from 1999. The financial opportunity to make such a promise arose once the Chancellor, Gordon Brown, had loosened the purse strings after adhering to Conservative spending plans for two years after the 1997 election. The political logic was the need to underscore Labour's anti-social behaviour programme, which was about public confidence rather than crime reduction. And public confidence – as reflected in opinion sampling – demanded the sight of police officers on the beat.

The debate about the correlation between police officer strength and the crime rate is a highly contested one. Figures produced by researchers in the House of Commons library in 2010 show that for most of the period between 1960 and 1995, police officer numbers went up and so did recorded crime.[10] Crime began to fall in 1995, although officer numbers did not begin to increase substantially until New Labour established the Crime Fighting Fund with a ring-fenced budget, which saw the overall number of police rise from 124,170 in March 2000 (Home Office 2001b) to 141,230 in July 2005 (Home Office 2005b). By July 2009, officer numbers in England and Wales had reached 143,770 (according to the Home Office), coinciding with a continued fall in most categories of recorded crime. Thus, as the election neared in 2010, the Home Office minister for crime and policing, David Hanson, had no qualms about praising the 'significant contribution of the increased numbers of police officers since 1997 on the overall reduction of crime'(*Guardian*, 18 February 2010).

Revealingly, he did not specify what contribution it had actually made. However, his claim was circumspection itself compared to this post-election blog by the Labour MP for Sheffield Central, Paul Blomfield:

Due to record investment in the police over the last decade, police numbers are up and this has resulted in crime in South Yorkshire falling for the last four years. Frontline job losses will undoubtedly cause crime to increase.[11]

No mention is made of the factors which almost certainly have a far bigger influence on crime rates, such as demographic and economic trends, employment levels, relative income inequality, as well as cultural and social fluctuations. If further proof is needed that the link between police numbers and the crime rate is an issue of political expedience rather than criminological evidence, it can be found in the response of the policing minister in the coalition administration, Nick Herbert, to a report by the think tank Civitas ('2011: the start of a great decade for criminals', Civitas, 7 January 2011) that the report 'makes a simple link between crime levels and police numbers, which the evidence does not support' (cited in the *Guardian*, 7 January 2011).

If the number of police on the beat does not correlate to reduced crime, then what is left as a justification for boosting officer strength? Clearly, the maintenance of public confidence. This, after all, was the message of the annual Audit Commission survey of performance indicators for 1999/2000, which found that only one in five people surveyed was happy with the number of police on the streets.[12] Frustratingly, the survey does not interrogate the underlying reasons for people's dissatisfaction and whether one of them might be the messages they take from the media. But Charles Clarke, who was a Home Office policing minister when the Home Secretary, Jack Straw, made his commitment to boost numbers in 1999, believes the media must take some responsibility:

> A whole debate took place at that time around police numbers. Many people, criminologists and others, believed it should not have been a key issue in policing, and it should not have been. The decisive issue was how you used intelligence and the resources you had. And that is still true today. But the power of the police lobby – faithfully recorded by the media – gets magnified and though I would not say that the media played the decisive role, it was a very significant one.
>
> Interview with author, 16 September 2010

In the face of the many profound challenges facing policing, a concentration on officer numbers, principally as a means of anchoring public confidence, was, at the very least, unhelpful. In 2008, the Chief Inspector of Constabulary, Sir Ronnie Flanagan, tried to puncture the balloon by stating that: 'I am persuaded that we would not be making the most effective use of resources dedicated to the police if police officer numbers were sustained at their current level' (cited in the *Guardian*, 8 February 2008). And he suggested that civilian staff could take over the roles of fully-sworn (i.e. warranted) officers in taking statements and some 'back office' functions. But although these were by no means unorthodox views within the police hierarchy, they did not fit the collusive narrative being nurtured by government and media. It is another example of Koch-Baumgarten and Voltmer's hypothesis that: 'The discursive hegemony of the media can limit the policy choices likely to engage public support' (2010: 218).

Charles Clarke's own policy priority was to oversee force mergers so that the existing structure of forty-three forces in England and Wales (forty-four if the City of London force is included) was reduced to a much smaller number. 'I never had a precise figure in mind but it would have been about fourteen or fifteen' (Interview with author, 16 September 2010). This failed to happen because there was not sufficient support within the police service itself, and both Number 10 and the Treasury had concerns about the financial implications. Both of these factors were well reflected in the media coverage and although it is absolutely certain that force amalgamations will return as a policy programme for a future Home Secretary because, evidentially, it makes sense, it will have to navigate its way past a mediated clamour first.

10 A changing media – and a new media

The previous chapter borrowed from Greer and McLaughlin's analysis of 'trial by media' which placed the Metropolitan Police Commissioner, Sir Ian Blair, in the dock. They define this phenomenon as: 'a dynamic, impact-driven, news media-led process by which individuals ... are tried and sentenced in the "court of public opinion"' (Greer and McLaughlin 2010b: 27).

The frequency with which individuals in public life – even if hardly household names – fall victim to this process is attested to by the fact that at least six of those interviewed for this book: David Blunkett, Charles Clarke, Brian Paddick, Tom Lloyd, Andy Hayman and David Scott, know first-hand what it is like to be the subject of *ad hominem* media attacks. There are a number of reasons for the attraction, to both media and audiences, of a targeted firestorm: one is the changing complexion of news media as it has morphed into a purveyor of opinion rather than fact, another is the voracious appetite of the 24-hour news machine, constantly looking for another morsel to devour. For David Blunkett, the policy implications are clear-cut:

> It is the seven-day-a-week, 24-hour multi-channel, satellite coverage which has made all the difference. Twenty years ago, we could have put out a statement saying 'we are reflecting, we will make a statement soon'. Now, you cannot do that because politicians who do not respond to the world moving on, which happens now almost instantaneously, are left high and dry as other people do respond.
>
> Interview with author, 8 October 2008

This mediatization of politics has manifested itself in a variety of ways. As Jones points out in a study of New Labour, even by 1998, the number of ministerial special advisers was almost double that of the Major administration (73 compared to 38) and their role had changed too. Previously hired as policy experts, they had become, in the words of the commentator, Hugo Young, 'the minister's personal familiars, whose prime talent, if any, lies in explaining what the minister wants to get across, and the messengers of perception' (cited in Jones 1999: 121).

In some cases, as we have seen, the policy advisers become ministers in their turn (Jack Straw and David Cameron, to name but two), which, in Simon Jenkins's view, has buttressed the media's agenda-setting function:

You have a class of politicians now who have very little experience to fall back on outside of politics – such as David Miliband – and it shows. Alastair Campbell was hugely influential but he had never been outside of a newspaper office, which is the most transient and ephemeral of contexts in which to formulate policy. All of these people have grown up in an environment in which the media played a large part and they find it very difficult to demote the media. When I was editor of *The Times* and went to see Margaret Thatcher, she did not even know which paper I edited. It was comical and I found it rather reassuring.

Interview with author, 21 June 2010

Substitute 'Tony Blair' for 'Margaret Thatcher' and that admission would be patently absurd. In the intervening period, politics has become communication. Charles Clarke is one of the few Home Secretaries to admit his limitations in courting the media and, in the case of the *Daily Mail* – 'I had a very low opinion of the editor Paul Dacre' (Interview with author 16 September 2010) – he tried none too hard, even if it was almost an article of faith amongst the Blairite faithful that tracking the concerns of the *Mail* was vital to continued electoral success.

Clarke is also at odds with many of his contemporaries in government in believing that some newspaper columnists, the so-called 'commentariat', wield an influence on policy.[1] Howell James, who had senior roles in both Downing Street and at the BBC, noted: 'When ministers believe they have a strong case for something, even when it will not be popular and will be difficult to get through, they usually decide to go ahead, even against the commentariat' (Hobsbawm and Lloyd 2008: 14).

Clarke's view is: 'Of course the commentariat is powerful. Any government committed to change needs to understand that the case for change can only be sustained through strong argument. Commentators reflect the strength of that argument' (ibid.: 11).

Clarke's belief that ministers need somehow to engage in intellectual combat in newsprint in order to press their case is a curiously old-fashioned one and takes insufficient account of the qualitative transformation in 'mainstream' media. The reason that he, like a number of other Home Secretaries, fell foul of media attack was not because they failed to present a robust argument but because New Labour's empathic sensibilities had diminished to the point where it was no longer a match for self-confident newspaper editors riding a tide of popular concerns, as the columnist, Peter Oborne, explains:

The reason that Paul Dacre is a great editor is not because he has political opinions. It is because he understands his own readers so well. So, when people attack the *Mail* as a kind of unelected, unaccountable force, what they are really doing is attacking the *Mail* readers, the ordinary, hard-working, lower middle class, often struggling to survive on low incomes, leading insecure lives and finding it hard to get access to decent public services. It is an elite concept and absolute nonsense that people who read the *Mail* are merely ciphers of Melanie Phillips or Richard Littlejohn.

Interview with author, 14 December 2010

For Mike Grannatt, it is the *Mail*'s ability to set the agenda for other influential parts of the media which is its biggest weapon:

> If broadcasters could express views, the game would change. The *Mail* influences a well-defined demographic. It has a very precise feel for what presses people's buttons. That is how successful papers work. Dacre has a vampire's eye for blood. So, what is a bunch of middle class people at the BBC going to do but be influenced by his agenda?.
>
> Interview with author, 12 October 2010

Reports of the *Mail*'s death may be exaggerated

If reading the previous section causes a gnashing of teeth and tearing of hair amongst the frontiersmen of new media, it was intended to do just that. To the cry, 'you are writing about the past, not mapping the future', the riposte is: this is the landscape of criminal justice politics between 1989 and 2010, which this book has tried faithfully to survey. Despite extravagant claims, the 2010 election was not the UK's 'first Internet election' and there is no empirical evidence that the digital world of blogs and websites, and social and interactive media, made a significant difference to the outcome. Nevertheless, currents are stirring, which suggest that our reading of the world is running at a deeper level as a result of Wikileaks exposures and the real-time exchange of information via Twitter and that this will have a profound impact on the ordering of society.

In February 2009, the Cabinet Office minister in the New Labour administration, Liam Byrne, was reported (but not in the *Daily Mail*) as telling the Commons public administration committee that 'The idea that the *Daily Mail* sets the agenda for government is in the past' (*Guardian*, 27 February 2009). He was responding to a committee member who had said that people believed crime was rising because of what they read in the *Mail*, and he accused ministers of allowing tabloids to set the agenda. Explaining why the government had created the post of director of digital engagement, at an annual salary of £120,000, Byrne said that:

> Tabloid newspapers … sell 22 million fewer copies than in 1997, while viewers on TV news channels have collapsed. The growth is in the new media, with 100 million [people] on Facebook, YouTube and freesheets, and it is these people the government has to reach.
>
> ibid.

As we have seen, New Labour's mastery of the 'old' media was central to its capture of power in 1997. Joy Johnson was the party's director of communications and campaigns from 1995 to1996, and in 1998, commented on the application of this skill:

> what is new with New Labour is the sheer volume of column inches ghosted by [Alastair] Campbell. His skill at tailoring the language to suit the paper, and the speed at which he can write articles, is his distinct and distinctive

advantage in the art of media management. Tony Blair's by-line has appeared in more copies of the *Sun* than any other newspaper and when the political and presentation imperative presents itself, he speaks to the people through the *Sun* readers.

Johnson 1998: 16

That was written only thirteen years ago yet both the language and the underlying assumption of a politician 'speaking to the people' in order to sell his prospectus, is redolent of a bygone era. Matthew Taylor, former head of the Downing Street policy unit, says political leaders must ground 'their appeal on a citizenship democracy rather than a consumer democracy' (*Guardian*, 3 June 2009). But perhaps Blumler and Coleman's analogy is more appropriate for a study of crime and justice: 'The public are no longer only voters to be seduced but potential witnesses to be managed' (Blumler and Coleman 2010: 147).

The literal image of the citizen as a 'witness to be managed' is being confronted almost daily in the workings of crime detection and justice. Increasingly, complaints against the police are supported by camera footage taken with a mobile phone, and appeals for information by the Independent Police Complaints Commission and others are made by Twitter. In December 2010, such was the enormous global interest in the case of the Wikileaks founder, Julian Assange, and his extradition battle with Sweden over allegations of rape, that a district judge allowed the 'tweeting' of a bail hearing by those inside the courtroom.[2] The issue had already been under consideration at a higher level and in February 2011, the UK Supreme Court issued guidance that, with a few exceptions (cases of family dispute or where reporting restrictions might apply), its own hearings would permit 'live text-based communications' (*Guardian*, 4 February 2011). Meanwhile, judges are having to grapple with the probability that some jurors in criminal trials are accessing the Internet when they get home to discover details about the case which the law does not permit them to know in the interests of the proper administration of justice.

As we saw in the previous chapter, the police have been lacerated over their handling of public order events as a result of the exploitation of new media. The holder of the national portfolio on public order for the Association of Chief Police Officers, at the time of the G20 protest, was the acting chief constable of Northumbria, Sue Sim. It was she, coincidentally, who was exposed to the pitiless scrutiny of social media during the hunt for the fugitive gunman, Raoul Moat, in July 2010.[3] Her appearance, when fronting televised news conferences, provoked vituperative comment. Here are two examples from the site mumsnet:

When she was on the news at the weekend, DH and I were nearly crying with laughter at her lilac eyeshadow and alarming blow-dry.

PlumSykes, 8 July 2010

It makes her look like the lovechild of Rod Hull and Madge off 'Neighbours'.

tawdryhepburn, 8 July 2010[4]

And some of the comments posted on the Yahoo 'answers' forum, in response to the question 'Does temporary Chief Constable, Sue Sim, need a makeover ?' were even more rancorous. It exemplifies Andrew Keen's jaundiced take on web discourse:

> An army of mostly anonymous, self-referential writers who exist not to report news but to spread gossip, sensationalise political scandal, display embarrassing photos of public figures and to link to stories on imaginative topics such as UFO sightings or 9/11 conspiracy theories.
>
> Keen 2007: 47

Take out the word 'anonymous' and how far removed is Keen's dystopian vision from much of the tabloid media? With a penchant for amplifying saloon-bar sentiment, it was no surprise that the *Daily Mail*'s columnist, Richard Littlejohn, joined the tormenters of Sue Sim:

> Judging by her haircut, she looked as if she had stepped straight out of *The Sweeney* [a 1970s UK television series about the Flying Squad] – more Margaret Beckett, circa 1975, than Farrah Fawcett-Majors in *Charlie's Angels* [a popular US television series]. She sounded like a soppy social worker, blathering on about her 'passion and commitment to policing our communities'.
>
> *Daily Mail*, 6 July 2010

Former police officers, too, were ready to join the media-led assault. Andy Hayman, despite suffering his own career vicissitudes, was quoted as saying of Sue Sim: 'She is probably a very nice person. She is in the wrong place at the wrong time. She is probably keeping the chair warm while the new chief is selected. She probably has not got the experience' (*Sun*, 13 July 2010).[5]

The Raoul Moat case was a perfect conjunction of social media being 'recruited' to give a new twist to a variety of familiar 'old' media crime narratives. One such trope is the homage to the victim of a serious crime – usually in the form of a bank of floral tributes left outside a home or by a roadside. In this instance, the twist was the revelation that, in addition to the physical shrine outside his house, 'friends' of Moat set up a virtual one by creating a Facebook page, lauding him as a heroic, anti-authority figure: 'RIP Raoul ur a legend! Never be forgotten. Wot a waste of life RIPXXX'; 'A man that lost everything. Just feel so sorry for him in the end' (cited in *Mail on Sunday*, 11 July 2010).

This encouraged the media to speculate on the psychological motivation behind such comments, supplementing, and in some cases replacing, the earlier narrative of a provincial police force perceived to be struggling in the national limelight. That same narrative inflection was evident in the coverage of the Soham murders when the Cambridgeshire force was heavily criticized for incompetence, although it later emerged that Ian Huntley and Maxine Carr had been identified by detectives as the perpetrators early in the inquiry. In a wider, non-policing context, Jürgen Habermas identifies a syndrome at work which: 'focuses the attention of an anonymous and dispersed public on selected topics and information, allowing citizens to focus on the same critically filtered issues and journalistic pieces at any given time' (Habermas 2006).

But the information stream from the multifarious blogs and websites of the digital world also encourage a generalized suspicion that the whole truth is not being revealed and this, in the view of the ACPO president, Sir Hugh Orde, feeds an urge to find someone to blame:

> In the case of Raoul Moat there was an obsessive attempt to get someone to say 'this was a disaster waiting to happen'. And this soaked up huge amounts of police time because they needed to provide reassurance that there had not been a cock-up. The acting chief constable [Sue Sim] was employed full time on briefing the media. But the consequence of that openness was an absolute belief in the minds of some journalists that the police were hiding something.
>
> Interview with author, 4 August 2010

The use of new media, especially social networking sites, as a virtual prop by newspapers in order to give their long-cherished, and often threadbare, frames of reference a makeover is another phenomenon worth recognizing. The *Daily Mail* has been taken to task by Facebook for connecting many of its crime-related stories to use of the site. A typical example was the headline 'How many more victims of Facebook sex gang?' (25 February 2010) over a story about the arrest of a man in Torbay, suspected of belonging to a paedophile ring. A similar tendency can be found in a growing number of stories about 'cyber-stalking', which seems to have replaced 'phishing' (a form of e-fraud) in the hierarchy of 'fear of crime' themes in the Internet era.

It is a sign of the intimate, almost incestuous, relationship between old and new media. Martin Clarke, the *Daily Mail* executive who runs *Mail Online* (the UK's most popular newspaper website) told the Society of Editors annual conference in November 2010 that 10 per cent of the website's traffic was generated by referrals from Facebook: 'The social networks are becoming increasingly important to us. If you want an engaging site, Facebook is not a threat or a parasite but a gigantic free marketing engine' (cited in Robinson 2010).

Newspapers are not the only organizations to spot an opportunity rather than whine about a threat. The Metropolitan Police used social media sites to engage with demonstrators on the TUC march against job cuts in March 2011 and were praised by some for seeking real-time feedback on how the protest had been policed.[6]

In October 2010, Greater Manchester Police put all of its emergency calls on Twitter for a 24-hour period (14 October) to demonstrate how much more they do than 'fight' crime. While in April 2011, West Midlands Police began what was described as the first 'tweet-a-thon' from a justice centre when they published the results of all the cases heard at Birmingham magistrates' court on Twitter. Crime maps, too, formally launched by the Home Office on 31 January 2011 (available by typing a postcode into the website: www.police.uk) are a use of new media to re-connect agencies of the state with the public, with the declared aim of achieving greater accountability.

It is clear, then, that the role of the 'traditional' media as gatekeeper of the information flow has already been augmented, if not replaced, in a myriad of ways. But the point was made in Chapter 1 of this study that too much information can be as restricting as too little, when we are without the tools and skills to make sense of it. The leak of material on MPs' expenses was a journalistic coup for the *Daily Telegraph*, as was the avalanche of confidential diplomatic cables shared by Wikileaks with the *Guardian*, amongst other newspapers. But such vast quantities of data could not have been turned into news stories of real import without the employment of researchers with the ability and experience to 'mine' it.

The founder of the Internet, Sir Tim Berners-Lee, has even predicted that the future of journalism lies with those who are comfortable with sifting and sieving this raw information, much of it in the form of statistics, and turning up nuggets of pure news. He offered this vision of the future at the launch in November 2010 of the first government datasets, releasing information on departmental spending of more than £25,000 (reported in the *MediaGuardian*, 22 November 2010). It is surely one of the more significant, and least heralded, indications of new media influence on government that, at time of writing (April 2011), 5,600 databases are available for scrutiny on the portal www.datagov.co.uk. The justice portal contains information ranging from advanced warning of upcoming new criminal justice IT contracts to analysis of all government criminal justice policies. If the Freedom of Information Act has turned out, because of the time delay in the release of material, to be of more use to authors than to journalists, then mining the datasets might provide a vital form of angioplasty for a media whose arteries are clogged with speculative comment and 'infotainment'.

Conclusion

Nearly half a century ago, one of the great pioneers of communication theory, Marshall McLuhan, wrote that the 'medium is the message' (McLuhan 1964). In 2005, after the 7/7 bombings, when every television news bulletin was enhanced by camera footage shot on mobile phones by members of the public, the executive editor of Sky News, John Ryley, echoed McLuhan by stating 'It is a real example of how news has changed as technology has changed' (cited in Allan 2006: 152).

The impact of new media technology on the practice and process of news making is indisputable. But that is not what this book is primarily about. It is about criminal justice policy, and, writing in 2011, with the exception of policing, it is hard to discern how the shape of policy formulation has been influenced by Web 2.0, Wiki disclosures and the ceaseless chatter of Internet forums, blogs and tweets. But inasmuch as there is a close connection between a changing style of media discourse – as this book has argued – and policy development, one must assume that the McLuhan of 2030 will look back on this period and conclude that something equally transformative as the 'global village' was being constructed.

11 Terrorism and the politics of response

Introduction

This chapter analyses the mediated policy responses of UK governments to terrorism since 1989, with the events of 9/11 as the fulcrum. Those who delight in ontological quests will be disappointed that no attempt is made to adjudicate between the many different deconstructions of terrorism. That contested field can happily be ceded to political theorists, philosophers and jurists. The crux of this inquiry is how governments of different persuasions responded to the violence employed by the Provisional IRA (henceforth referred to as PIRA) on the British mainland. And to make comparisons with the challenge posed by Islamist or jihadist militants (so-called 'new' terrorism), with the consequence that 'policy goals have shifted further towards anticipatory responses ... criminal justice has been increasingly moulded towards early intervention' (Walker 2009: preface).

This chapter will put forward the proposition that, contrary to Tony Blair's famous war cry, 'Let no-one be in any doubt, the rules of the game are changing',[1] a reaction to the later attacks on 7 July 2005, New Labour's 'precautionary response to threats' (Furedi 2009: 197) can best be understood as part of a continuum of coercive policy which had begun in the mid-1990s. That was the period when the party began incubating ideas which would lead to the largely bi-partisan 'rulebook' of crime, justice and civil rights being re-written, so that, by 2001, it was an ideal template for applying to the changed circumstances of twenty-first century terrorism. Two of the key signposts along this trail have been glimpsed in previous chapters: a securitization of policymaking and a media prepared to see due process marginalized. A third has not: the prominence of think tanks in contesting the 'public sphere'.

Like a Russian doll, this under-explored 'back story' to the response to Islamist terrorism conceals another one – which might be called the 'crisis of insecurity' pre-9/11 that manifested itself in fears about asylum and immigration and the breakdown of community cohesion. This was reflected in the electoral popularity of far-right parties and, in the summer of 2001, riots in towns and cities with large Muslim communities: Oldham, Bradford and Burnley. Both Blair and Blunkett attest to the impact on the 'ruling elite' of these events (see, for example, Blair 2010; and Blunkett 2006). Thus, whereas the PIRA's mainland campaign was addressed as predominantly a security threat, Islamist terrorism led to the controversial Prevent strategy to combat radicalization and opened up an unresolved mediatized debate about multi-culturalism and identity.

Priming the response – the crisis of insecurity pre-9/11

Imagining a parallel universe post-9/11, Richard Jackson writes:

> Authorities could have … tried to reassure that it was an atypical event; could have pointed out all the measures taken to ensure security while stressing that the terrorists are tiny groups of people with few resources who have never yet managed to overthrow a democracy.
>
> Jackson 2005: 120

Douglas Hurd was Home Secretary when the PIRA resumed its mainland campaign, after a four-year hiatus, by bombing the Royal Engineers Inglis Barracks at Mill Hill in North London in August 1988, killing one serviceman. Thirteen months later, in September 1989, eleven Royal Marine bandsmen were killed when their barracks at Deal in Kent was blown up. Naturally, the amount of news coverage devoted to PIRA terrorism expanded during this period but a textual analysis of reporting in *The Times*, *Sun*, and *Daily Mirror* shows that it did not stray much beyond the traditional discourse of political response ('another act of infamous cowardice' was the reaction of the Labour leader, Neil Kinnock, to the Mill Hill bomb)[2] with the focus largely on lapses in physical security at both bases, which the bombers had exploited. There are cursory calls for tighter border checks (*Sun*, 23 September 1989) and for longer jail sentences and a vague and unspecified change to the rules on interrogation (*Daily Mirror*, 25 August 1988) but nothing which could be called a sustained campaign for fresh legislation.

Although some of the papers suggested that defence ministers might have to pay a price for security weakness, there was little or no ratcheting up of the pressure on the Home Secretary:

> It surprised me that there was not more media or public pressure over the IRA. I felt under less media pressure on terrorism than I did over violent crime. There was no real feeling that the IRA could overwhelm us all, even if the Prime Minister had been knocked out in the Grand Hotel bombing [in Brighton in 1984], life would go on. We thought the law was about right.
>
> Douglas Hurd, interview with author, 21 July 2008

Taking Jackson's point that 9/11 was an atypical (indeed, unique) event, it is evident that the media–politics response was to assume that it was going to become a 'typical' event and to deal with it on that basis by way of increasingly draconian legislation. Whereas Hurd and the political class of the early to mid-1990s knew that PIRA violence was a typical event – after all, in its various manifestations, they had lived with it for nearly a quarter of a century – but they did not respond with legislation, other than the annual renewal of the Prevention of Terrorism Act. Mike Grannatt, who became head of the Cabinet Office's Civil

Contingencies Secretariat in 2001, argues that there was a qualitative difference in the ministerial handling of the two terrorist campaigns:

> There was a period [in 2004], before David Blunkett left office, when ministers were veering between a desire to jack up people's interest and awareness in security and a complete paranoia about generating fear. During one week close to Christmas, both Blair and Blunkett made speeches about terrorism and pushed fear levels way up. And it was not clear why they had done that. This was not about warning the public. It was about politics ... i.e. we are better than the Tories at protecting you ... Nothing was being done at that period to equip the public effectively to help deal with terrorism. If you think back to the PIRA days, think of the number of times the media was told [by the police] 'we need people to report groups of young men in flats, renting lock-ups for cash, this is the anti-terrorist hotline number, ring it if you see anything suspicious.' That was sound advice which, over the years, has probably led to the arrest of more terrorists than anything else ... That was not happening during the [post-9/11] period. Stories about terrorism were being jacked up for political reasons and then damped down again.
>
> Interview with author, 12 October 2010

Since 9/11, the normative answer to this critique is that *pace* Blair, the rules of the game have changed by virtue of suicide bombing (leaving to one side the scope of the jihadist 'agenda', which has amorphous global ambitions, unlike the concrete aim of a united Ireland being pursued by PIRA).[3] And politicians, in the UK as elsewhere, are responding to a new reality: 'It is that uncontrollable risk is now irredeemable and deeply engineered into all the processes that sustain life in advanced societies' (Beck 2002: 46).

The question is whether this risk-informed reality is a by-product of 9/11 or whether the response to 9/11 was itself the outcome of a process which had begun independently of terrorism (either 'new' or 'old'). In Chapter 1, Barry Richards's model of 'emotional governance' was cited as a means of better understanding some of the criminal justice policy developments of the 1990s. What he identifies as 'psycho-cultural reserves of anxiety', in relation to the nature of terrorist attacks (Richards 2007: 136), is a useful litmus test for exploring the state of the world immediately before the 9/11 attacks, as recalled by Huw Evans, David Blunkett's special adviser:

> Britain had changed very significantly, along with a lot of the other most industrialized democracies, and some of the symptoms of that change were labour market movement and the vast numbers from a range of different countries coming into Britain, the development of broadband and mobile communications and so on. These things were great advantages but they also fuelled an underlying sense of insecurity. So, when you had unprecedented attacks, like 9/11, or a computer that could run at amazing speeds, or people being trafficked across continents, all of these things blended together [to

create] a world that is changing very quickly and which you cannot necessarily understand.

Interview with author,10 February 2010

The criminologist, Richard Garside, has also noted these destabilizing effects of modernity, associated with 'the rise of individualism, technological innovation and the disorienting impact of globalisation' (Garside 2007: 32). Seen from within government, David Blunkett says that 'the media was both picking up on and fuelling this insecurity – especially around immigration and asylum' (Interview with author, 8 October 2010). His immediate reference point is the events at the Sangatte camp in Calais during July and August 2001, when refugees from the developing world were pictured nightly in television news broadcasts making determined attempts to reach the UK by any means possible. Newspaper headlines – especially in the *Daily Mail* and the *Sun* – described the Sangatte 'immigrants' as a mass of 'illegals', who were 'swarming', 'plaguing' and 'flooding' Calais in an effort to come to 'soft touch' Britain. As we saw in Chapter 2, in relation to the media's coverage of the summer riots of 1991, policymakers find it hard to escape the 'ground-tone' (Wayne *et al.* 2008) set by media imagery over a sustained period, not merely because the pictures and stories have impact but because of the sub-text they carry about policy. In 2001, the commentary related to New Labour's perceived failure to take a grip on the issues of asylum and immigration during its first term, as Jack Straw concedes:

> I had not let the issue drift, as sometimes alleged, but I had made a judgment while we were in opposition that, because we were having to turn around so much on crime, I had better 'travel light' on asylum. I published a White Paper and introduced the 1999 Immigration Act, which was starting to bite. … the other thing I did, which I should not have done, and I regret it now, was to agree to a write-off for about 30,000 asylum seekers, which was essentially an amnesty. It did send out a [wrong] message.

Interview with author, 21 September 2010

As described in an earlier chapter, Straw's replacement by Blunkett after the 2001 election was Tony Blair's message that he was going to regain 'control' over the contentious issue of immigration which had become the most insistent source of media criticism of government. Blunkett himself was under severe pressure, as he acknowledged in an authored piece for the *Observer*, published only two days before 9/11:

> Some seem to think that because there is a flood of publicity, I should produce a rabbit out of the hat … We have reached a point in the media circus where a minister cannot pause for careful thought without being branded 'uncertain' or, in the words of one leader writer, 'bewildered'.

Observer, 9 September 2001

But, as with many ministerial assertions of independence, there is often a 'hidden hand'. In this case, the commentator, Peter Oborne, says it was the tabloids:

> The Downing Street grid [showed] a collaboration between Blunkett and the *Sun* when it was running a campaign to crack down on immigration. The grid says '*Sun* to launch anti-immigrant campaign' – and on the third/fourth days, Blunkett is wheeled out to say: '*Sun* readers are right about immigration'.
>
> Interview with author, 14 December 2010

This critical period of the summer of 2001 – critical, that is, for the future direction of a range of policies touching on crime, migration and terrorism – crystallizes the argument put forward by Baumgartner and Jones that 'media attention sometimes precedes and sometimes follows changes in attention by government agencies ... each can affect the other, reinforcing the pattern of positive feedback and punctuated equilibrium' (Baumgartner and Jones 1993: 125). This is the platform on which Jones and Wolfe (2010) have constructed their 'detection theory', described in Chapter 1, and which is a more plausible model for explaining the securitizing of policy actions on immigration and asylum in the post-9/11 period than the claim that politicians were deliberately exploiting fear for the purposes of expedience.[4]

Nevertheless, it is also the case that a government that had been in power for more than four years, and which had been developing a distinctive approach to crime and justice for a further four years before that, had its own repository of policy principles to draw on when faced with the crisis of 9/11 and was not merely tossed about like a cork on turbulent waters. The Crime and Disorder Act, with its empowerment of hearsay evidence and anonymous witnesses, provided a means of short-circuiting some of the lengthy and cumbersome criminal justice processes of which the tabloid media had complained since the early 1990s and was the first large brick prised loose from the edifice of due process built up over many lifetimes. The Regulation of Investigatory Powers Act, 2000 – on the face of it, an attempt to place a mish-mash of powers available to agencies such as MI5 on a statutory footing – proved eminently malleable in a host of unforeseen circumstances (e.g. local authorities spying on householders, surveillance of terrorist suspects). The Terrorism Act 2000, which gave the police strengthened powers to seek the forfeiture of assets of organized crime, became the basis on which Gordon Brown rushed through emergency orders against suspected terrorist funding within weeks of 9/11.[5] In short, 9/11 was by no means the beginning of the journey to summary justice, the surveillance society and the curtailment of *habeas corpus*, but merely a refuelling point.

If this hypothesis holds good, it suggests that studies such as that by Mythen and Walklate examining 'how the communication of the terrorist risk meshes into broader cultural formations of crime and (in)security' (Mythen and Walklate 2006: 123) are in danger of lifting the wrong end of the telescope to view the UK experience. Although they are correct in stating that the 'war against terrorism seems not to consist of a coherent and precise set of achievable objectives' (ibid.: 129), their assumption that the concept 'is not simply extending into national policies about immigration, detention, identity cards, policing and surveillance; it actually appears to be driving them' should be reversed. In fact, it is policies and ideas conceived to address issues of crime and justice which 'appear to be driving' policies on terrorism rather than vice versa. Indeed, it is often forgotten that ID cards were first proposed by Michael Howard in the context of a speech on crime ('punishment with a purpose' was his catchphrase that year) to the Conservative Party conference in 1994 and that it progressed as far as a Green Paper before falling by the wayside.

Coincidentally, or perhaps not, this was the period when the work of those responsible for counter-terrorism, especially the security service, MI5, and the Metropolitan Police anti-terrorist branch, began to receive greater media exposure as a result of decisions by government (especially in the case of MI5) to foster accountability through de-mystification. The naming of Stella Rimington as Director-General of MI5 in November 1991 – the first British intelligence head whose appointment was publicly announced – led to something of a media frenzy, and the pursuit of Rimington by photographers, in her own words, 'became ludicrous' (Andrew 2010: 775). Six months later, in April 1992, MI5 was given the lead role in combating PIRA. With the anti-terrorist branch, too, beginning to hold more regular off-the-record briefings for journalists, the amount of news and comment about terrorism in all forms of media expanded considerably. It may be speculative to suggest that such exposure heightened public anxiety but it probably did little to dampen it down, even if the 'political class' felt it served the purpose of greater transparency and thus accountability.

It is certainly the case that opening the Pandora's Box of comment led to suspicions of an ulterior motive every time a Director-General of MI5 voiced his or her opinion in a forum where they knew they were going to be quoted. Thus when Eliza Manningham-Buller gave an interview in 2006, she felt obliged to insert a disclaimer:

> My officers and the police are working to contend with some 200 groupings or networks, totalling over 1600 identified individuals (and there will be many we don't know) who are actively engaged in plotting, or facilitating, terrorist acts here and overseas ... I do not speak in this way to alarm (nor as the cynics might claim to enhance the reputation of my organisation) but to give the most frank account I can of the Al-Qaida threat to the UK.
>
> *The Times*, 10 November 2006

Terrorism and 'community cohesion'

In her study of media representations of British Muslims, Elizabeth Poole writes that: 'Islam is deemed an alien culture, with the allegiances of its people held elsewhere' (Poole 2009: 250). A comparison of policy responses to the PIRA mainland campaign of terrorism with the violence associated with Islamist extremism can be attempted on a number of levels: addressing objectives, tactics, cultural assumptions about the allegiances of 'host' communities, the place of those communities within the wider polity of the UK, and so on. But a book tracing the lineaments of media influence need not apologize for taking discourse as its starting point. In their comparative study on the construction of 'suspect' communities, Nickels *et al.* found:

> religious difference is a key element of the contrast between the representations of the Irish and Muslim experiences, with Catholicism/Protestantism being made invisible or assimilated in news discourse, and Islam/Muslims being made highly visible and constructed as outside British culture.
>
> Nickels *et al.* 2010: 17

It is useful to break down this analysis into its two constituent parts. First, the issue of religion. As Poole points out, citing Jacobson (1997) and Modood *et al.* (1997): 'Increasingly, researchers are finding that religion is a more significant source of identity than ethnicity for young Muslims' (Poole 2009: 224).

Whether this self-referential marker explains the nature of much of the policy discourse post-9/11 is not entirely clear but some argue that over-focusing on religion, at the expense of security – in contrast to the response to the PIRA threat – took the Preventing Violent Extremism (PVE) strategy down some curious byways. One of those who take this view is Douglas Murray, director of the conservative-leaning Centre for Social Cohesion:

> I think the [New Labour] government made errors from the very beginning in deciding that it should 'do' theology. I am sceptical of government being competent at very much and of all the things it *can* do, one of them is not theology, and certainly not a theology which it understood nothing about … Why would it be the job of a Prime Minister or US President to talk about what a religion is or is not? … And once the political class has … decided on the register in which the discussion should be had, it is beyond most mainstream politicians to get off that register.
>
> Interview with author, 27 April 2010

That may be an over-simplification although it is the case that, while neither media nor government routinely referred to 'Catholic' PIRA terrorists, jihadist violence, whether labelled 'Islamic' or 'Islamist', is seen as the expression of a religious fundamentalism.

The journalist, Martin Bright, argued that it had led the government into a trap: 'Instead of tackling the ideology that helps to breed terrorism, Whitehall has embraced a narrow, austere version of the religion … it is pursuing a policy of appeasement towards radical Islam that could have grave consequences' (Bright 2006: 12).

Following the Rushdie affair, successive governments, both Conservative and New Labour, encouraged the creation of the Muslim Council of Britain (MCB) as the 'official' voice of Muslim opinion and Bright argues that was a mistake because the MCB was too closely aligned to a Jamaat-e-Islami view of Islam.[6] In the preface to the Policy Exchange pamphlet, the journalist Jason Burke spreads the blame to the media:

the Western media often privileges those who shout loudest, have the most guns, hold the most animated demonstrations or are responsible for the most violence, at the expense of the vast silent majority who merely want a quiet life that assures them a modest degree of prosperity, security and dignity.

ibid.: 8

But, in giving the MCB so much print space and airtime, the media, in effect, provided more than enough rope to hang it, according to Mahan Abedin, former director of research at the Centre for the Study of Terrorism:

A good example of this was the MCB's continued opposition to Holocaust Memorial Day. It gave the media a chance to attack it and it was a stupid tactic because any organization seeking representation has to buy into the discourse of the state. Any state has a certain minimum acceptable level of values which you have to buy into – otherwise why would the state accommodate you? By criticizing the MCB over Holocaust Memorial Day, the media was able to portray Muslims as the 'other' and almost as treasonable.

Interview with author, 19 March 2010

There are plenty of examples of the media searching out individuals to represent as the 'other'; these range from obsessive coverage of the hook-handed cleric, Abu Hamza – a ready-made cartoon 'baddie' – every time he took Friday prayers outside Finsbury Park mosque in North London, to demonization of the so-called 'Tottenham Ayatollah', Omar Bakri Mohammed, who Abedin insists is:

a real pussycat and has the heart of a mouse. The idea that he was in any way serious about terrorism or confronting the state is a total joke. He is a fraud and a buffoon but the media built him up into this mad mullah character, bent on terrorism and at the epicentre of everything which was evil about the Muslim community. It was a total fabrication.

ibid.

Loyalty tests

The media's infatuation with Jungian archetypes (good and evil, etc.), as we have seen in relation to crime reporting, is a constant factor in British discourse and, by constricting the space for debate and decision, is one of the influences on policymakers. It can be likened to a form of unspoken loyalty test imposed on both audiences and protagonists. It says to them: if you adopt a contrary view to this 'characterization', then take a long hard look at yourself because you are dangerously out of kilter with received and responsible opinion, and that carries consequences. Unlike, say, the McCarthyite era in the United States in the 1950s, which spawned the House Committee on Un-American Activities, it does not have an overt, concrete manifestation, and that makes it hard to skewer and dissect. Nevertheless, it is there as a presence.

As suggested above, what gave the post-9/11 debate its unique flavour is that it was about 'values' and not purely terrorist violence. The role of the MCB in public discourse crystallizes this well. Dr Daud Abdullah is director of the Middle East Monitor and former deputy director-general of the MCB:

> Muslims have always been called upon to explain whether they are British first and Muslim second. We do not ask Catholics to do it. We do not ask Jews to do it. They go to Palestine and fight in the Israeli army and some of them have committed war crimes, in Gaza. But when it comes to Muslims, they have to demonstrate their loyalty. This is the problem. There is an unwillingness to accept Muslims as equal citizens, with equal rights and responsibilities.
>
> Interview with author, 26 April 2010

Abdullah knows the personal cost of the 'loyalty test'. In March 2009, the *Observer* broke a story that, while attending a conference on Gaza, held in Turkey, he signed a declaration which could have been interpreted as a call to Muslims to attack the Royal Navy. The story, headlined 'British Muslim leader urged to quit over Gaza', referred to the MCB's boycott of Holocaust Memorial Day – an implicit test of subscription to British 'values' – in the third paragraph, even though it had nothing to do with the subject matter, and continued:

> Abdullah ... was a member of the Mosques and Imams National Advisory Board, the body endorsed by the government that trains imams and was set up to curtail the activities of extremist clerics. In January, he briefed the home secretary, Jacqui Smith, and communities secretary, Hazel Blears, on the situation in Gaza and its likely impact on social cohesion in the UK ... A spokeswoman for the Department of Communities and Local Government [Hazel Blears's ministry] said: 'If it is proven that the individual concerned had been a signatory, we would expect [the MCB] to ask him to resign and to confirm its opposition to acts of violent extremism.
>
> *Observer*, 8 March 2009

Abdullah denies having endorsed calls for Muslims to attack the Royal Navy and was astounded when the published story was read over to him (he was in Gaza when it was published):

> It concluded with a call from the secretary of state that I should be dismissed. This was unprecedented. No formal investigation had taken place but she had already delivered that verdict. As the controversy unfolded, we asked 'Did you ever treat another organization, such as the British Board of Deputies, in a similar manner? Have you ever intervened in the affairs of the Board and said to them that you must dismiss an elected official?' It really depicts the type of attitude and approach to Muslims and their organizations, that they are not seen as independent. And, by the way, the MCB has never been in receipt of government funds for its 'co-operation', only for special projects.
>
> ibid.

One of the many, and obvious, differences between the Board of Deputies and the MCB is the former's attunement, born of many more years' experience, to signals from national government, whether sent directly, or via the media. In this instance, less than a fortnight before the disputed declaration in Turkey, Hazel Blears had semaphored a change of strategy towards 'extremist' groups. In a speech at the London School of Economics, widely trailed by the media, she promised a more robust response to non-violent groups which opposed homosexuality, rejected democracy and sought to infringe women's rights: 'There is a need for moral clarity, a dividing line rooted in our overriding sense of what is right and wrong. Engagement is not the same as endorsement' (*Guardian*, 25 February 2009).

It was felt necessary to 'put on notice' groups who might fail the 'loyalty test' because so many more bodies had been brought within the embrace of the PVE agenda. Having 'promoted' the MCB as the representative voice of British Muslims up to 2004/5, the government was happy to see the creation of other organizations, such as the Sufi Muslim Council and the British Muslim Forum, and more overtly, the Quilliam Foundation, to reach a wider section of opinion. In retrospect, it was a case of ministers and advisers floundering as they sought the best direction to take, according to Robin Richardson, who helped author the landmark Runnymede Trust report on Islamophobia in 1997:[7]

> As I understand it, in 2003, when it was preparing to invade Iraq, the government tried to influence organizations like the MCB to 'deliver the Muslim vote'. But it was a non-starter, it could not be done. We then saw an enormous attack on the MCB in an attempt to de-legitimise it. We saw an alliance between the government and journalists like Martin Bright and John Ware, who did a *Panorama* on the MCB ... If there are radicalized, alienated young people, you talk to people who know them and are close to them – not people who say they represent Islam but who may be from a different generation. The government ended up listening to the wrong people.
>
> Interview with author, 15 April 2010[8]

The Policy Exchange pamphlet written by Martin Bright was the product of a set of documents leaked to him when he was a correspondent at the *Observer* by officials within the Foreign Office. They were unhappy that engagement with groups, such as the Muslim Brotherhood, abroad was infecting strategy at home. At around the same time, in 2006, the *Guardian* reporter, Vikram Dodd, was also the beneficiary of a leak – the first draft of the PVE strategy which, *inter alia*, suggested that the government wanted university staff to inform on suspect students. The ensuing controversy led to the draft being changed. Dodd also distilled his findings and misgivings about government policy into a Policy Exchange publication.

Thus, the media and a plethora of think tanks – Policy Exchange, the Quilliam Foundation, the Centre for Social Cohesion, Demos and others – were all contesting the 'public sphere', with the aim of influencing policy, illustrating Jones and Wolfe's information-processing model that: 'Attention is a scarce good, can be allocated only in pieces rather than continuously, and is a necessary condition for policy change. As a scarce resource, actors in politics struggle to process, understand and manage it' (Jones and Wolfe 2010: 29–30).

Rarely, if ever, can such a cacophony of fractious voices have been heard on an issue of public policy as in the debate over preventing violent extremism and there were consequences. Shortly before she made the well-trodden journey from newspaper journalist to director of a think tank (Demos), Madeleine Bunting wrote: 'The danger is that as the government's "community cohesion" policy flounders, there is no shortage of media commentators pouring out a flood of venomous advice on exactly why no Muslim is worth talking to anyway' (*Guardian*, 16 August 2006). This not only created confusion and division among policymakers – witness the conflict in government over whether the radical group, Hizb-ut-Tahrir, should be proscribed – but uncertainty within the security agencies. Dr Robert Lambert, formerly of the Metropolitan Police, set up the Muslim Contact Unit at Scotland Yard in 2002 and attests to the impact of media representation:

> The unit helped install a new trustee body at the Finsbury Park mosque after the removal of Abu Hamza's supporters in 2005. But immediately, a reporter from *The Times* door-stepped one of the new trustees at his home and 'established' that he had a background linked to Hamas. The headline in *The Times* was, 'one group of extremists replaced by another'. The response of the borough commander, Barry Norman, was 'if we worried about everybody's views in the area, I'd never leave the office' ... But the reporting of what we thought was a 'good news' story was disappointing.
>
> Interview with author, 14 June 2010

The broad-brush approach of much of the media to such sensitive issues has been a perennial concern to the think tanks, whose object is to influence policy. The Quilliam Foundation was set up with government funds so, at times, acted almost like an intravenous drip feeding ideas into New Labour. But the media's influence can never be discounted, says its deputy director of research and communications, James Brandon – another former journalist:

> If we do a report saying 'this is the problem and it needs to be dealt with by government or civil society intervention', we publicise it through the media. This is how you get clout, impact. But if you send out a press release saying 'Hizb-ut-Tahrir is running some schools' or whatever, you never quite know how it is going to be treated in the *Mail*, *Express* or *Telegraph*. You might get some hugely inflammatory coverage which, OK, makes your point and gets you publicity, but might actually undermine a lot of the good work you are trying to do ... And, at times, those papers are printing stuff which is generically anti-Muslim. They are saying 'it is Muslims and their religion which is the problem'. It is the same as Islamists arguing that 'Western society is the problem, Western governments are out to get us'. It is a kind of mirror image.
>
> Interview with author, 29 April 2010

Having dealt with religion *per se*, it is worth interrogating the second part of the analysis by Nickels *et al.*, that Muslims have been 'constructed as outside British culture' (2010: 17). That points up a distinctive difference from the response to the PIRA campaign, which, conspicuously, did not lead to any state-sanctioned introspection about British identity. By contrast, the mediatized debate around Islamist radicalism, from its earliest manifestation during the controversy over the publication of Salman Rushdie's *The Satanic Verses*, assuredly has:

> The regular appearance in the headlines of the words, 'Rushdie', 'Veil', 'Race' and 'Riot(s)' suggests that Muslim communities are portrayed as a symbolic threat to British values in the news. Indeed, the issues raised by the fatwa on Salman Rushdie, the 2001 riots [in Oldham, Burnley and Bradford] and Jack Straw's comments on the acceptability of the full-face veil strongly relate to the suitability of multiculturalism as a viable policy for the British state.
>
> ibid.[9]

Contrast that with the response to the bombing of the Royal Marine barracks at Deal in 1989. Even though in numbers killed it was the most devastating attack of PIRA's mainland campaign, it was presented and dealt with as an existential security threat to the British state. And while the campaign of violence warped policymaking to the extent that the Thatcher government unwisely implemented a broadcast ban on representatives of Sinn Fein (1988–94), it had no other legislative consequences. The fatwa issued by Ayatollah Khomeini against the author of *The Satanic Verses* in the same year heralded something more profoundly troubling for Britain's relationship with itself. The media coverage: 'suggested that Muslims outside Britain were dictating the agenda for Muslims in Britain, that Muslim (foreign) values were impinging on British society and were a constant reminder of the global menace' (Poole 2009: 79).

Thus, the first link in the chain leading to a 'community cohesion strategy,' the PVE agenda and the Terrorism Act 2006, which took the law into uncharted territory by outlawing 'glorification', was the fatwa against Rushdie. Iranian-born Mahan Abedin, of the Centre for the Study of Terrorism, dates the political 'mobilization' of British Muslims from this point:

> It was a huge consciousness-raising moment for British Muslims. The groups at the forefront of that mobilization were the Sufis, especially in Birmingham. For the media, these were the 'bad' guys. And the tabloids reacted very strongly to the fact that a foreign head of state, like Khomeini, could have such an impact in this country. This was a new development. Then, in the 90s, the issue of Palestine began to radicalize UK Muslims.
>
> Interview with author, 19 March 2010

The travails of Bosnia, fighting to preserve an independent identity amid the violent break-up of Yugoslavia, was also a recruiting catalyst for young British Muslims, especially those attracted to the radical creed espoused by Hizb-ut-Tahrir.

One such, Ed Husain, who later founded the Quilliam Foundation, says the media played an important role:

> Nothing gave us greater motivation than to hear our ideas being amplified in the national media, reaching new audiences of millions ... We were resigned to biased reporting but we knew that there was a crucial constituency of Muslims who would look upon us as their leaders, their spokesmen against the attacks of the infidels.
>
> Husain 2007: 103

But the media amplification of ideas did not lead to a more informed understanding of the subversive effects of such thinking on British Muslim minds set on making a point on their own soil. Even in 2001, the assumption in policy circles was that a terrorist attack would come from outside. An examination of the parliamentary debates on the Anti-Terrorism, Crime and Security Bill, in the immediate aftermath of the shock of 9/11, shows this to be the dominant mood. As Huysmans and Buonfino have found:

> the policy that is being justified and mostly taken for granted, is one of externalizing terrorist dangers. The threat, whether existential or not, comes from outside the UK, both in terms of its geographical origins and in terms of the nationality of the 'dangerous' individuals.
>
> Huysmans and Buonfino 2008: 773

Hence, the most controversial section of the bill, Part 4, which provided for the indefinite detention of foreign-born terror suspects and required the UK to derogate from the European Convention on Human Rights. This takes us on to the fiercely contested politics of the legislative response to 9/11 and its home-grown equivalent, 7/7.

Pick a number – 28, 42 or 90?

A key thesis, set out in Chapter 1 of this book, is that under the influence of Tony Blair, New Labour re-defined the notion of civil rights from the mid-1990s. Despite attacks on discrete elements of its crime and justice programme, from the Crime and Disorder Act onwards, it took the crisis of 9/11 and the response to 'new terrorism' for the critique to cohere. The defining moment was the co-ordinated bombings in London on 7 July 2005 by four British suicide terrorists. That was the point at which the government dramatically raised the stakes by proposing that the maximum time limit for holding a suspect before charge should be raised from 14 to 90 days. Blair's declaration that 'the rules of the game are changing' (5 August 2005) ensured that the discursive contestation of this issue would go to the heart of the argument about civil liberties and security.

Writing after the 90-day proposal had been thrown out by the Lords (Blair's only parliamentary defeat), the Home Secretary, Charles Clarke, rounded on media critics of the government's authoritarian counter-terrorism agenda and, significantly, framed his argument in more or less exactly the same terms as Blair had outlined his version of the communitarian programme in the 1990s: 'my appeal is to urge our media to come to terms with a modern concept of rights and responsibilities ... to accept the modern reality that human rights are wider than those that the individual possesses in relation to the state' (*Guardian*, 25 April 2006).

Having stated (or, more accurately, re-stated) the government's interpretation of human rights – and explicitly contrasted it with the European Convention's code – Clarke elaborated on those 'rights' that New Labour had determined were crucial to the contract between citizen and state:

> The right to go to work safely on the tube. The right not to be killed by someone who has served his sentence for violent crime but remains danger-ous. The right to live at home without being disturbed by antisocial behaviour outside the front door ... None of them removes the obligation on the state to operate in accordance with its national and international obligations under law. But when we respond, for example, with counter-terror legislation or proposals to control those criminals who are dangerous to society, many in the media retort that we are destroying democracy and constructing tyranny.
>
> ibid.

By bracketing together anti-social behaviour and terrorism, Clarke was rein-forcing the argument which underpins this book: that 'the rules of the game' did not change with the events of 7/7 but when Tony Blair first glimpsed the possi-bility of power and decided that the best way to achieve it was through the prism of criminal justice:

> fighting crime was a personal cause, it completely fitted a new politics beyond old right and left, and since no Labour person had ever made anything of it ... the field was mine to play on ... It achieved enormous traction. It showed leadership. I took a traditional Labour position, modernized it, made it popular and upended the Tories with it.
>
> Blair 2010: 55

Part of the 'new politics' was an instrumental use of the media, achieved by employing an empathic style and discourse as 'a rhetorical device to reach out past the office [of the Prime Minister] in order to connect at an imagined "more human" level' (Gaffney 2001: 131). This congruence of form and content can be seen most famously in Blair's response to the death of Diana in 1997 ('the people's princess') but also in the picture, displayed in virtually every newspaper on the day after the 7/7 bombing, of the Prime Minister, head bowed but somehow resolute even in shock, at the Gleneagles G8 summit.

The media academic, John Tulloch, is in a unique position as both a victim of 7/7 – he was in the carriage of the tube train which was blown up at Edgware Road – and commentator on the response. He writes of the Gleneagles image: 'My immediate thought was that it was a performance, a photo opportunity to gain empathy by a politician ... who is deeply unpopular' (Tulloch 2006: 48–9). His reasons for deducing that are entirely circumstantial but he may be on firmer ground when commenting on the use of his own bloodied, bandaged image by the *Sun*, under the exhortatory headline: 'Terror Laws: Tell Tony he's right' (*Sun*, 8 November 2005), the day before the Commons voted on the 90-day detention proposal:

> The juxtaposition of my face with those words was obvious: this victim of 7/7 representing all victims, was begging the public to support Blair in the House of Commons vote on the anti-terror law the following day ... I believe ... this *Sun* incident is an example of media manipulation, demonstrating the close and causal links between the Murdoch empire and New Labour's leadership.
>
> ibid.

In the event, of course, even as powerful an alliance as Blair and Murdoch failed to carry the vote, partly, one suspects, because the government's case was seen as over-inflated. Charles Clarke wrote in a newspaper article, two days before the vote, that:

> the very strong police view is that the current 14-day period is no longer enough to allow proper investigations to be conducted and successful prosecutions to be mounted. Their considered professional opinion, formed with the prosecutors who are their colleagues and on the basis of their unique experience, is that a maximum of 90 days detention may be needed for a very small number of cases.
>
> *Evening Standard*, 7 November 2005

Although the impression may have been given at the time, and it suited the government to give it, that law enforcement was uniformly in favour of the 90-day proposal, that was not the case. It later became clear that, both on the police and prosecutorial side, there were doubters. When Gordon Brown revived attempts to extend the detention time limit (to 42 days) in 2008, the splits within ACPO, and between ACPO and government, became apparent. The deputy chief constable of Avon and Somerset, Rob Beckley, who had been ACPO lead on communities and counter-terrorism until 2007, told a conference of the Muslim Safety Forum:

> It would be wrong to think that there is a uniform professional view within the police service. I, and I know other chief officers, do not see the necessity of 42 days; we can see the desirability, but at this stage, I do not see the professional necessity. The issue now, unfortunately, has become very toxic and political, and we are moving away from a rational debate because of the politics that now envelop the subject, not least of all, the role and position of the government and prime minister and all the other dimensions we read about in the press.
>
> *Guardian*, 13 June 2008[10]

Three months later, Lord Goldsmith, who had been Attorney General until 2007, and thus responsible for the 'prosecutorial side' referenced by Clarke, wrote of the proposal for a 42-day detention limit before charge:

I regard it as not only unnecessary but also counter-productive; and we should fight to protect the liberties the terrorists would take from us, not destroy them ourselves ... During my time as Attorney General, I studied the issue of how long suspects can be held before being charged, and was closely involved (sic) with a number of the terrorist plots with which the bill is designed to deal. I had been a solitary voice in government questioning 90 days. I am confident that it is a wrong-headed and dangerous approach to extend still further the time for pre-trial detention.

Guardian, 13 October 2008

And early the previous year, the Director of Public Prosecutions, Sir Ken Macdonald, questioning the 'war on terror' rhetoric, told the Criminal Bar Association that he supported a 'culture of legislative restraint' (*Guardian*, 24 January 2007). None of those expressing scepticism about the need for a longer period of pre-trial detention singled out the media for pushing policy in that direction, though it may have been lurking in their minds. But the point was later made explicit by Sir David Omand, who, in 2002, became the first permanent secretary and security intelligence co-ordinator in the Cabinet Office: in other words, the principal architect of the post-9/11 strategy. Speaking on the Radio 4 *PM* programme in 2010, he said:

People have found it hard to accept the necessity for some of the measures ... the 90-day period of detention was not appropriate to the kind of threat we actually faced ... the influence of the media here is not always positive. Is there time for arguments to be put, debates to be had? [The media] presses early decisions on government when sometimes, it is wiser to take time to establish all the facts ... A secretary of state wakes up to discover on your programmes the trailing of some announcement of a change in policy before the system, the process, has caught up with it. This has led to a divorce between policymaking and the executive because those who have to implement the policies on the ground are not fully consulted, so not surprisingly, when the announcement is made, they are critical of it.

PM programme, 8 June 2010

His implication that secretaries of state wake up to surprise announcements on the radio rather than announcements heavily 'spun' in advance by their special advisers, will bring a wry smile to those who work in the media. But it is clear from what has been said by key policy actors since 7/7 that, far from there being a solid bloc of law enforcers behind an extension of the detention limit, there were deep misgivings. Indeed, it now appears that one of the few to 'keep the faith' throughout this period was the Metropolitan Police Commissioner, Sir Ian Blair. In November 2006, he gave a speech in Berlin – press released in its entirety by

Scotland Yard – in which he conducted a *tour d'horizon* of the security landscape, including discussion of 'Britishness', and explained why 'the rules of the game were changing':

> The UK spent over 30 years dealing with Irish terrorism and yet did not need an exceptionally different legal framework in this area. However, particularly at the end of their 30 year campaign, the IRA could be characterized in four ways: with the odd exception, they did not want to cause mass casualties, they gave warnings, they themselves did not want to die in attacks and they were heavily penetrated by British intelligence. This meant that the police in Britain could take a certain degree of risk with Irish active service units, letting them get very close to carrying out a bombing before they were arrested, so that evidence available against them was maximized. None of these four conditions exist at present in relation to the international terrorist threat … I believe that an extension to the 28 days time for detention will have to be examined again in the near future.
>
> Blair 2006

His distinction between the threat of Islamist extremism and that of PIRA was, of course, made repeatedly by government ministers, in parliament, in print and on the airwaves. But those who had 'seen it all before' remained unconvinced. Lord King of Bridgewater, who, as Tom King, had been both Northern Ireland secretary and defence secretary in the Thatcher and Major administrations, spoke in the Lords debate on the Prevention of Terrorism Bill in March 2005:

> From my time, in Northern Ireland … I know that it is often said that if the security services make proposals to you, then who are you to resist them? … But the reality is that, in facing up to terrorism, we have a responsibility to ensure that we approach it in the most constructive way … Proposals … were made to me by the police, by the RUC, by the army and by the security services … But it is the minister's job – it is what he is there for – to decide which ones are sensible and helpful. Anyone in Northern Ireland gets a fairly good training in recognizing a recruiting sergeant for terrorism when he sees it coming down the road. I share the fears expressed by others about the way in which some of the implications of this legislation may affect the attitude of the Muslim community, as the nationalist republican community was affected when internment without trial was introduced in Northern Ireland. Against that background, simply passing a law, sounding resolute and taking decisive action is not enough. It is the responsibility of us all … not simply to embark on it and hope that it comes out all right in the end.
>
> HL Deb 2005

The views of Sir Ian (now Lord) Blair and Lord King do not merely reflect the differing perspectives of a policeman and a politician but speak to the changed temper of their times. Blair represented the mediated politicization of policing and security which became such a feature of the New Labour era. King and Douglas Hurd were not merely faced with a different kind of terrorism but were under less pressure to respond amid the full glare of television cameras and the thunder of leader and comment columns. Asked, on the fifth anniversary of the 7/7 bombings, to reflect on whether New Labour had taken some legislative decisions out of a sense of obligation to act, the former Home Secretary, Alan Johnson, had this to say:

> Yes, I have said this when people have asked me to reflect honestly, perhaps there was a knee-jerk reaction … you have to remember what things were like on 9/11. It changed everything. We did not know where the next attack was coming from. We did not know what was going to happen. These were people, unprecedented, who would take as many lives, kill and maim as many people as they could and kill themselves at the same time … did we have to do 42 days, did we have to try and go to 90 days? Probably not. Did we have to declare the whole of London under Section 44 [of the Terrorism Act 2000], an area where you could stop and search? Probably not, in rational judgment and the benefit of hindsight.
>
> Interview with author, 7 July 2010

Conclusion

Hindsight also suggests that it would have been far more productive if issues such as detention time limits, control orders and the use of telephone intercepts as evidence in trials had been debated as matters of technical procedure rather than partisan politics, with all the emotion that entails. That would have made it less likely (though not impossible) that the *Sun*, reporting Tony Blair's 'rules are changing' declaration, would have run the headline 'Victory for *Sun* over new terror laws' (*Sun*, 6 August 2005). Robert Lambert, founder of the Muslim Contact Unit at Scotland Yard, and now an academic, believes that what has been lacking from the debate is a source of truly independent and disinterested advice to government:

> Home Secretaries have security advisers, those advisers have academic associates and they believe they are getting the best possible advice. But there is not a great deal of independent, academic expertise on terrorism to draw on. There are also so-called 'experts' on terrorism who pop up on the media who have never done a day's counter-terrorism work in their lives. It is an issue worthy of some study itself – that cosy relationship between politicians, the security world and hand-picked academics. If the issue was a medical one, the government would feel the need to consult the British Medical Association, in other words, a powerful, independent voice that it has, at least, to think about and negotiate with. Whereas, with terrorism, the government does not have to worry about a powerful, independent academic voice that might challenge it. It does not have to overcome that hurdle.
>
> Interview with author, 14 June 2010

The lesson from this troubled period is that, invariably, it is painstaking, and narrowly focused, counter-terrorist policing, which frustrates terrorist plots and not grand-standing or poorly conceived strategies to inculcate 'British' values and isolate extremists. Andy Hayman, former Assistant Commissioner, Terrorism, has little time for the Preventing Violent Extremism agenda:

> You show me any substantial outcomes from all the time and investment put into the programme in five years since 7/7. Is life any different now to five years ago? No, it is not. We are not getting any community intelligence in. None of the successful interdictions have come from that. They are all from other sources. And that is a terrible indictment. Apart from tackling radicalization, nothing else is paying dividends.
>
> Interview with author, 20 April 2010

12 Conclusion

The *Daily Telegraph* journalist, Philip Johnston, has calculated that 'between 1851 and 1996, there were 122 pieces of criminal justice legislation, 39 of them primary measures or Acts of Parliament; between 1997 and 2009, there were 212 pieces of legislation, 26 of them primary'(Johnston 2010: 89).[1] In a breezy joust against the culture of political correctness and over-zealous officialdom, Johnston concludes that 'Our commonsense has been stolen. We want it back' (ibid.: 309).

As an experienced home affairs editor and commentator, Johnston knew better than to flout the old Fleet Street convention that 'dog does not eat dog', and his book does not explore what role the media may play in persuading policymakers that it is better to legislate even when it is against their better judgment and that of their officials. Of course, had he done so, it would have been a very different kind of book, probably with a thesis not dissimilar to that of Walgrave and Lefevere:

> that the media's impact on the public policy simply is too broad a question to be answered. It can only be dealt with when split up into small and theoretically and empirically manageable sub-questions: which media, which politics and what impact?
>
> Walgrave and Lefevere 2010: 44

Steered by this cautionary advice, the present study has not sought to replicate the efforts of other researchers in communications and political science who have struggled to find direct causal connections between media and policy. Instead, it has chosen themes spanning a 21-year period, in which the media undoubtedly underwent qualitative and quantitative change, to draw inferences, using as a guide Jones and Wolfe's detection theory, which posits: 'a complex systems framework focusing on information flows, which implies non-linear, interactive relationships' (Jones and Wolfe 2010: 17).

The added ingredient, here, is interviews with key participants. Of course, the reflections of politicians and their advisers tend to be self-serving. Reputations matter more than they should, even years after the event. But what is sometimes missing from studies of criminal justice policymaking is the feel for politics in the raw and how options are viewed at the time decisions are taken, before they are weighed and found wanting in the cold light of scholarly hindsight.

It is also the case that what the former Prime Minister, Harold Macmillan, is supposed to have described as the greatest challenge to a statesman, 'events, my dear boy, events' have an impact on ministerial time and attention which, in retrospect, can seem distorting and disproportionate.[2] One such event was undoubtedly 9/11, as David Blunkett's special adviser, Huw Evans, concedes:

> I think criminal justice was the big loser of David's time as Home Secretary, in terms of his 'head space' and attention span and his ability to deliver a multi-faceted approach ... Before 9/11, responsibility for counter-terrorism occupied probably about 10 per cent of the Home Secretary's time and about 1 per cent of his brain power ... Within a few months of his taking office, that side of the job was taking up at least a quarter of his time and a significant amount of his personal effort and energy ... His ambitions for a modernized reform of the criminal justice system ... never came to fruition and I think that is the big tragedy in terms of his public perception. I know for a fact, and remember from the conversations I had with him back in those first few weeks in office, that he was absolutely passionate about it and wanted it to be part of his legacy as Home Secretary. The 9/11 disaster, and everything that followed, completely scuppered his ability to spend the time and energy on it that he wanted to.
>
> Interview with author, 10 February 2010

Many of the Home Secretaries of the past two decades were strong personalities (although some were conspicuously not) who brought to the post more than a few traces of their own lived experience. For example, Jack Straw, who, with Blair, set the course of New Labour policy on crime and disorder, was heavily influenced in his thinking about anti-social behaviour by his own upbringing on an Essex council estate:

> There were some neighbours who were really difficult to all those around, including my mother, who was on her own and bringing up five kids. And the police would not do anything. They would not intervene. In the end, my mother took this woman to court. Moving on to the 1990s, we had an awful, very disruptive family in Blackburn and looked at every measure that could be taken ... And I developed the idea of anti-social behaviour orders in the then chief superintendent's office with him. We called them community safety orders originally.
>
> Interview with author, 21 September 2010

This is personal reminiscence, yes, but deserves to be considered alongside the somewhat reductive hypothesis that 'faced with a declining crime rate, the Labour government discovered, so to speak, a new territory of concern, and a beguiled public found a new crime wave replacing the old' (Mooney and Young 2006: 399). Indeed, the experience of Alun Michael, another key, if unsung, architect of New Labour's youth justice strategy, as a youth and community worker and magistrate in Cardiff, was arguably as influential as the Audit Commission's 1996 report, 'Misspent Youth', which became a blueprint for the incoming government (Audit Commission 1996).

David Blunkett's performance as Home Secretary, even if it fell below his own expectations, was undoubtedly shaped by his background in the municipal politics of Sheffield and the highly competitive instinct of a blind man making his way in a sighted world:

> What's the point of being here as Home Secretary if we are not going to change the world? I could have done what [previous Labour Home Secretary] Roy Jenkins did and achieved things by encouraging private members bills dealing with the major social/liberal measures and giving them a fair wind with government support. That is one way of doing things. But we chose not to. We chose to get our arms up to the elbow in the mire, saying you cannot just ignore what people out there are seeing and what they are reading, because they are our taskmasters. I overdid it, no question, and I would not do it in the same way again – but it was for a very good reason.
>
> Interview with author, 8 October 2008

The fact that it is hard, if not impossible, to measure the role that the media plays in the policy process should be a spur rather than a discouragement. It seems evident, from what Blunkett and others have said, that what counts in this 'information processing' environment, and thus what is worth investigating, is the signal being transmitted and received on an issue, and the ability of the media to 're-weight' it: 'The stronger the signal, the clearer and more urgent the message, the more likely government will respond, and the larger the response' (Jones and Wolfe 2010: 38).

Thus, in crime and justice, that signal was perceived to be at its strongest in the early 1990s, culminating in the murder of James Bulger and post-2001 in relation to public protection. In the field of security, the 'tipping point' was 9/11. At the very least, that was how the policymakers saw it.

But there are many aspects of modern mediated governance which defy simple linear analysis. One is the 'damned if I do, damned if I don't' aspect of politics. For example, if a minister, or indeed a party leader in opposition (*pace* Ed Miliband) is seen to have too low a public profile, he or she is often perceived as being at the mercy of media agenda-setting (as well as attacked for being ineffective). If they are too conspicuous, it is because they are manipulating media attention for their own ends. Huw Evans says it is a misreading of the political realities:

> A lot of the times that David [Blunkett] ended up commenting on things were when he was already doing an interview about an announcement we were making and something else had happened and he was asked about it. Either he could not resist answering or felt that it would be too politically damaging to side-step and that he was better off saying something than nothing. I do not think that was always appreciated sufficiently.
>
> Interview with author, 10 February 2010

But this is where political actors, and their representatives, tend to downplay their own responsibilities. Perhaps it is not realistic to expect politicians to do what Simon Jenkins urges and 'take the media as it is and bend it to their will' (Interview with author, 21 June 2010) but Home Secretaries who pull a criminal justice lever because it is within reach and will win them some short-term 'credit' when they know it is, at best, tangential to the solution of a social or cultural problem and, at worst, a pandering to shallow populism, are doing a calculated disservice to good governance.

And what about the civil servants who keep the motor of government running? Phil Wheatley's time in the prison service and offender management spans the entirety of the period under consideration and he argues that modern mediated governance has had the effect of infantilizing society:

> You could criticize quite a lot of what is done in government around media handling as being reactive rather than proactive. [It reflects] the nervousness about the media. The view 'we will not do that because they will definitely throw something at us if we do that' is probably damaging good governance. Actually we need a much more active 'this makes sense and this is how we are going to explain it' approach. That would involve treating us more like grown-ups. But that would probably involve the media behaving as if we were grown-ups. I do worry about the media in this present, very competitive age.
>
> Interview with author, 18 June 2010

In examining late modern policymaking in crime and justice, this book has attempted to unpick a complex mélange of influences: a self-confident tabloidized media, expert in binary simplification; politicians whose self-validation, in a 'citizen' democracy, derives from being seen to respond by 'feeling the pain'; the insecurity of globalization. It is the very interconnectedness which defies structural modelling and analysis, and which, one hopes, has made the quest for answers so worthwhile.

Appendix: List of interviewees

Dr Daud Abdullah, director of the Middle East Monitor, former deputy secretary general of the Muslim Council of Britain, 26 April 2010.

Mahan Abedin, former director of research at the Centre for the Study of Terrorism, 19 March 2010.

Vera Baird QC, former Labour MP for Redcar (2001–10), former Solicitor General (2007–10), 5 July 2010.

Rt Hon. David Blunkett, Labour MP for Sheffield Brightside and Hillsborough, former Home Secretary (2001–4), 8 October 2008.

James Brandon, director of research and communications at Quilliam Foundation, 29 April 2010.

Eric Carlin, former member of the Advisory Council on the Misuse of Drugs (ACMD), 13 May 2010.

Rt Hon. Charles Clarke, former Labour MP for Norwich South (1997–2010), former Home Secretary (2004–6), 8 July 2008 and 16 September 2010.

Julian Corner, former head of crime strategy at the Home Office, 6 August 2008.

Philippa Drew, former senior civil servant at the Home Office, 23 December 2008.

Huw Evans, former special adviser to the Prime Minister Tony Blair (2005–6), former special adviser to the Home Secretary David Blunkett (2001–4), 10 February 2010.

Matt Foot, criminal defence solicitor and the coordinator of Asbo Concern, 10 September 2010.

Fiona Fox, director of the Science Media Centre, 11 June 2010.

Rt Hon. Lord Goldsmith QC, former UK Attorney General (2001–7), 14 November 2008.

Mike Granatt, former director-general of the Government Information and Communication Service at the Cabinet Office (1998–2003), 12 October 2010.

Sheila Gunn, former press advisor to Prime Minister John Major, former political correspondent for *The Times*, 29 September 2008.

Andy Hayman, former assistant commissioner and head of counter-terrorism in the London Metropolitan Police, 20 April 2010.

Rt Hon. Lord Howard of Lympne QC, former Conservative MP for Folkestone and Hythe (1983–2010), former Home Secretary (1993–7), 9 July 2008.

Rt Hon. Lord Hurd of Westwell, former Conservative MP for Mid Oxon (1974–1983) and for Witney (1983–1997), former Secretary of State for Northern Ireland (1984–5), former Home Secretary (1985–9), 21 July 2008.

Sue Jago, former head of the Home Office Prostitution Review Team, 7 July 2008.

Sir Simon Jenkins, journalist and columnist at the *Guardian* and the *Sunday Times*, 21 June 2010.

Rt Hon. Alan Johnson, Labour MP for Kingston upon Hull West and Hessle, former Home Secretary (2009–10), 7 July 2010.

Dr Les King, former head of the Drugs Intelligence Unit in the Forensic Science Service, former member of the Advisory Council on the Misuse of Drugs (ACMD), 22 June 2010.

Danny Kushlick, director of Transform Drug Policy Foundation, 25 May 2010.

Dr Robert Lambert, former head of the Muslim Contact Unit (MCU) in the London Metropolitan Police, 14 June 2010.

Sir David Latham, chairman of the Parole Board for England and Wales, Vice-President, Court of Appeal (Criminal Division) (2006–9), 17 November 2010.

Tom Lloyd, former chief constable of Cambridgeshire police, 2 June 2010.

Douglas Murray, director of the Centre for Social Cohesion, 27 April 2010.

Martin Narey, former chief executive of the National Offender Management Service (NOMS), 10 September 2008.

Andrew Neilson, head of public affairs and policy at the Howard League for Penal Reform, 21 July 2008.

Prof. David Nutt, former chairman of the Advisory Council on the Misuse of Drugs (ACMD), 13 May 2010.

Peter Oborne, journalist and columnist at the *Daily Telegraph*, 14 December 2010.

Richard Offer, former head of media at the Independent Police Complaints Commission (IPCC), 19 February 2010.

Prof. Pat O'Hare, honorary president of International Harm Reduction Association (IHRA), former director of the Mersey Drug Training and Information Centre in Liverpool, 4 June 2010.

Sir Hugh Orde, president of the Association of Chief Police Officers (ACPO), 4 August 2010.

Ed Owen, former adviser to Home Secretary Jack Straw (1997–2001), 1 October 2008.

Brian Paddick, former deputy assistant commissioner in the London Metropolitan Police, 23 September 2010.

Robin Richardson, former director of the Runnymede Trust, 15 April 2010.

Jeremy Sare, former secretary to the Advisory Council on the Misuse of Drugs (ACMD), former head of drug legislation at the Home Office, 15 June 2010.

David Scott, former head of the London Probation Service, 26 October 2010.

Harry Shapiro, director of communications and information at DrugScope, 22 June 2010.

Rt Hon. Jack Straw, Labour MP for Blackburn, former Home Secretary (1997–2001), 21 September 2010.

Julian Walker, former assistant private secretary to Home Secretary Kenneth Clarke (1992–3), former speech writer to Home Secretary Michael Howard (1995–6), 12 September 2008.

Phil Wheatley, former director general of HM Prison Service, former director-general of the National Offender Management Service (NOMS), 18 June 2010.

Rt Hon. Lord Woolf of Barnes, former Lord Chief Justice of England and Wales (2000–5), 11 May 2009.

Notes

Chapter 1

1 The phrase was coined by the Canadian press magnate, Roy Thomson, when he was awarded the franchise to run Scottish Television in 1957.
2 For confirmation of Tony Blair's attachment to home affairs, see his memoir entitled: *A Journey* (2010: 54).
3 The phrase was uttered during the coverage of the MacTaggart Lecture at the Edinburgh TV Festival, August 2007.
4 Tony Blair used the phrase in a speech to a Labour Party audience in Wellingborough on 19 February 1993.
5 In a 30-year career at the Home Office, Faulkner held various posts and was until 1990, Deputy Secretary in charge of the influential Criminal Research and Statistics Department.
6 This is a reference to Michael Howard's speech to the annual Conservative Party conference, 6 October 1993.
7 As distinct from concerns such as repeat victimization, which criminologists, such as Ken Pease, were studying much earlier in the decade.
8 The funding for extra officer numbers, announced in September 1999 was 'ring-fenced' under the Crime Fighting Fund.
9 The encounter with Gillian Duffy on 28 April 2010 was caught on a Sky News microphone and is thought have been a defining point in the election campaign.
10 The suggestion that 11 September 2001, was 'a good day to bury bad news' was made by Jo Moore, special adviser to the Transport Secretary, Stephen Byers.
11 A copy of this letter was provided to the author in confidence.

Chapter 2

1 This phrase was uttered during Kenneth Clarke's statement to parliament on the government's plans for dealing with juvenile crime: HC Deb (1993) 2 March 1993 vol. 220 cc 139–50.
2 *Doli incapax* is the presumption that a child between the age of ten and fourteen was incapable of knowing the difference between right and wrong, and was abolished in the Crime and Disorder Act, 1998.
3 The attack on Hampstead liberals came in a speech to the Institute of Public Policy Research on 13 January 2000 and was a response to legal opposition to the Criminal Justice (Mode of Trial) Bill.
4 One version of the full quotation, 'Success has a thousand fathers; failure is an orphan' comes from President Kennedy's response to the Bay of Pigs disaster in April 1961.
5 Given the American influence, it is appropriate that the phrase, which Blair generously attributes to Gordon Brown, was dreamed up when the two men were having

a brainstorming session about crime policy in a New York hotel in 1992 (Blair 2010: 56).
6 R v Secretary of State for the Home Department, *ex parte* Cheblak (1991) 1 WLR 890, 894.
7 From the US Declaration of Independence, 4 July 1776.

Chapter 3

1 Sir Brian Leveson appeared on the Victoria Derbyshire programme on Radio 5 Live on 8 March 2011.
2 On 10 July 2006, the Attorney-General decided that the sentence was not 'unduly lenient' and he would not refer it to the Appeal Court.
3 John Reid applied that description to the Immigration and Nationality Directorate when he appeared before the Commons Home Affairs Committee on 23 May 2006.
4 This information was supplied confidentially to the author by an official.
5 This is a reference to the Sherlock Holmes mystery, *Silver Blaze*, in which the fact that a dog did not bark during the night was an important clue.
6 Lord Falconer's comment was made on the BBC *Question Time* programme on 15 June 2006.
7 An example is those cases of environmental or other forms of protest, where defendants have pleaded guilty but are found not guilty by a jury after the defence of 'lawful excuse' has been considered.
8 See *A* v *Secretary of State for the Home Department* [2004] UKHL 56, [2005] 2 AC 68.

Chapter 4

1 Megan's Law, which varies in application from state to state, was introduced after the murder of 7-year-old Megan Kanka in New Jersey in 1994 by a released paedophile.
2 Sarah's Law is a reference to a campaign for 'community notification', along US lines, launched after the murder of 8-year-old Sarah Payne by convicted paedophile Roy Whiting in 2000.
3 Changes in recording standards and arguments about the relative merits and flaws of the BCS and police recorded figures make this a treacherous issue for comparisons.
4 See, *R (F) (by his litigation friend F)* v *Secretary of State for the Home Department* [2010] UKSC 17 [updated].
5 Comments made during his address to the annual conference of the Criminal Solicitors Association, 12 November 2004.
6 As an indication of the rise in sentence lengths, the Sentencing Statistics 2005 (see Home Office press release 010/2007 on 30 January 2007) showed that the average custodial sentence for an indictable offence at Crown Court rose by 25 per cent from 1995 to 2005.
7 OASys and ViSOR are risk assessment databases used by the probation and prison service (in the case of OASys) and the police (in the case of ViSOR).
8 *R* v *Johnson* and other appeals [2006] EWCA Crim 2486 at [3].
9 House of Commons Standing Committee, 11 February 2003 (Hansard col. 917).
10 Parliamentary answer, 10 May 2007 (Hansard col. 438W).
11 Nichol gave the projected figure in a lecture at the Centre for Crime and Justice Studies, King's College London on 9 January 2007.
12 *R* v *C* [2005] EWCA Crim 3533; (2006) 1 Cr App R 28.
13 Figures from: Parole Board press release PR/08/2006, 20 July 2006.
14 Carter's report 'Managing Offenders – Reducing Crime' was published on 6 January 2004.

Chapter 5

1   The Home Office was located at Queen Anne's Gate from 1978 to 2004.
2   See 'Prison Disturbances April 1990: Report of an Inquiry' by Lord Justice Woolf and Sir Stephen Tumim, published on 25 February 1991.
3   See 'Press at the Prison Gates: Report of the inquiry' by the Press Council into press coverage of the Strangeways Prison Riot and related matters, published on 17 January 1991.
4   See Chapter 1 for biographical details on David Faulkner.
5   The term originated with New York sociologist, Professor Robert Martinson, whose 1974 study of 231 prison systems around the world found that rehabilitation results amongst offenders were roughly the same, whatever strategies were followed.
6   The crime rate also fell in many other jurisdictions without a rise in prison numbers, indicating that the reasons were more to do with the economy and demography than penal policy.

Chapter 6

1   The proposal was made during a speech to the inaugural session of the Global Ethics Foundation on 30 June 2000.
2   The proposal was contained in the report: 'Reducing re-offending by ex-prisoners' (Social Exclusion Unit 2002).
3   The Lord Chief Justice, Lord Woolf, held this view (Interview with author, 11 May 2009).
4   Birt had a degree in engineering (third-class) and Jack Straw said: 'Birt thought he could use a systems approach to re-engineer criminal justice. I was highly sceptical about that' (Interview with author, 21 September 2010).
5   Blunkett disagrees with Stevens's version of this 'threat' (see, Blunkett 2006: 350).
6   Nick Ross, presentation to the annual conference of the Probation Boards Association, June 2002.
7   Ibid.
8   See press release 182/2003 (Home Office 2003) for a fuller version of Blunkett's remarks.
9   The full title was: 'Paying the Price: A Consultation Paper on Prostitution', 16 July 2004, London: Home Office.
10 Alastair Campbell concedes this point in his 2002 article, 'It's Time to Bury Spin', in the *British Journalism Review* 13(4): 17.
11 Campbell's insinuation that Brown had 'psychological flaws', one of the best-known examples of this, found its way into the public prints in a column by Andrew Rawnsley in the *Observer* in 1998.

Chapter 7

1   This adage is attributed variously to Alfred Harmsworth, the British newspaper magnate and to the American journalists and editors, Charles A. Dana and John B. Bogart.
2   Angus Macqueen wrote and directed a series of documentary films for Channel 4 entitled *Our Drugs Wars*. The series contained three episodes: 'Everyone's at It', first broadcast on 2 August 2010; 'The Life and Death of a Dealer', first broadcast on 9 August 2010; and 'Birth of a Narco-State', first broadcast on 16 August 2010.
3   The drug mephedrone is part of a family of drugs called cathinones which are closely related to amphetamines.
4   For the purpose of this research, the author carried out a keyword search of 'mephedrone' in the UK press via the newspaper database, NewsBank. The results revealed

that the *Sun* referred to mephedrone in 205 of its articles between September 2009 and March 2010; the *Daily Telegraph* contained 39 references to the term between November 2009 and March 2010; and the *Daily Mail* made 76 mentions in the same period. Putting aside the obvious need to examine the context in which mephedrone was discussed, the figures, as they stand, provide an indication of the frequency in which this issue was discussed in the national press.

5 A class B drug carries a maximum penalty for possession of five years in prison, and 14 years for a dealing offence.

6 The *Sun's* obsession with mephedrone was such that it carried a story on 27 November 2009: 'Sex-tear injury on "cat" drug', which reported that a man from Durham had ripped off his own scrotum under the influence of the drug. Later investigation showed that the story was a hoax picked up, without verification, from a website (see, for example, 'The Anatomy of a Media Drug Scare' in the *Guardian*, 6 April 2010).

7 On 28 May 2010, the *Times Online* reported that the 'Teenagers' deaths were not caused by "legal" high mephedrone'. Indeed, toxicology results established that neither of the two men had taken mephedrone prior to their deaths.

8 Although Professor Nutt delivered his lecture on 14 July 2009, his paper was not published until 29 October 2009 (on the Centre for Crime and Justice Studies, King's College London website: www.crimeandjustice.org.uk).

9 Jacqui Smith's reprimand of Professor Nutt most notably occurred during Home Office questions in the House of Commons on 9 February 2009 (HC Deb 2008–2009).

10 The *Science and Society Third Report* was published on 14 March 2000. The Report concluded that there was a need to promote expert information on science especially when it is under attack in the news media (House of Lords Select Committee on Science and Technology 2000).

Chapter 8

1 See the comments, later in this chapter, of Charles Clarke, another core 'Blairite', on also being given a free rein by the Prime Minister when he wrestled with the decision on leaving cannabis a Class C drug in 2006.

2 It is worth mentioning that Gordon Brown told the Labour Party conference on 24 September 2007 that under his administration 'drugs are never going to be decriminalized' (Brown 2007).

3 Particularly because from 1974 to 1995, Ruth Runciman was a member of the ACMD.

4 The Drug Equality Alliance (DEA) is a not-for-profit organization which campaigns (according to its mission statement) for a 'rational and objective legal regulatory framework on drugs' (www.drugequality.org/).

5 The author received two letters from the Office of John Reid (on 17 September 2008 and 7 September 2010), both of which stated that Mr Reid had declined to be interviewed.

6 At the time of writing (January 2011), the Report is available on the Drug Equality Alliance website: www.drugequality.org.

Chapter 9

1 The website Fitwatch – so named because it monitors the police Forward Intelligence Teams – carries out this function in a literal sense (see: www.fitwatch.org.uk).

2 Metropolitan Police press bureau statement, 1 April 2009.

3 See HMIC report, *Policing Public Order: An Overview of Progress Against the Recommendations of 'Adapting to Protest' and 'Nurturing the British Model of Policing'*, published 9 February 2011.

4 Bramshill (in Hampshire) is the staff college for higher police training.

5   *Wood* v *Commissioner of Police for the Metropolis* [2009] EWCA Civ.414; [2009] HRLR 25. 21 May 2009.
6   Available HTTP: www.urban75.com (accessed 4 May 2011).
7   Boris Johnson also used this sobriquet in the *Daily Telegraph*, 11 July 2002, when writing about the controversy over the Brixton cannabis experiment (detailed in Chapter 8).
8   Mike Todd subsequently became chief constable of Greater Manchester and died in November 2008.
9   The Asian victim, Balbir Matharu, was killed trying to prevent thieves stealing goods from his van. But one reason for the comparatively little publicity was a reluctance by the borough police to speak to the media. This led to friction between the Commissioner and the Crime Reporters Association (private source).
10 Cited by Mark Easton, Home Editor, *BBC News*, 28 April 2010. Available HTTP: www.newsvote.bbc.co.uk/mpapps/pagetools/print/news/.bbc.co.uk/1/hi/uk_politics/ (accessed 4 May 2011).
11 Available HTTP: www.paulblomfield.co.uk/index, 6 December 2010 (accessed 4 May 2011).
12 Available HTTP: www.audit-commission.gov.uk/pages/default.aspx (accessed 4 May 2011).

Chapter 10

1   The term is usually attributed to the late *Daily Telegraph* writer, Frank Johnson.
2   The hearing, before senior district judge Howard Riddle, took place at City of Westminster magistrates' court on 14 December 2010.
3   Raoul Moat, from Newcastle, murdered one person and seriously wounded two others (including a police officer) and later killed himself after an intensive manhunt by the Northumbria force.
4   Both comments can be found at: www.mumset.com/Talk/style_and_beauty/998531-can-we-talk-about acting-chief-constable-Sue-Sim-please (accessed 31 August 2010).
5   Andy Hayman was wrong in that prediction. Sue Sim was appointed chief constable of Northumbria – the first woman to head a metropolitan force – on 21 April 2010.
6   But they were criticized as well because the website they had set up crashed fairly quickly. See timmymc.blogspot.com/2011/03/policing-of-tuc-march.html.

Chapter 11

1   Tony Blair made this statement during his monthly press conference on 5 August 2005.
2   This was reported in *The Times* on 2 August 1988.
3   Interestingly, MI5 archives reveal that as early as 1991, the worst-case scenario envisaged by the security service was that the PIRA would employ the tactics of suicide bombing (Andrew 2010: 773).
4   This is the general thesis of Peter Oborne's pamphlet, 'The Use and Abuse of Terror', published by the Centre for Policy Studies in February 2006.
5   Later moves by the Chancellor to freeze assets via an order-in-council, thus by-passing parliament, were ruled unlawful by the UK Supreme Court in 2010.
6   Jamaat was founded by Maulana Maududi in Pakistan and is committed to the establishment of an Islamic state ruled by sharia law.
7   The report, entitled 'Islamophobia: A Challenge for Us All', was published in November 1997.
8   The BBC *Panorama* programme, first broadcast on 21 August 2005, was called 'A Question of Leadership'.

9 David Blunkett's essay in the publication 'Reclaiming Britishness', published in September 2002, touches on some of these issues.
10 On behalf of ACPO, in December 2005, Beckley also criticized powers in the Counter Terrorism Bill to allow the police to shut down mosques suspected of terrorist links.

Chapter 12

1 The figures were arrived at by interrogating a number of sources, mainly the parliamentary website and National Archives.
2 According to the *Oxford Dictionary of Quotations* (1999) the remark is 'attributed' to Macmillan but the date and circumstances in which he said it are uncertain.

References

ACMD (2010) *Consideration of the Cathinones*, London: Home Office.

ACPO (2003) *Cannabis Enforcement Guidance*, Press Release, Can/guide/03, 12 September 2003, London: ACPO.

Adebowale, V. (2005) 'Smoking Gun', *Community Care*, 5–11 May 2005: 30.

Aitkenhead, D. (2010) 'David Nutt: "The Government Cannot Think Logically About Drugs"', *Guardian*, 6 December 2010. Online. Available HTTP: <http://www.guardian.co.uk/uk/2010/dec/06/david-nutt-drugs-alcohol> (accessed 12 January 2011).

Allan, S. (2006) *Online News: Journalism and the Internet*, Maidenhead: Open University Press.

Andrew, C. (2010) *The Defence of the Realm: The Authorised History of MI5*, London: Penguin.

Audit Commission (1990) *Effective Policing – Performance Review in Police Forces*, Police Papers No. 8, London: The Stationery Office.

Audit Commission (1996) *Misspent Youth: Young People and Crime*, London: Audit Commission.

Baumgartner, F.R. and Jones, B.D. (1993) *Agendas and Instability in American Politics*, Chicago: University of Chicago Press.

BBC Four (2008) *Prime Ministers and Press Barons*, Television Documentary, 10 March 2008.

BBC News Online (2006) Media 'Dictates Paedophile Plans', 19 June 2006. Online. Available HTTP: <http://news.bbc.co.uk/1/hi/5096542.stm> (accessed 3 May 2011).

BBC News Online (2010) Ex-minister Bob Ainsworth: Make Drugs Legally Available, 16 December 2010. Online. Available HTTP: <http://www.bbc.co.uk/news/uk-12005824> (accessed 12 January 2011).

Beck, U. (2002) 'The Terrorist Threat: World Risk Society Revisited', *Theory, Culture and Society*, 19(4): 39–55.

Becker, H. (1967) 'Whose Side are We On?', *Social Problems*, 14(3): 234–47.

Bennett, W.L. (1990) 'Toward a Theory of Press–State Relations in the United States', *Journal of Communication*, 40(2): 103–25.

Bingham, T. (2003) *Judging Today*, Ditchley Foundation Lecture XXXIX, Lecture, 11 July 2003, Chipping Norton, UK. Online. Available HTTP: <http://www.ditchley.co.uk/page/178/lecture-xxxix.htm> (accessed 4 May 2011).

Bingham, T. (2010) *The Rule of Law*, London: Allen Lane.

Blair, I. (2006) *Speech Delivered to the Urban Age Summit*, Speech, 11 November 2006, Berlin, Germany. Online. Available HTTP: <http://content.met.police.uk/News/Commisioners-Urban-Age-Summit-Speech/1260267603090/1257246745756> (accessed 27 April 2011).

Blair, T. (2007a) *Speech Delivered at Reuters Headquarters*, Speech, 12 June 2007, London, UK. Online. Available HTTP: < http://uk.reuters.com/article/2007/06/12/uk-blair-speech-idUKZWE24585220070612> (accessed 16 February 2011).

Blair, T. (2007b) 'Blair: Shackled in War on Terror', *Sunday Times*, 27 May 2007.

Blair, T. (2010) *A Journey*, London: Hutchinson.

Blumler, J. and Coleman, S. (2010) 'Political Communication in Freefall: The British Case – and Others?', *International Journal of Press/Politics*, 15(2): 139–54.

Blunkett, D. (2001) *Politics and Progress: Renewing Democracy and Civil Society*, London: Politico's Publishing.

Blunkett, D. (2006) *The Blunkett Tapes: My Life in the Bear Pit*, London: Bloomsbury.

Boland, P. (2008) 'British Drugs Policy: Problematizing the Distinction Between Legal and Illegal Drugs and the Definition of the "Drugs Problem"', *Probation Journal*, 55(2): 171–87.

Bottoms, A.E. (1995) 'The Philosophy and Politics of Punishment and Sentencing', in C.M.V. Clarkson and R. Morgan (eds) *The Politics of Sentencing Reform*, Oxford: Clarendon Press.

Boyd-Caine, T. (2010) *Protecting the Public?*, Cullompton: Willan.

Bratby, L. (1999) 'New Scheme Highlights Link Between Drugs and Crime', *Police Review*, 15 January 1999.

Bridges, A. (2008) *Need for More Light and Less Heat in Public Discussions about the Criminal Justice System*, Press Release, 15 July 2008, London: HM Inspectorate of Probation. Online. Available HTTP: <http://www.justice.gov.uk/inspectorates/hmiprobation/docs/annual-report-2007-08-rps.pdf> (accessed 28 March 2011).

Bright, M. (2006) *When Progressives Treat with Reactionaries: The British State's Flirtation with Radical Islamism*, London: Policy Exchange.

Brown, G. (2007) *First Speech to the Labour Conference as Party Leader*, Speech, 24 September 2007, Bournemouth, UK. Online. Available HTTP: <http://news.bbc.co.uk/1/hi/uk_politics/7010664.stm> (accessed 16 January 2011).

Brown, R. (2010) 'The Media and the Policy Process: A Policy Centric Approach', in S. Koch-Baumgarten and K. Voltmer (eds) *Public Policy and Mass Media: The Interplay of Mass Communication and Political Decision Making*, London: Routledge.

Campbell, A. (2002) 'It's Time to Bury Spin', *British Journalism Review*, 13(4): 15–23.

Campbell, B. (1993) *Goliath: Britain's Dangerous Places*, London: Methuen.

Carlin, E. (2010) *Eric Carlin's Letter of Resignation from the ACMD*, Letter, 2 April 2010. Online. Available HTTP: <http://news.bbc.co.uk/1/hi/uk/8600929.stm> (accessed 17 January 2011).

Charles, N. (1998) *Public Perceptions of Drug Related Crime in 1997, Home Office Research and Statistics Directorate, Research Findings No. 67*, London: The Stationery Office.

Chibnall, S. (1977) *Law and Order News*, London: Tavistock.

Clarke, C. (2007) 'New Labour and the Media: Ten Years On', Speech to the Royal Television Society, 28 March 2007.

Cohen, N. (1999) *Cruel Britannia: Reports on the Sinister and the Preposterous*, London: Verso.

Cohen, N. (2003) *Pretty Straight Guys*, London: Faber.

Cohen, S. (2002) *Folk Devils and Moral Panics*, London: Routledge.

Commons Home Affairs Committee (2004) *Draft Sentencing Guidelines 1&2, Fifth Report, Session 2003–2004 HC1207*, London: Stationery Office.

Coomber, R., Morris, C. and Dunn, L. (2000) 'How the Media Do Drugs: Quality Control and the Reporting of Drug Issues in the UK Print Media', *International Journal of Drug Policy*, 11(3): 217–25.

Cottle, S. (2004) *The Racist Murder of Stephen Lawrence: Media Performance and Public Transformation*, Westport, CT: Praeger Publishers.

Crick, M. (2005) *In Search of Michael Howard*, London: Simon and Schuster.

Critcher, C. (2003) *Moral Panics and the Media*, Buckingham: Open University Press.

Cross, S. (2007) 'Under a Cloud: Morality, Ambivalence and Uncertainty in News Discourse of Cannabis Law Reform in Great Britain', in P. Manning (ed.) *Drugs and Popular Culture: Drugs, Media and Identity in Contemporary Society*, Cullompton: Willan.

Davies, N. (2009) *Flat Earth News*, London: Vintage.

Davis, A. (2007a) 'Investigating Journalist Influences on Political Issue Agendas at Westminster', *Political Communication*, 24(2): 181–99.

Davis, A. (2007b) *The Mediation of Power*, London: Routledge.

Dearing, J.W. and Rogers, E.M. (1996) *Communication Concepts 6: Agenda Setting*, Thousand Oaks, CA: Sage.

Department of Health (1998) *Tackling Drugs to Build a Better Britain: The Government's Ten-year Strategy for Tackling Drugs Misuse*, London: The Stationery Office.

Downes, D. and Morgan, R. (2002) 'The Skeletons in the Cupboard: The Politics of Law and Order at the Turn of the Millennium', in M. Maguire, R. Morgan and R. Reiner (eds) *Oxford Handbook of Criminology*, Oxford: OUP.

Dunbar, I. and Langdon, A. (1998) *Tough Justice: Sentencing and Penal Policies in the 1990s*, London: Blackstone Press.

Easton, M. (2010) *Tension at Heart of Drug Classification*, BBC Weblog, 12 July 2010. Online. Available HTTP: <http://www.bbc.co.uk/blogs/thereporters/markeaston/2010/07/tension_at_heart_of_drug_classification.html> (accessed 18 January 2011).

Entman, R.M. (1993) 'Framing: Toward Clarification of a Fractured Paradigm', *Journal of Communication*, 43(4): 51–8.

Etzioni, A. (1995) *The Spirit of Community: Rights, Responsibilities and the Communitarian Agenda*, London: Fontana Press.

Fairclough, N. (2000) *New Labour, New Language?*, London: Routledge.

Fellows, C. and Madden, P. (2004) *Trends in London Arrest Referral April 2000 – February 2004*, London: The London Health Observatory and the Centre for Research on Drugs and Health Behaviour, Imperial College.

Forsyth, A. (2001) 'Distorted? A Quantitative Exploration of Drug Fatality Reports in the Popular Press', *International Journal of Drug Policy*, 12(5): 435–53.

Furedi, F. (2009) 'Precautionary Culture and the Rise of Possibilistic Risk Assessment', *Erasmus Law Review*, 2(2): 197–220.

Gaffney, J. (2001) 'Imagined Relationships: Political Leadership in Contemporary Democracies', *Parliamentary Affairs*, 54(1): 120–33.

Galtung, J. and Ruge, M. (1973) 'Structuring and Selecting News', in S. Cohen and J. Young (eds) *The Manufacture of News: Social Problems, Deviance and the Mass Media*, London: Constable.

Garland, D. (2001) *The Culture of Control: Crime and Social Order in Contemporary Society*, Oxford: OUP.

Garside, R. (2007) '"Punitiveness" and "Populism" in Political Economic Perspective', in R. Roberts and W. McMahon (eds) *Social Justice and Criminal Justice*, London: Centre for Crime and Justice Studies. Online. Available HTTP: <http://www.crimeandjustice.org.uk/opus408/socialjusticecriminaljusticeweb.pdf> (accessed 28 March 2011).

Gossop, M. (1996) *Living With Drugs*, Aldershot: Arena.

Great Britain (1971) *Misuse of Drugs Act 1971* (c. 38), London: The Stationery Office.

Great Britain (2010) *The Misuse of Drugs Act 1971 (Amendment) Order 2010 Statutory Instruments 1207 2010*, London: The Stationery Office.

Greer, C. and McLaughlin, E. (2010a) 'We Predict a Riot? Public Order Policing, New Media Environment and the Rise of the Citizen Journalist', *British Journal of Criminology*, 50(6): 1041–59.

Greer, C. and McLaughlin, E. (2010b) '"Trial by Media": Policing, the 24-7 News Mediasphere and the "Politics of Outrage"', *Theoretical Criminology*, 15(1): 23–46.

Habermas, J. (2006) 'Towards a United States of Europe', Acceptance Speech for the Award of the Bruno Kreisky Prize, Speech, 27 March 2007. Online. Available HTTP: <http://www.signandsight.com/features/676.html> (accessed 29 April 2011).

Hagell, A., Hazel, N. and Shaw, C. (2000) *Evaluation of Medway Secure Training Centre*, London: Home Office.

Hajer, M. (2009) *Authoritative Governance: Policymaking in the Age of Mediatization*, Oxford: OUP.

Hall, S., Critcher, C., Jefferson, T., Clarke, J.N. and Roberts, B. (1978) *Policing the Crisis: Mugging, the State and Law and Order*, London: Macmillan.

Halliday, J. (2001) *Making Punishments Work: A Review of the Sentencing Framework for England and Wales*, London: The Stationery Office.

Hardwick, S. and King, L. (2008) *Home Office Cannabis Potency Study 2008*, London: The Stationery Office.

Harrington, V. and Mayhew, P. (2001) *Mobile Phone Theft, Home Office Research Study No. 235*, London: Home Office.

HC Deb (1993) 02 March 1993 vol. 220 cc 139–150.

HC Deb (2009) 9 February 2009 vol. 487 cc 1091–1095.

HL Deb (2005) 10 March 2005 vol. 670 cc 1040–1041.

HM Inspectorate of Probation (2006) *Serious Further Offence Review: Anthony Rice*, HMIP: Home Office.

Hobsbawm, J. and Lloyd, J. (2008) *The Power of the Commentariat: How Much do Commentators Influence Politics and Public Opinion?*, London: Editorial Intelligence Ltd in association with the Reuters Institute for the Study of Journalism.

Home Affairs Select Committee (2002) *The Government's Drug Policy: Is it Working? Third Report, Session 2001–2002 HC 318*, London: The Stationery Office.

Home Office (1990) *Crime, Justice and Protecting the Public, Cm. 965*, London: Home Office.

Home Office (2001a) *Blunkett to Focus on the Menace of Hard Drugs*, Press Release, 255/2001, 23 October 2001, London: Home Office.

Home Office (2001b) *Largest Increase in Police Numbers for More Than a Decade*, Press Release, 076/2001, 22 March 2001, London: Home Office.

Home Office (2002a) *Justice for All, Cm. 5563*, London: Home Office.

Home Office (2002b) *All Controlled Drugs are Harmful, All Will Remain Illegal*, Press Release, 192/2002, 10 July 2002, London: Home Office.

Home Office (2003) *Vital to Help Victims of Prostitution Break Out of Violent Circle of Abuse* – David Blunkett, Press Release, 182/2003, 27 June 2003, London: Home Office.

Home Office (2004) *£1 Million Cannabis Information Campaign Begins*, Press Release, 020/2004, 17 January 2004, London: Home Office.

Home Office (2005a) *Cannabis Reclassification*, Press Release, 002/2005, 28 January 2005, London: Home Office.

Home Office (2005b) *Police Numbers Reach Record High*, Press Release, 113/2005, 25 July 2005, London: Home Office.

Home Office (2006a) *Crime in England and Wales: Quarterly Update to December 2005*, Press Release, 069/2006, 27 April 2006, London: Home Office.

Home Office (2006b) *Annual Parole Board Lecture*, Press Release, 073/2006, 22 May 2006, London: Home Office.

Home Office (2006c) *Government Says No to Managed Prostitution Zones*, Press Release, 006/2006, 17 January 2006, London: Home Office.

Home Office (2010) *Drug Strategy 2010 Reducing Demand, Restricting Supply, Building Recovery: Supporting People to Live a Drug-free Life*, London: The Stationery Office.

Home Office Crime and Drug Strategy Directorate (2006) *Review of the UK's Drugs Classification System – A Public Consultation*, London: Home Office. Online. Available HTTP: <http://www.drugequality.org/files/Review_of_Drugs_Classification_Consultation_Paper.pdf> (accessed 18 January 2011).

Home Office Standing Conference on Crime Prevention (1989) *Report of the Working Group on the Fear of Crime*, London: Home Office.

Hough, M. and Mitchell, D. (2003) 'Drug-Dependent Offenders and Justice for All', in M. Tonry (ed.) *Confronting Crime: Crime Control Policy Under New Labour*, Cullompton: Willan.

House of Commons Science and Technology Committee (2006) *Drug Classification: Making a Hash of It?*, Fifth Report of Session 2005–2006, HC 1031, London: The Stationery Office.

House of Lords Select Committee on Science and Technology (2000) *Science and Society Third Report, Session 1999–2000 HL 38*, London: The Stationery Office.

House of Lords Select Committee on the Constitution (2007) *Relations between the Executive, the Judiciary and Parliament, Sixth Report of Session 2006–2007 HL 151*, London: The Stationery Office.

House of Lords Select Committee on the Constitution (2010) *The Cabinet Office and the Centre of Government, Fourth Report of Session 2009–2010*, London: The Stationery Office.

Howard, M. (1996a) *Letter from Michael Howard to the Director General of the BBC*, 7 February 1996, London: BBC Archives.

Howard, M. (1996b) *Letter from Michael Howard to the Director General of the BBC*, 9 April 1996, London: BBC Archives.

Hurd, D. (2003) *Douglas Hurd: Memoirs*, London: Little, Brown.

Husain, E. (2007) *The Islamist*, London: Penguin.

Huysmans, J. and Buonfino, A. (2008) 'Politics of Exception and Unease: Immigration, Asylum and Terrorism in Parliamentary Debates in the UK', *Political Studies*, 56(4): 766–88.

Innes, M. (2004) 'Crime as a Signal, Crime as a Memory', *Journal for Crime, Conflict and the Media*, 1(2): 15–22.

IPCC (2007) *Independent Police Complaints Commission Stockwell 2 Report: An Investigation into Complaints About the Metropolitan Police's Handling of Public Statements Following the Shooting of Jean Charles de Menezes on 22 July 2005*, London: IPCC.

IPCC (2009) *Commissioner's Report Following IPCC Independent Investigation into Metropolitan Police Service Response to the Prison Recall Notification of Dano Sonnex*, London: IPCC.

Jackson, R. (2005) *Writing the War on Terrorism*, Manchester: Manchester University Press.

Jacobson, J. (1997) 'Religion and Ethnicity: Dual and Alternative Sources of Identity among Young British Pakistanis', *Ethnic and Racial Studies*, 20(2): 238–56.

Jameson, N. and Allison, E. (1995) *Strangeways 1990: A Serious Disturbance*, London: Larkin Publications.

Johnson, A. (2009) *Letter to Professor David Nutt*, Letter, 30 October 2009. Online. Available HTTP: <http://www.bbc.co.uk/blogs/thereporters/markeaston/2009/10/nutt_gets_the_sack.html> (accessed 17 January 2011).

Johnson, J. (1998) 'Rupert's Grip?', *British Journalism Review*, 9(1): 13–19.

Johnston, P. (2010) *Bad Laws: An Explosive Analysis of Britain's Petty Rules, Health and Safety Lunacies and Madcap Laws*, London: Constable.

Jones, B.D. and Baumgartner F.R. (2005) *The Politics of Attention: How Government Prioritizes Problems*, Chicago: University of Chicago Press.

Jones, B.D. and Wolfe, M. (2010) 'Public Policy and the Mass Media: An Information Processing Approach', in S. Koch-Baumgarten and K. Voltmer (eds) *Public Policy and Mass Media: The Interplay of Mass Communication and Political Decision Making*, London: Routledge.

Jones, N. (1999) *The Sultans of Spin: The Media and the New Labour Government*, London: Victor Gollancz.

Jordan, B. (1999) 'Bulger "Back to Basics" and the Rediscovery of Community', in B. Franklin (ed.) *Social Policy, the Media and Misrepresentation*, London: Routledge.

Keane, J. (2009) *The Life and Death of Democracy*, London: Simon and Schuster.

Keen, A. (2007) *The Cult of the Amateur: How Today's Internet is Killing our Culture*, New York: Currency.

Koch-Baumgarten, S. and Voltmer, K. (eds) (2010) *Public Policy and Mass Media: The Interplay of Mass Communication and Political Decision Making*, London: Routledge.

Lang, K. and Lang, G. (1955) 'The Inferential Structure of Political Communications: A Study in Unwitting Bias', *Public Opinion Quarterly*, 19(2): 168–83.

Lawrence, R.G (1996) 'Accidents, Icons and Indexing: The Dynamics of Coverage of Police Use of Force', *Political Communication*, 13(4): 437–54.

Lewis, D. (1997) *Hidden Agendas: Politics, Law and Disorder*, London: Hamish Hamilton.

Loader, I. (2006) 'Fall of the Platonic Guardians: Liberalism, Criminology and Political Responses to Crime in England and Wales', *British Journal of Criminology*, 46(4): 561–86.

MacKenzie, D. and Uchida, C. (1994) *Drugs and Crime: Evaluating Public Policy Initiatives*, Thousand Oaks, CA: Sage.

Manning, P. (ed.) (2007) *Drugs and Popular Culture: Drugs, Media and Identity in Contemporary Society*, Cullompton: Willan.

Mark, R. (1978) *In the Office of Constable*, London: Collins.

Mathieson, T. (1997) 'The Viewer Society: Foucault's Panopticon Revisited', *Theoretical Criminology*, 1(2): 125–34.

May, T., Warburton, H., Turnbull, P.J. and Hough, M. (2002) *Times They Are A-changing: Policing of Cannabis*, York: Joseph Rowntree Foundation.

McCombs, M.E. and Shaw, D.L (1972) 'The Agenda-Setting Function of the Press', *Public Opinion Quarterly*, 36(2): 176–87.

McLuhan, M. (1964) *Understanding Media: The Extensions of Man*, New York: McGraw Hill.

Meyer, T. and Hinchman, L. (2002) *Media Democracy: How the Media Colonize Politics*, Cambridge: Polity.

Modood, T., Berthoud, R., Lakey, J., Nazroo, J., Smith, P., Virdee, S. and Seishon, S. (1997) 'Ethnic Minorities in Britain: Diversity and Disadvantage', Fourth National Survey of Ethnic Minorities, London: Policy Studies Institute.

Monaghan, M.P. (2008) 'Appreciating Cannabis: The Paradox of "Evidence" in Evidence-Based Policy-Making', *Evidence and Policy*, 4(2): 209–31.

Mooney, J. and Young, J. (2006) 'The Decline in Crime and the Rise of Anti-Social Behaviour', *Probation Journal*, 53(4): 397–407.

Mulgan, G. (2003) 'Government, Knowledge and the Business of Policy-making', Facing the Future Conference, Canberra, 23–24 April. Online. Available HTTP: <http://www.odi.org.uk/rapid/Bibliographies/Research_Policy/Documents/Mulgan_2003.pdf> (accessed 14 February 2011).

Mullins, R. (2009) *Letter from the Home Office FOI Unit to J. Silverman Concerning the Outcome of a Request for Information Under the FOIA (Case Ref. 12713)*, Letter, 19 October 2009, London: Home Office.

Mythen, G. and Walklate, S. (2006) 'Communicating the Terrorist Risk: Harnessing a Culture of Fear?', *Crime Media Culture*, 2(2): 123–42.

Nash, M. (2006) *Public Protection and the Criminal Justice Process*, Oxford: OUP.

Newburn, T. (1996) 'Back to the Future? Youth Crime, Youth Justice and the Rediscovery of "Authoritarian Populism"' in J. Pilcher and S. Wagg (eds) *Thatcher's Children?: Politics, Childhood and Society in the 1980s and 1990s*, London: Falmer Press.

Newburn, T. and Jones, T. (2005) 'Symbolic Politics and Penal Populism: The Long Shadow of Willie Horton', *Crime Media Culture*, 1(1): 72–87.

Nickels, H.C., Thomas, L., Hickman, M.J. and Silvestri, S. (2010) 'A Comparative Study of the Representations of "Suspect" Communities in Multi-Ethnic Britain and of their Impact on Irish Communities and Muslim Communities – Mapping Newspaper Content', London: Institute for the Study of European Transformations, London Metropolitan University. Online. Available HTTP: <http://www.londonmet.ac.uk/fms/MRSite/Research/iset/Working%20Paper%20Series/WP13%20.pdf> (accessed 31 March 2011).

Nutt, D. (2009a) 'Equasy – An Overlooked Addiction with Implications for the Current Debate on Drug Harms', *Journal of Psychopharmacology*, 23(1): 3–5.

Nutt, D. (2009b) 'Estimating Drug Harms: A Risky Business?' Eve Saville Lecture 2009, The Centre for Crime and Justice Studies (CCJS), King's College London. Online. Available HTTP: <http://www.crimeandjustice.org.uk/opus1714/Estimating_drug_harms.pdf> (accessed 12 January 2011).

Nutt, D., King, L., Saulsbury, W. and Blakemore, C. (2007) 'Development of a Rational Scale to Assess the Harm of Drugs of Potential Misuse', *The Lancet*, 369(9566): 1047–53.

Poole, E. (2009) *Reporting Islam: Media Representations of British Muslims*, New York: I.B Tauris.

Reiner, R. (2002) 'Media Made Criminality: The Representation of Crime in the Mass Media', in M. Maguire, R. Morgan and R. Reiner (eds) *Oxford Handbook of Criminology*, Oxford: OUP.

Reiner, R. (2007) *Law and Order: An Honest Citizen's Guide to Crime and Control*, Cambridge: Polity Press.

Reuter, P. and Stevens, A. (2008) 'Assessing UK Drug Policy from a Crime Control Perspective', *Criminology and Criminal Justice*, 8(4): 461–82.

Richards, B. (2007) *Emotional Governance: Politics, Media and Terror*, Basingstoke: Palgrave Macmillan.

Robinson, J. (2010) 'Facebook Generates 10% of Mail Online's UK Traffic', *Guardian Online*, 15 November 2010. Online. Available HTTP: <http://www.guardian.co.uk/media/2010/nov/15/mail-online-uk-traffic-facebook> (accessed 29 April 2011).

Robinson, P. (2002) *The CNN Effect: The Myth of News, Foreign Policy and Intervention*, London: Routledge.

Roshier, B. (1973) 'The Selection of Crime News by the Press', in S. Cohen and J. Young (eds) *The Manufacture of News*, London: Constable.

Rozenberg, J. (1994) *The Search for Justice: An Anatomy of the Law*, London: Hodder and Stoughton.

Rozenberg, J. (2005) 'Not the Usual Channels', *Daily Telegraph*, 10 November 2005. Online. Available HTTP: <http://www.telegraph.co.uk/news/uknews/1502611/Not-the-usual-channels.html> (accessed 13 April 2011).

Runciman, R. (2000) *Drugs and the Law: Report of the Independent Inquiry into the Misuse of Drugs Act 1971*, London: Police Foundation.

Ryan, M. (1999) 'Criminology Re-engages the Public Voice', *Criminal Justice Matters*, 34: 11–12.

Sanders, T. (2005) 'Blinded by Morality? Prostitution Policy in the UK', *Capital and Class*, 29(2): 9–15.

Sare, J. (2010) 'Flawed Thinking on Mephedrone', *Guardian*, 9 April 2010. Online. Available HTTP: <http://www.guardian.co.uk/commentisfree/2010/apr/09/flawed-thinking-mephedrone> (accessed 19 January 2011).

Schlesinger, P. and Tumber, H. (1994) *Reporting Crime: the Media Politics of Criminal Justice*, Oxford: Clarendon Press.

Scott, D.M. (2010) 'Who's Protecting Who?', *Probation Journal*, 57(3): 291–5.

Scraton, P. (2004) 'Streets of Terror: Marginalization, Criminalization and Authoritarian Renewal', *Social Justice*, 31(1–2): 130–58.

Seddon, T. (2000) 'Explaining the Drug–Crime Link: Theoretical, Policy and Research Issues', *Journal of Social Policy*, 29(1): 95–107.

Shapiro, H. (2011) *The Media Guide to Drugs: Key Facts and Figures for Journalists*, London: DrugScope. Online. Available HTTP: <http://www.drugscope.org.uk/resources/Media+Guide > (accessed 13 January 2011).

Silverman, J. and Wilson, D. (2002) *Innocence Betrayed: Pedophilia, the Media and Society*, Cambridge: Polity.

Silverstone, R. (2007) *Media and Morality: On the Rise of the Mediapolis*, Cambridge: Polity.

Simmons, J. and Dodd, T. (2003) *Crime in England and Wales, 2002/2003, Home Office Statistical Bulletin No. 07/03*, London: Home Office.

Smith, D. (2003) *The Nature of Personal Robbery, Home Office Research Study No.254*, London: Home Office.

Social Exclusion Unit (2002) *Reducing Re-offending by Ex-Prisoners*, London: Social Exclusion Unit.

Stevens, A., Berto, D., Heckmann, W., Kerschl, V., Oeuvray, K., van Ooyen, M., Steffan, E. and Uchtenhagen, A. (2005) 'Quasi-Compulsory Treatment of Drug Dependent Offenders: An International Literature Review', *Substance Use and Misuse*, 40(3): 269–83.

Stevens, J. (2006) *Not for the Faint-Hearted*, London: Orion Books.

Taylor, S. (2008) 'Outside the Outsiders: Media Representations of Drug Use', *Probation Journal*, 55(4): 369–87.

Thomas, D. (2010) 'The Government's Green Paper on Sentencing is to be Welcomed', *Guardian*, 8 December 2010. Online. Available HTTP: <http://www.guardian.co.uk/law/2010/dec/08/green-paper-sentencing-welcomed> (accessed 13 April 2011).

Thomas, T. (2009) 'The Sex Offender Register: Some Observations on the Time Periods of Registration', *Howard Journal of Criminal Justice*, 48(3): 257–66.

Tonry, M. (2003) 'Evidence, Elections and Ideology in the Making of Criminal Justice Policy', in M. Tonry (ed.) *Confronting Crime: Crime Control Policy Under New Labour*, Cullompton: Willan.

Tonry, M. (2004) *Punishment and Politics: Evidence and Emulation in the Making of English Crime Control Policy*, Cullompton: Willan.

Tulloch, J. (2006) *One Day in July: Experiencing 7/7*, London: Little, Brown.

Walgrave, S. and Lefevere, J. (2010) 'Do the Media Shape Parties' Agenda Preferences?', in S. Koch-Baumgarten and K. Voltmer (eds) *Public Policy and Mass Media: The Interplay of Mass Communication and Political Decision Making*, London: Routledge.

Walgrave S. and Van Aelst, P. (2006) 'The Contingency of the Mass Media's Political Agenda Setting Power: Toward a Preliminary Theory', *Journal of Communication*, 56(1): 88–109.

Walker, C. (2009) *Blackstone's Guide to the Anti-Terrorism Legislation*, Oxford: OUP.

Warburton, H., May, T. and Hough, M. (2005) 'Looking the Other Way: The Impact of Reclassifying Cannabis on Police Warnings, Arrests and Informal Action in England and Wales', *British Journal of Criminology*, 45(2): 113–28.

Wayne, M., Henderson, L., Murray, C. and Petley, J. (2008) 'Television News and the Symbolic Criminalisation of Young People', *Journalism Studies*, 9(1): 75–90.

Windlesham, D. (1993) *Responses to Crime*, Oxford: Clarendon Press.

Index